Go
and make
disciples

THE
GOAL
OF THE
CHRISTIAN
TEACHER

Go
and make
disciples

JANE L. FRYAR

CPH.
SAINT LOUIS

To Mom and Dad
who first brought me to the Lord Jesus
and
to
Miss Bahls
Mrs. Volk
Mr. Roell
Mrs. Fredrickson
Pastor Schaefer
and
Pastor Sylwester
who taught me to know and love Him

Contents

Acknowledgments

"All of us are smarter than one of us!" That's what the sign on Arnold Schmidt's desk proclaimed the first morning I reported to work at the Board for Parish Services. Arnold really believes that. He works that way. His example has taught me volumes about team ministry.

Although my name appears on the title page as author, this book in reality represents a team effort by literally dozens of God's people. Again and again as I worked, I found myself overwhelmed with the magnanimity and Christian love with which so many of my brothers and sisters in the faith shared themselves, their knowledge, their time, and their resources. Our Lord truly has blessed His church with gifts—people gifts!

As I began my work, a group of Christian day school teachers, Sunday school teachers, and principals sat with me to brainstorm the topics that were eventually included in these pages. Dr. Steve Carter, Debbie Fitzpatrick, Ruthann Gieseke, Linda Luebbe, Gregg Pinick, Ed Schlimpert, and Debbie Stroh saw to it that I started off down the right path. I may have strayed from it after that, but, if so, not because their guidance was faulty.

Many people found time to read and to react in detail to all or parts of the original outline and the chapters from the first few drafts of the manuscript itself. I found their critiques invaluable:

- Dr. Arthur Bacon
- Dr. Marian Baden
- Viola Bahls
- Dr. Gary Bertels
- Dr. Rudy Block
- Dr. Tom Doyle
- Ralph Geisler
- Dr. Mel Kieshnick
- Dr. Priscilla Lawin
- Keith Loomans
- Dr. Gerhardt Meyer
- Dr. Emily Moore
- Dr. Carl Moser
- Tim Peters
- Rodney Rathman
- Rev. Ted Schroeder
- Dr. James M. Unglaube
- Dr. Joseph Glass

Dr. Larry Sohn provided invaluable help as he read and reacted to a large portion of the manuscript, and as he suggested resources as I researched specific topics. Most of all, though, I found myself thanking God for Larry's excitement about the project and for all his encouragement. What a blessing from our Lord he has been to me!

Meredith Dornemann (MSW) and Carol Henning (MSN) both brainstormed with me as I outlined the chapters on ministry with individual children, ministry with families, and team ministry. They each suggested valuable resources. God smiled on Northwest Lutheran School in Milwaukee and Word of Life Lutheran School in St. Louis when He sent these servants of His to minister in those communities, and He smiled on me when He brought them into my life as friends and colleagues.

During the past 11 years, Dr. Earl Gaulke has taught me to appreciate the heritage members of The Lutheran Church—Missouri Synod share in our doctrine of Law and Gospel. He not only writes of it and teaches it, he lives it. Earl critiqued the first drafts of several chapters, providing both helpful comments and much-welcome encouragement. He also worked with me to find a way I could spend time away from the office to finish this book. I thank God for you, Earl, more than I can say!

As I worked on this manuscript, Shari Siemsen did the impossible again and again. Without her help in locating resources, I would have given up in despair. Based on the barest scraps of information (a few words from a title here, a misspelled author's name there), she often found books or films I needed. She also brought helpful materials to my attention, resources I would certainly not have accessed on my own. Her skills and her servant's heart have humbled me more than once.

Other colleagues on the Board for Parish Services offered encouragement, suggestions, and their ongoing support. To Don, Martha, Dale, Ron, Marilynn, and Jim, thank you!

Dr. William Weinrich, Rev. Jerald Joersz, Rev. Dirk van der Linde, and Rev. Jim Winsor shared of their time and wisdom as I sorted through various doctrinal issues, in particular the doctrine of the holy ministry. I thank God for their patience and for their insights.

Don Fick, my accountant and a dear brother in the Lord, took time during the busyness of tax season to discuss financial stewardship and some of the specific aspects of tax law as they apply to church workers. You have been a blessing, Don!

Chuck and Janet Beasley listened patiently while I talked through many of the concepts presented on these pages. Our Lord used their incisive comments and grace-based suggestions to put me back on course countless times as I wrote during the past year. How I thank God for their ongoing ministry in my life.

More people than I can mention, probably even more people than I know, have had a hand in this manuscript by virtue of their prayers for it and for me. I could not have survived the past months without the prayers of God's saints.

Last, but by no means least, I thank God for Ruth Geisler, editor par excellence! Her confidence in me, all the leg work she did, her understanding and flexibility with deadlines, her kindness, her skills, and her love have meant more than I could ever say.

While my brothers and sisters in the faith counseled, guided, and helped me throughout the writing process, nevertheless, the responsibility for any mistakes, misstatements, or errors rests, of course, solely on my own shoulders.

Jane L. Fryar

CHAPTER 1

Called to Be Disciples, Disciplers

A seven-year-old ragamuffin—let's call him Jon—stood in the entryway outside the principal's office. He clung to his mother's hand and looked down at his feet, scuffing his shoes back and forth impatiently.

Jon's father had walked out on his family during the last days of July. Jon and his mom had not heard from Dad, and as a matter of fact, they would never hear from him again, though they did not know that then. Mom sensed Jon's pain. In her own loneliness, she knew she could not reach deeply enough inside herself to help her son. So, led by dim memories of her own childhood experiences with a neighborhood Sunday school, Jon's mom brought him to the principal's office to enroll her son for the year in a Christian day school.

Like Jon, she stood with her head slightly down, avoiding eye contact. She spoke softly, almost too softly to hear at times. But just before she left the office, she looked up into the principal's eyes. Her words came out firm and clear. "Teach him about Jesus," she said. Then she turned around quickly and walked away.

As the school year began, Jon blended into the woodwork of the second grade classroom. But after a few months, his reading skills showed some improvement. He began to write little stories and share them with his teacher. Once or twice a day, he would smile a slow smile. Sometimes on the playground he would even laugh out loud.

Thanksgiving . . . the Christmas service . . . third quarter parent conferences . . . basketball season . . . Easter—the school year slipped by.

Late one Friday afternoon in early spring, the telephone rang in the principal's office. It was Jon's mom. Jon would not be coming back to school. A drunk driver. A crumpled bicycle. A mangled little body.

At the funeral home, Mom let the principal hold her close as the two cried together. "I'm so sorry, so very sorry," choked the principal. "I wish we could have . . ."

"No, don't . . . don't apologize," the grieving woman whispered through her tears. "I asked you to tell Jon about Jesus. And you did. You did what I asked. Jon is with Jesus now. And we will be, too, someday. Thank you. Thank you for what you gave him. For what you gave me."

Follow Me!

That invitation rang out from Jesus' lips as He called His first disciples. The small band of people He gathered together in first century Palestine would change the world forever. Jesus called and discipled people who would, in turn, disciple others. You and I, Jon and his mom, millions of saints, thousands of martyrs, countless Christian teachers,[1] principals, pastors, and students all form part of a long procession of disciples and disciplers, a procession that stretches in an unbroken chain back through 20 centuries, back to the 12 apostles and to our Lord Jesus Himself.

What attracts people to that man? That question must have raced through the minds of Jesus' enemies hundreds of times. They watched, helpless, as Jesus' popularity mushroomed. They saw thousands follow Jesus out into the countryside to listen, transfixed by His teaching. They heard, to their dismay, a roar of hosannas on Palm Sunday. Jesus taught thousands, fed thousands, healed thousands.

Yet Jesus had much more than simply a first century ministry to the masses. Jesus deeply touched individual hearts and lives:

- At Jesus' call, James and John dropped the nets they were washing and walked away from the fishing business they shared with their father, Zebedee.
- Matthew heard Jesus' call, closed up his tax collector's booth, and forever turned his back on the huge profits possible to the publicans of his day.
- Nicodemus heard Jesus challenge, "You must be born again." The

words burned in his heart as he wrestled with their meaning. A respected and powerful member of the Sanhedrin, Nicodemus put his position on the line for Jesus more than once—and that, so far as we know, after a single, private conversation with Christ.

And so it went. Martha. Zacchaeus. Thaddaeus. Peter. Mary. John. Simon the Zealot. Jesus touched something deep within each of them. Some responded immediately. Some wrestled with His call. But each of them knew life could never be the same again. His call, His touch, changed them forever.

Radical Discipleship

Many rabbis of first century Israel had disciples; Greek philosophers also drew disciples into their sphere of influence—but neither the rabbis nor the philosophers touched the lives of their followers in the powerful way Jesus did.

Christ's concept of discipleship differed radically from the ideas and practices of His day. Disciples often chose rabbis for themselves from whom they hoped to gain deeper insights into the meaning of the Torah. Among the Gentiles, especially the Greeks, young disciples frequently chose gifted philosophers and gathered around them to gain deeper intellectual insights. The disciples of philosophers sometimes even paid for the privilege.

In contrast to all this, Jesus told His disciples, "You did not choose Me, but I chose you . . . to go and bear fruit" (John 15:16). Jesus did the choosing. Jesus did the calling.

More radical still, Jesus called His disciples to a lifetime commitment. He taught no new philosophy. Rather, Christ called people to a new relationship—a relationship with Himself. As Dietrich Bonhoeffer observed, "When Christ calls a man, He bids him come and die."[2]

Jesus called His disciples to die to themselves. He called them to share in His work and in His suffering. He called them to a life of repentance and to a life of abundant joy. Jesus did not claim to be the head of a new school of thought, but rather the living Lord of their lives.[3]

We can call Jesus' view of discipleship *radical* in the deepest sense of that word—it cut to the root of all human existence and

15

all human relationships. It cut to the root of our relationship with God Himself.

In our Lord's own words, He came to "seek and to save what was lost" (Luke 19:10). To understand the radical nature of Christ's mission, we need to look back at Eden and at the heavenly Father's intention when He created human beings.

The Scripture tells us that God made Adam and Eve in His own image. That means, among other things, that Adam and Eve shared God's character. They loved with God's self-forgetful love. Their hearts overflowed with God's perfect justice and mercy. Adam and Eve walked in God's gentleness, kindness, truth, and compassion. They enjoyed unbroken fellowship with their Creator and with each other. God, the Giver, gave to His human creatures complete joy and unimaginable pleasure in His presence. Living in our present, fallen state, we can scarcely imagine their lives. Adam and Eve received an uninterrupted flow of God's goodness, and they reflected that goodness to one another and back to Him.

Satan, of course, hated that relationship. Imagine it! Hundreds, thousands, maybe eventually millions of human beings—each loving as God loves, each reflecting God's holiness, each part of a perfect family that brings perfect worship, honor, and glory to God. The possibilities made hell shudder. And so, Satan crept into Eden to tell the poisonous lie that led to the first human sin.

But sin did not shatter God's dream of creating a family. Even as He went to find Adam crouching in shame and fear behind one of the trees in Eden, God was setting in motion the plan of restoration the Trinity had agreed upon even before the creation.

Many centuries later, Jesus came—not just to rescue, but also to restore. Jesus came so our sins could be forgiven, yes, but also so that God could recreate His image in us. Jesus came to make it possible for each of us to be "little Christs." Jesus came to bring salvation—wholeness—to a world of people broken by sin. The apostle Paul describes it this way:

> For those God foreknew He also predestined to be conformed to the likeness of His Son, that He might be the firstborn among many brothers. And those He predestined, He also called; those He called, He also justified; those He justified, He also glorified. (Rom. 8:29–30)

16

That sums up God's plan for Christian discipleship. We are Jesus' disciples because of what He has done for us, not because of what we have done or could ever do for Him.

At the cross, God placed our sin on Jesus. He then placed the full righteousness of His perfect, dearly loved Son on us. We are—right now—as justified, as forgiven, as loved by God as we ever will be. By our heavenly Father's grace, by our Savior's death and resurrection, by the Holy Spirit's call to us in our Baptism, the core of our being has been transformed. We are God's new creation. We have become disciples, disciples in whom the Holy Spirit works. He molds, shapes, and transforms us until that day we become fully like our Father, fully like our brother, Jesus.

Jesus, the Discipler

Parents delight in a newborn baby, yet they expect that infant to grow and develop. In the natural course of things, that's exactly what happens. Infants become children who become teens who grow into adults. The maturing process continues throughout life.

When Jesus walked on earth, He called disciples to Himself and then began the process of discipling them, of helping them grow up, mature, into His image. As our Lord nurtured the spiritual growth in His disciples, He used specific techniques—teaching techniques, discipling techniques. Good teachers have always relied on techniques like these, but Jesus used them with more skill, more wisdom, and more consistent, life-changing power than any teacher before or since.

Jesus shared His life with His disciples. He did not limit His influence to a 55-minute class period. He did not conceptualize discipling as a six-hour-a-day process. In his gospel, Mark reports that Jesus called the Twelve "that they might be with Him" (Mark 3:14). Even more than the mission to which He called them, Jesus valued the relationship to which He called them. He knew that this relationship would sustain them through the firestorm of persecution they would later face for Him and for His Word.

And so, Jesus ate, drank, slept, laughed, prayed, worked, walked, shivered, and sweated with His disciples. They watched Him up close—all day, every day.

Jesus modeled the attitudes and behavior He wanted to

17

see in His disciples. And it worked! One morning, for example, the Twelve approached Him and asked, "Lord, teach *us* to pray" (Luke 11:1). What prompted this request? What brought about this teachable moment? Jesus had just finished a time of personal prayer. The disciples saw firsthand the comfort and joy that Jesus received from spending time in the Father's presence, and they coveted that kind of power and joy in their own lives.

This modeling process touched the disciples' lives in other ways too. In his gospel, the apostle John often refers to himself as "the disciple whom Jesus loved." John doesn't swagger over that little phrase, boasting about it as a title by which he hopes to prove that He was Jesus' favorite disciple. Rather, John uses these words in utter humility. It's almost as though the thought overwhelmed him: *Jesus loved him—John!*

Astonished by that love, overcome by wonder at the personal love that the Lord of lords so freely offered, John's heart slowly melted. The young zealot who once volunteered to call down fire from heaven on some inhospitable Samaritans became the apostle of love (Luke 9:51ff.).

You see, the love John received from his Teacher carried with it the motivation and the power that enabled him to respond in love toward others. It enabled him to pass that legacy of love on, even to disciples who would live centuries after him. The epistles of John, written toward the end of the apostle's life, repeat again and again these words: "Little children, let us love one another."

Jesus scheduled classroom time with His disciples. As He spent time teaching the disciples, Jesus often told stories—terse, hard-hitting stories. He explained concepts and principles and gave practical examples of how these principles work out in everyday situations. He crafted His lessons so that they touched the heart as well as the head, the spirit as well as the intellect. Then He answered the disciples' questions. And did they have questions!

"Lord, how many times should I forgive my brother when he sins against me?"

"Lord, why do you speak to the people in parables?"

"Lord, if this is the situation between a husband and wife, it is better not to marry!"

"Lord, we've left everything to follow You! What then will there be for us?"

18

CALLED TO BE DISCIPLES, DISCIPLERS

"Lord, what will be the sign of Your coming and of the end of the age?"

"Lord, will You at this time restore the kingdom to Israel?"

Jesus patiently answered all these and many more like them. He often bumped up against the limits of His disciples' abilities to understand, but He continued to teach, to explain, to share new examples. The evangelist Mark records Jesus' parable of the mustard seed and then goes on to say, "With many similar parables Jesus spoke the word to [the crowds], as much as they could understand. He did not say anything to them without using a parable. But when He was alone with His own disciples, He explained everything" (Mark 4:33–34).

Jesus gave His disciples meaningful, practical assignments. Luke tells of a time Jesus gave a very explicit set of directions to 72 of His disciples and then sent them, two by two, into the towns and villages He would soon visit in person. These disciples had watched Jesus' healing ministry. They had observed firsthand the methods He used in dealing with demons. They had absorbed His teaching. After all this, the Lord sent them out to practice what they had observed.

This was no meaningless, busywork assignment. Each pair of disciples functioned as an advance team for the Lord. They prepared the towns and villages for His arrival. Their ministry bears many of the same marks as that of John the Baptizer.

Jesus praised and encouraged His disciples when they experienced success. All good teachers find deep satisfaction when their students show the ability to use outside the classroom what they have learned in class. Jesus found that same satisfaction, and He told His disciples about His pleasure at their progress. Luke details what happened when the 72 returned from the assignment Jesus had given them:

> The seventy-two returned with joy and said, "Lord, even the demons submit to us in Your name."
>
> He replied, "I saw Satan fall like lightning from heaven. I have given you authority to trample on snakes and scorpions and to overcome all the power of the enemy; nothing will harm you. However do not rejoice that the spirits submit to you, but rejoice that your names are written in heaven."

At that time, Jesus, full of joy through the Holy Spirit, said, "I praise You, Father, Lord of heaven and earth, because You have hidden these things from the wise and learned, and revealed them to little children . . ."

Then He turned to His disciples and said privately, "Blessed are the eyes that see what you see. For I tell you that many prophets and kings wanted to see what you see but did not see it, and to hear what you hear but did not hear it." (Luke 10:17–24)

Jesus set His disciples up for success. He gave them the tools and the knowledge they needed to succeed. When they returned, He shared in their joy at the victories they had seen the heavenly Father win for them.

Jesus went on to reinforce some of the important concepts they had learned and practiced. Then the Savior encouraged His disciples to keep their perspective. After all, their names were written in heaven! They were seeing and hearing things that prophets and kings had missed! What honor the Father had given them! How thankful they could be for God's grace and power at work in their lives!

Can't you just see Peter, Thomas, and the rest glow in response to their Lord's words? Can't you imagine the eagerness in their eyes as they awaited their next assignment?

Jesus asked His disciples questions and encouraged them to apply what they already knew. We catch a glimpse of this on the day the Savior fed the 5,000. Almost any Sunday school child remembers Jesus' question to Philip, "Where shall we buy bread for these people to eat?" The Lord already knew what He would do, but He wanted to give Philip a chance to grow as he thought about his Teacher's question.

Even when Philip fumbled, Jesus patiently went on to do what He had planned all along. All four gospel writers tell us that the disciples picked up 12 large baskets of pieces after everyone had eaten a full meal. Can't you see Philip and the others, a bit red in the face, trying to remain inconspicuous as they gather up the pieces and count the dozen baskets of leftovers—one basketful for each of them? Wouldn't you like to have caught a glimpse of Jesus' lesson plan book? How skillfully our Lord used one big problem and one short question to teach a powerful lesson in trust!

Jesus confronted the disciples with their sin. The Savior came to our earth as the "friend of sinners" (Matt. 11:19). That doesn't mean, however, that He overlooked or ignored sin in the lives of His disciples. He sharply scolded Peter on one occasion when this disciple tried to dissuade Christ from His appointment with death by crucifixion (Matt. 16:21ff.).

More than once Jesus took the disciples aside to cool tempers that flared in argument over who would hold the position of greatest honor in the Lord's coming kingdom. Jesus pointedly confronted the disciples' pride. His words must have stung. Yet when the Law had done its work, Jesus spoke words of healing and grace to the disciples.

Jesus prayed for His disciples. That alone must have comforted them beyond words. John invites us to eavesdrop on one of those prayers. Who wouldn't find powerful encouragement in hearing the Son of God intercede for them with words like these:

> [Father,] I have revealed You to those whom You gave Me out of the world. They were Yours; You gave them to Me and they have obeyed Your word. . . . I gave them the words You gave Me and they accepted them. They knew with certainty that I came from You, and they believed that You sent Me. I pray for them. I am not praying for the world, but for those You have given Me, for they are Yours. All I have is Yours, and all You have is Mine. And glory has come to Me through them. . . . Holy Father, protect them by the power of Your name—the name You gave Me—so that they may be one as We are one. . . .

> I pray also for those who will believe in Me through their message, that all of them may be one, Father, just as You are in Me and I am in You. May they also be in Us so that the world may believe that You have sent Me. I have given them the glory that You gave Me. (John 17:6, 8–11, 20–22)

Called to Become Disciplers

Called by Christ to discipleship, the disciples went on, in turn, to disciple others. Even as Jesus prayed for the apostles in the hours before His arrest and crucifixion, He continued to plant within their hearts the seeds of that call: "I pray for those who will believe in Me *through their message.*"

Jesus' call to disciple others did not imply that their own growth in discipleship was now complete. The Lord knew each of them had much more growing to do. Yet He had shown them that He would work through them. He had shared His glory, His power, His love with them. That enabling power would continue to flow into their lives and through their lives to others. The same mighty power on which He relied for His ministry would, at Pentecost, be poured out on them.

They need never doubt their adequacy, their sufficiency, their worthiness. All these things came, not from themselves, but from Him.

The Christian Teacher—Disciple, Discipler

Still today, Jesus gathers disciples to Himself. He shares His life with us. He has given us the Scriptures, which make it possible for us to study His attitudes, His actions, His character. Our Teacher sets up both "lecture" and "lab" experiences for us. He nurtures both our intellectual understanding and our ability to apply His Word in everyday life. He welcomes our questions and gives us assignments. He encourages us as we succeed, even as He reminds us that He empowers our success. He confronts us with our sin. He comforts us with His precious Gospel of forgiveness. He prays for us.

Just as Jesus' first disciples, we grow in His grace. We learn how to use the power He has given us. We learn to love as He loves. We learn how to respond under pressure. We learn how to rely on Jesus as our Rock when the waves of circumstances come crashing in on our lives. Not perfectly, of course. Not always with the consistency we (or Jesus) would like. But still, we continue the process of growth. Jesus continues to work with us, to correct us, to mold and shape us so that little by little, we become more and more closely conformed to His image.

Exciting and challenging as that is, our Lord has even more in mind for us! If Christ has called you to teach in a Christian classroom, He challenges you to think of that calling as one in which—by His grace—you can participate in the discipling process of the students whose lives you touch. He sends you to children like Jon, to parents like Jon's mom. He sends you as His ambassador, as His representative in their lives.

Are you adequate? In yourself, no. Are you worthy? In yourself, no. Is your talent, your ability sufficient? No, and it never will be.

But you don't teach alone! You don't disciple alone! You don't walk into the classroom, the teachers' lounge, the parent conference alone! As our dear brother and fellow disciple, Paul, once wrote:

> Such confidence as this is ours through Christ before God. Not that we are competent in ourselves to claim anything for ourselves, but our competence comes from God. He has made us competent as ministers of a new covenant—not of the letter, but of the Spirit; for the letter kills, but the Spirit gives life. (2 Cor. 3:4–6)

Throughout the rest of this book, we will explore several specific facets of the discipling process:

- We will examine in more detail the methods our Lord uses to enable our own personal discipleship.
- We will learn how we can respond more effectively to our Savior as He nurtures our growth in grace.
- We will explore the reasons Christian teachers need to think of themselves primarily as disciplers.
- We will discover practical ways we can use Jesus' discipling methods in our own classrooms as we participate in the discipling process our Lord directs in the lives of each of our students.

But before we dig into all that, you need to answer an important question. A question of both challenge and joy: Why do I want to teach in a Christian classroom? The next chapter will help you explore that question.

To Think About

1. Think of two or three believers who have discipled you in the Christian faith. How did God use these people in your life? How might you thank these people?
2. Jesus came to rescue and also to restore. He came so our sins could be forgiven, but also so that God could recreate His image in us. How have you seen both Jesus' rescuing work and His restoring work in your own life?
3. If you do not already teach in a Christian classroom, do you want to do so? If you do teach in a Christian classroom, do you want

to continue? Write your reasons for answering as you did. Then share your thoughts with someone you trust before you read chapter 2.

Notes

1. Throughout this text, I have tried to use the phraseology "those who teach in Christian schools" rather than the term "Christian teachers." Literally millions of Christ's people teach in public and private schools around the world; no one would deny they are Christian teachers, or that they witness to our Lord in powerful ways. We thank God for their ministry and for their witness. At times, though, it has seemed wise for the sake of simplicity of language in this work to use "Christian teacher" as a shorthand way to refer to those who serve the church in the called, public ministry.
2. Dietrich Bonhoeffer, *The Cost of Discipleship,* rev. and unabridged (New York: The Macmillan Company, 1963), 99.
3. Gerhard Kittel and Gerhard Friedrich, eds., *Theological Dictionary of the New Testament,* abridged ed. (Grand Rapids: Eerdmans Publishing Company, 1985), 552–62.

CHAPTER 2

Called to Serve
the King's Kids

Suppose that some Saturday morning, as you sit at the breakfast table, you hear the doorbell ring. Suppose you open the front door to see your letter carrier standing outside. He hands you a registered letter, a letter sent by a great and powerful ruler—an emir or king from an oil-rich emirate in the Middle East. As you glance down at the letter, you note that it has your name on it; it is addressed to you—personally.

Now, you do not know this king. But the letter makes it obvious that the king knows you! The letter tells of his concern for you and for your struggles, your problems, your abilities, and your joys. But the letter goes further. The king offers to use all the resources at his command to help you with every struggle you face. And, just for good measure, he closes off his letter by inviting you to become an adopted member of his family.

Something that fantastic could never happen, could it? But, of course, it already has. It has happened—to you and to me.

The King of the entire universe has sought us out, has tracked us down. He has seen our struggles and our problems. He knows each of us intimately. And the King cares—cares desperately—about us as individuals. The psalmist tells us that our King cherishes each one of us so very much that He keeps careful count of our tears, bottling each one (Ps. 56:8).

This King commands wealth and authority beyond our wildest dreams. So great is His power that He flung our universe into existence by simply speaking. His creative Word still holds the universe together (Heb. 1:3).

Most remarkable of all, this King has chosen to call Himself our heavenly Father! He has adopted us as members of His family and has made us His very own heirs—"heirs of God and co-heirs with

Christ" (Rom. 8:17). Just think of it! We share Christ's inheritance with Him!

> You are all sons of God through faith in Christ Jesus, for all of you who were baptized into Christ have clothed yourself with Christ. . . . If you belong to Christ, then you are Abraham's seed, and heirs according to the promise. . . .

> When the time had fully come, God sent His Son, born of a woman, born under law, to redeem those under law, that we might receive the full rights of sons. Because you are sons, God sent the Spirit of His Son into our hearts, the Spirit who calls out, "*Abba,* Father." . . . and since you are a son, God has made you also an heir. (Gal. 3:26–29; 4:4–7)

United with Jesus, our Brother, in Baptism, we have fallen heir to the riches of heaven. Our King has thrown the doors of His throne room open wide to us and invites us to come in, to come home.

Such lavishness is astonishing beyond belief. As Martin Luther once commented on the opening words of the Lord's Prayer, "Our Father who art in heaven":

> If I understood these words in faith—that the God who holds heaven and earth in his hand is my Father—I would conclude that therefore I am lord of heaven and earth, therefore Christ is my brother, therefore all things are mine, Gabriel is my servant, Raphael is my coachman, and all the other angels are ministering spirits sent forth by my Father in heaven to serve me in all my necessities, lest I strike my foot against a stone.[1]

But how could God even think of doing all this for us? After all, He has revealed Himself in the Scriptures as the holy Judge, the one who sees our every act, who hears our every word, who knows our every thought, who understands our every motive. How could God, the all-knowing one, possibly want us in His family? Would an earthly king adopt a traitor? Would an earthly king invite a gang of criminals to join his family?

Certainly not! But that is exactly what we were. Traitors. Rebels. Thieves. Murderers. We hated God. We lived as enemies of the King, enemies quite literally hell-bent for destruction. The Scripture says, "Once you were alienated from God and were enemies in your minds because of your evil behavior" (Col. 1:21).

But the story, praise God, does not end there:

Now He has reconciled you by Christ's physical body through death to present you holy in His sight, without blemish and free from accusation. (Col. 1:22)

Once enemies of the King, we have now become not only His friends, but His children, His heirs—holy, without blemish, free from accusation before the court of heaven. Our King has dropped all charges against us! You see, our King is also our Redeemer. Jesus Christ died for us, and in doing so, paid the price so that now He can rule in our hearts by the Word of His grace. By that grace, He has forgiven our sins.

By that same grace, He has restored our relationship with our heavenly Father. Our Lord now holds His arms open wide to us in invitation. "Come home," He says, "Come, eat at My table. Feast on My love. Drink the wine of My goodness. Let Me hold you close. You are Mine, My precious possession. Please do not doubt My love. Please do not doubt My forgiveness. I want you right here beside Me, receiving My love, forever and ever and ever."

When we see the truth—really see it—God's lavish, forgiving love overwhelms us. It drives us to our knees. It forces us to fall flat on our faces in worship. For you see, the King sacrificed His Son, His own Son, His only Son. For you. For me.

A Picture of Love: Service

Tucked away in a quiet corner of the Old Testament lies the description of a poignant ceremony. This ceremony paints for us one picture of God's lavish love and of the response we, in turn, offer Him:

If you buy a Hebrew servant, he is to serve you for six years. But in the seventh year, he shall go free, without paying anything. If he comes alone, he is to go free alone; but if he has a wife when he comes, she is to go with him. If his master gives him a wife and she bears him sons or daughters, the woman and her children shall belong to her master, and only the man shall go free.

But if the servant declares, "I love my master and my wife and children and do not want to go free," then his master must take him before the judges. He shall take him to the door or the doorpost and pierce his ear with an awl. Then he will be his servant for life. (Ex. 21:2–6)

Slavery was an accepted institution in nearly every culture on earth at the time God led Israel out of Egypt. Because of the hardness of His people's hearts, God allowed the institution to stand in ancient Israel.[2] However, God laid out very specific laws to regulate slavery. These laws made the lives of slaves in Israel much less harsh and dehumanizing than the lives of slaves in surrounding nations.

Even so, only under unusual circumstances could one of God's people become a slave. For instance, sometimes Israelites convicted of theft were sold into slavery. Then, too, those who could not pay their debts could sell themselves. God's law provided, though, that after seven years Hebrew slaves could walk away free—their debt paid, their crime forgotten.

The possibility remained, however, that a slave would become attached to a particularly generous master. Perhaps the master treated the slave kindly and took good care of him. Perhaps during the seven years of service the slave would marry, settle down, and have children. Perhaps the slave would wake up one morning to discover his life better than it had ever been, better than he had ever thought it could be. Suppose that when his years of slavery ended, the slave didn't want to leave. Suppose he had come to love his master? What then?

At that point, slave and owner would present themselves before the authorities. These judges would, doubtless, interrogate the slave. Once satisfied that the arrangement was voluntary, the judges would then order the master to take the slave to the doorpost and, using an awl, pierce the slave's ear. Perhaps a ring of some kind was involved, perhaps not. But either way, the slave had willingly become his master's servant. In love, he would serve his master for life.

In certain ways, this provision in Israel's civil law reflects our relationship of service to our Savior. Seeing His love, experiencing His care, living in His protection, we simply do not want to live for ourselves any more. God's Spirit has led us to the heartfelt conviction: "I love my Master! I do not want to go 'free!'"

God's Spirit has revealed to us the essence of true freedom. God's Spirit has revealed to us the meaning of Jesus' riddle: "Whoever finds his life will lose it, and whoever loses his life for My sake will find it" (Matt. 10:39). We no longer want to live for ourselves and for the trinkets of life that at one time seemed so important.

In his epistles, the apostle Paul often uses words like these to introduce himself: "Paul, a slave of Jesus Christ." Contemporary Bible translations frequently substitute the word *servant* for *slave,* but the original Greek is unmistakably clear; Paul thought of himself as Christ's slave. Yet how wonderful he found his bondage: "I consider everything a loss compared to the surpassing greatness of knowing Christ Jesus, my Lord" (Phil. 3:8). Bound by the King's love, Paul surrendered himself to the King in willing service.

Today—this minute—our King continues to extend His love to His human creatures. Having received that love, we each can respond in joy, "Lord, pierce *my* ear!" Loved, we serve.

A Second Picture of Love: Lives Broken and Poured Out

Do you remember the day Mary of Bethany anointed Jesus' feet while He attended a dinner held in His honor at the home of Simon the leper? It happened shortly after Jesus raised Lazarus, Mary's brother, from the dead. Mary came to Jesus carrying an alabaster jar filled with expensive perfume. She knelt at His feet, broke the jar open, and began to pour its contents on His head and feet. The beautiful fragrance filled the whole house.

The disciples, especially Judas Iscariot, looked on aghast. Then they began to sputter, "Why was this fragrant oil wasted? For it might have been sold for more than three hundred denarii and given to the poor" (Mark 14:4–5 NKJV).

From a human standpoint, we can understand their dismay. A denarius represented a day's pay. In a few fleeting moments, Mary had lavished on Jesus an offering worth a year's wages! Some scholars have suggested the perfume may have been her dowry. Mary's sacrifice left most of those present numb with astonishment. But not the Savior. He received the sacrifice as Mary intended it, as an act of deep adoration.

Jesus would soon pour out His blood, His life, for Mary and for all the Father's disobedient children. He allowed her the honor of breaking the alabaster jar and pouring it out on Him as an expression of love and commitment.

Mary had perhaps only a nebulous idea of what Jesus was about to do for her; we have seen our Savior nailed to the cross, broken

29

for us. Mary had perhaps barely begun to understand the freedom her Savior would win for her; we have experienced the intoxication of that freedom—freedom from the power of sin and Satan.

The Holy Spirit works in our hearts even as He worked in Mary's, and we respond in ever-deepening worship and ever more willing service to our King. As the Spirit works within us, we long to pour out our lives for Him and for His kingdom.

Set Apart for the Gospel

God intends that kind of dedication, that kind of "set apartness," for all His people, regardless of their age, occupation, abilities, or gifts. He wants all of His disciples to grow into the kind of self-forgetful, sacrificial love that serves the King by serving others.

To equip and encourage all of His people to grow in the discipleship and service to which He has called them, God has chosen, gifted, and called some of His disciples into a unique kind of service—public ministry.[3]

But what does this service involve? How does the King make His will known regarding those whom He has chosen to serve others in His name and in the name of His church? Acts 6:1–7 points us in the right direction as we look for answers to these two critical questions. The incident, rare in its clarity about the specific procedures the early New Testament church followed in setting aside workers for public ministry, provides a classic case study:

> In those days when the number of disciples was increasing, the Grecian Jews among them complained against the Hebraic Jews because their widows were being overlooked in the daily distribution of food. So the Twelve gathered all the disciples together and said, "It would not be right for us to neglect the ministry of the Word of God in order to wait on tables. Brothers, choose seven men from among you who are known to be full of the Spirit and wisdom. We will turn this responsibility over to them and will give our attention to prayer and the ministry of the Word."

> This proposal pleased the whole group. They chose Stephen, a man full of faith and of the Holy Spirit; also Philip, Procorus, Nicanor, Timon, Parmenas, and Nicolas from Antioch, a convert to Judaism. They presented these men to the apostles, who prayed and laid their hands on them.

So the Word of God spread. The number of disciples in Jerusalem increased rapidly, and a large number of priests became obedient to the faith.

If we analyze the text closely, we note that the workers identified here received God's call to perform public ministry—ministry on behalf of the Lord and His church—in this way:

- The believers and the apostles together identified a specific ministry need (the distribution of food to the Grecian widows). Up to this time, the task had apparently resided in the apostles' portfolio. God had given the ministry to the church, and the congregation acknowledged this. On the other hand, the Lord held the apostles, as His representatives, responsible for seeing to it that the ministry was done. The congregation acknowledged and honored that too.

- The congregation's spiritual leaders (the apostles), concerned for both God's people and for quality ministry, did not "lord it over" the other believers, but rather asked the congregation to select specific believers who met certain criteria ("full of the Spirit and wisdom").

- The family of believers identified seven men who met the qualifications set up by their spiritual leaders. Presumably the church based its selection on the past words and actions of the seven they chose. Having been faithful in little, the seven were now asked to assume a task that would require that they be faithful in much.

- The apostles concurred with the congregation's recommendation, prayed for the workers, laid hands on them, and set them into active service. By virtue of their ongoing responsibility of oversight before God for the work of His church, the apostles certainly retained some degree of supervision. However, the seven received full authority to do the work which God, through His people, had called them to do. By God's grace, they had been set apart for the Gospel.[4]

The seven carried out a wide variety of work on behalf of the congregation. They functioned in ways similar to those whom the New Testament later calls "deacons," though that specific Greek word does not appear in this particular text. Certainly they administered the daily food distribution to the church's needy as they had

31

been commissioned to do. But at least two of these servants participated also in the church's outreach work:

- The Scripture tells us that Stephen, "full of God's grace and power" (Acts 6:8), performed miracles and proclaimed the message of the Gospel. His witness brought so much consternation to the enemies of the cross that they eventually martyred him.
- Philip also worked as an evangelist—at first in the region of Samaria. Many people came to believe in Christ and to receive Baptism as a result of Philip's witness. So many, in fact, that the church in Jerusalem sent Peter and John to investigate. Even then, the Lord had not finished with Philip. Later on, the Holy Spirit dispatched him to the desert road to intercept the Ethiopian official and to share the Gospel with him so that the official could carry the Good News back to Africa. From there, God sent Philip, the evangelistic deacon, to Azotus. Philip apparently then worked as an itinerant missionary, ministering along the coast of Palestine from one end to the other.

These servants were not unique to the church's ministry. The New Testament mentions many other "deacons"—and "deaconesses" too—who apparently performed various kinds of service on behalf of the Lord Jesus and at the request of His church. Paul, in 1 Tim. 3:8–13, lists the formal qualifications for these workers, qualifications inspired by God's Spirit.

Acts 6, while not meant as a step-by-step how-to manual for congregational organization, does set a precedent and exemplify an important principle: In the early church, the apostles together with all the believers felt free to create the office of "deacon" to make more effective ministry possible. Our Lord approved of their action and evidenced His approval by later formalizing His expectations for workers who, in the name of the church and of Christ, are commissioned to public ministry. We may conclude from this, I believe, that the church today can exercise the same freedom our Lord granted in the first century.

As God's people minister in Christian schools today, our office and ministry please and honor our Lord Christ. Chosen by God and set apart by His people for service, teachers who serve in Christian schools

- realize they belong to the holy Christian church and, as such, treasure the position of priesthood God has given to them and to all believers;
- recognize the church's authority to set aside certain "priests" from their number to perform public ministry;
- acknowledge Christ's call on their own personal lives to share publicly in the ministry God has given His people in that place;
- perform in the name of the congregation specific tasks of service the congregation and its spiritual leadership have identified as part of its mission, Christ's mission, in that place;
- serve in Christ's name, at Christ's command, and in Christ's stead;
- rely on the power and wisdom only the Holy Spirit can provide as they faithfully carry out the ministry entrusted to them.

Teachers who minister publicly in Christian schools share Jesus' love in a holistic way with their students. We care about their faith and we care about their families. We care about their physical needs and about how they get along with others. We plan ways to help them to grow in discipleship and ways to help them grow in their appreciation for God's creation. Who could help but have a sense of excitement and joy in this kind of call! We touch lives forever. We minister on behalf of our King. We serve the King's people. What a fantastic privilege.

But how does God call someone into this work? Or, to personalize the question: How do *I* know if God has set *me* apart for full-time service in public ministry as a teacher in a Christian school? Will I hear God speak to me audibly? Will I see a vision or dream a dream? Will I "just know," down deep in my heart?

Throughout both the Old and New Testaments, we see the King's call come to certain servants directly. The Lord spoke to Moses in the burning bush. Jesus said to Andrew, "Follow Me." Isaiah and Jeremiah saw visions and heard God describe their commission in an audible voice.

Yet down through history the call to public ministry has come to most servants of the King in quieter, less spectacular ways. Take David, for example. The prophet Samuel came to Jesse's family under a cloak of strict secrecy. As the anointing oil ran silently down the young shepherd's head, Samuel solemnly announced God's call. Samuel told David that he would reign as Israel's king—someday.

God's Word through Samuel came true, even though David waited for its fulfillment through a preparation period that lasted 15 years.

Just as quietly, Paul took Timothy under his wing, discipled him for a period of time, and eventually left him in Ephesus as pastor of the church there.

Still today God calls some from among the priesthood of all believers into a full-time, public office. Note that always the initiative rests in God's hands. God chooses. God calls. God sets each of His people as individuals aside for His specific purposes. He gifts and equips each of us in unique ways for unique kinds of service.

How very kind our Lord is! He wants each of His baptized people to experience the maximum degree of effectiveness in their service to Him. He knows that only then will we experience the maximum degree of joy He wants us to have as we live in His kingdom of grace here on this earth. For that reason—because He wants to bless us—He wants each of us to serve in ways that are just right for us.

Martin Luther first tied the idea of "vocation" with the doctrine of the priesthood of all believers. He taught that the members of the holy Christian church serve Christ as priests regardless of the work they do to support themselves financially. A stable boy could see himself as *God's* stable boy—even while he cleaned out stalls. A scullery maid could see herself as *God's* scullery maid—even while she cleaned the dirt off the garden vegetables and as she washed the dishes. Centuries earlier, the apostle Paul had put it like this:

> Whatever you do, work at it with all your heart, as working for the Lord, not for men, since you know that you will receive an inheritance from the Lord as a reward. It is the Lord Christ you are serving. (Col. 3:23–24)

We serve the Lord Christ! We serve a great King, the one who redeemed us! Whatever we do, we do it as to Him. God receives much more glory from a plumber who enjoys her work and who does it well than from a preacher who does not have the temperament to work with his people nor the ambition to study and prepare adequate sermons and Bible class material.

We dare not enter public ministry merely on our own whim or because we find ourselves swept away on a wave of emotion after we hear a missionary speak to our Sunday school class. We dare not stumble into public ministry simply because we think we might like the fringe benefits we imagine we will receive. How terrible it would be if God's purpose for a congregation were disrupted for a minute, let alone for years or decades, because a saint with good intentions presumed—in error—that God had called him into public ministry as a director of Christian education. How terrible it would be if some of God's children wasted most of a school year with a well-meaning Christian teacher who could not teach. How sad for God's people—all of them, the DCE and teacher included.

If our Lord's call to disciple others through full-time public ministry rests on our lives, we certainly would not want to walk away from that call. We would not want to resist the honor He wishes to give us. We would not want to bypass the challenge and joy of that kind of ministry. On the other hand, we want to avoid the sin of presumption. We want to serve the King where and when He asks us to serve.

How can we know?

Some Key Questions

Knowing God's will for our service, like everything else in our walk with our King, depends upon His grace. When we feel unsure about God's direction for our lives, we can ask Him to make it clear. If you think God may be calling you into a public, teaching-discipling ministry in His kingdom, trust Him to guide you as you pray and as you think your way through some basic questions:

What do I enjoy doing? What do I do well?

That may sound a bit frivolous or "unspiritual." Can God possibly care about what I would *like* to do in His kingdom? Yes!

At the risk of repeating myself too many times, I say it again: The King loves us! Our Creator made the entire universe for us with an eye toward beauty and toward bringing us delight (Ps. 104). Our Redeemer told the Twelve in no uncertain terms that He had come so that as His people, we could have life—abundant life (John 10:10). Our Sanctifier marks His presence in our lives at least in part by producing in us the fruit of joy (Gal. 5:22).

The God who created the heavens and the earth does not waste what He has made. If He has given you an aptitude for math, you probably enjoy working with figures and puzzling over equations. If He has given you verbal skills, you probably enjoy writing words that sing on the page or making speeches that move your audience to tears and to action. If He has created you with an eye for beauty, you may have the ability to sculpt, to paint, to draw, and to teach others how to do these things. Whatever abilities your Creator has given you, He wants to help you wring your best work from your mind, your heart, and your hands. He wants you to enjoy all the pleasure, all the ecstasy, that process can involve.

Of course, no one who has served in Christ's kingdom for very long will deny that our King sometimes asks us to do some unpleasant things. However, unhappiness is *not* the hallmark of effective ministry, and it is *not* our Lord's wish to force His servants into a lifetime of misery!

So as you ask yourself whether or not the Lord's call to teach in a Christian school rests on your life, take a close look at your natural interests, talents, and abilities. If you do not like spending time with young children, God is probably not asking you to teach in a Christian preschool. If you have trouble when you try to balance your checkbook, God probably will not ask you to teach math in a Christian high school. On the other hand, if you learn foreign languages with ease, your King may be calling you to teach English on the foreign mission field or to teach Spanish in a Christian high school.

What does God seem to be saying to me through His Word?

Jesus promised that the Holy Spirit would lead His people into all truth. He does that as He works through His Word. As you read through the Scriptures, perhaps certain texts seem to burn themselves into your heart. A passage that I still find particularly meaningful is recorded in 1 Samuel 1 and 2—the birth of Samuel.

Elkanah, Samuel's father, came from the tribe of Ephraim, not Levi, or so some Bible scholars think, based on 1 Samuel 1:1–2. Thus Samuel's mother may have known her son could never become a priest—the law of Moses limited that office to the descendants of Levi. Still, even before her son was born, Hannah dedicated Him to God's service: " 'I give him to the Lord. For his whole life he will be given over to the Lord.' And he [Samuel] worshiped the Lord" (1 Sam 1:28).

The text goes on to record Hannah's hymn of praise, a breathtakingly beautiful description of our Lord in His mercy and majesty.

Every time I read this text, even in elementary school, the Lord spoke to my heart through it. Still today at times when I find myself tired or doubtful about God's purpose for my life, the Lord comforts me with these words. He assures me of His call, and I pray the words of Hannah's hymn back to Him.

Do you sit up a little straighter in the pew when your pastor preaches about Isaiah's call (Isaiah 6)? Does the account of Jeremiah's ministry tug at your heart? Does God seem to shout as you read Jesus' call to the Twelve or His Great Commission? Do you find yourself drawn to other parts of Scripture in which God seems to be telling you of His purpose for your life?

If so, don't ignore it! Read those texts carefully. Study them. Pray about the words. Ask God to reveal His will. Ask Him to keep you on track as you gather more evidence and as you continue to rely on His guidance.

What do other, more mature Christians who know me say about me? Do they see ministry gifts in me and will they help me grow in these gifts?

Maybe your pastor has noticed that you seem to have a gift for communicating Jesus' love to young children or for encouraging senior adults in their faith. Maybe the DCE in your congregation feels confident in asking you to help out with a VBS or Sunday school class. Maybe others in your congregation have seen God-given ministry gifts in you. Perhaps they have not said anything to you. You need to ask.

Make an appointment with someone whose Christ-centered wisdom you respect. Give those people who know you well an opportunity to share their observations with you. Urge them to be honest. Ask them to pray with you and for you.

What kind of results do I see when I use the abilities God has given me?

Ask God to help you find a way to try out specific kinds of ministry. Ask that He send one or more gifted mentors into your life, people who can guide you and who can give you specific feedback on your performance. Then draw upon God's grace as you serve faithfully in small ways. Gradually, as you mature in your abilities, God will find a way to increase your responsibilities.

During the weeks and months of service that follow, you may become more and more aware of the joy and peace of the Holy

Spirit rising in your own heart. The work may be difficult. Perhaps no one will thank you for what you have done; maybe they will not even notice you. But if you experience God's joy with some consistency, and if you begin to see other believers bear more fruit as a result from your work, take that as an additional piece of evidence that God may be calling you to that kind of service.

Will those to whom we minister always bear more and more fruit? We must answer that question with a cautious no. The scriptural precedents demonstrate that God sometimes places His servants into fields of ministry which seem infertile. In fact, the Bible points on rare occasions to those who go on serving even though they never live to see the results of their ministry.

For example, Bible scholars often call Jeremiah "the weeping prophet." Despite many decades of ministry, Jeremiah's powerful preaching seemingly achieved very little—so little, in fact, that the prophet often wept in frustration and discouragement.

Nevertheless, several decades after Jeremiah had gone home to be with His Lord, Daniel read and believed Jeremiah's prophetic words—God's promise that Judah would return to the Promised Land. On the basis of that prophecy, Daniel began to pray that God would fulfill His Word (see Dan. 9:1ff.). Shortly thereafter, the remnant of God's people began their return from exile. The exiles, Daniel included, held God's promises through Jeremiah close to their hearts. Still today Jeremiah's words confront God's people with their sins and comfort God's people with His grace.

Jeremiah's ministry was not futile, despite outward appearances to the contrary. All those whom God has called can confidently assert with St. Paul that our "labor in the Lord is not in vain" (1 Cor. 15:58). The King's servants need not always see a bumper crop of fruit.

However, under ordinary circumstances God will let His servants see some of the fruit that results from the ministry into which He has called us and for which He has gifted us. We work with the most potent, life-changing force in the universe—God's Word. The Scriptures often speak of the harvest that Word germinates, nurtures, and ripens in the hearts and lives of those touched by it. The prophet Isaiah encourages the servants of the Word with this promise:

> As the rain and the snow come down from heaven, and do not return to it without watering the earth and making it bud and

flourish, so that it yields seed for the sower and bread for the eater, so is My Word that goes out from My mouth: It will not return to Me empty, but will accomplish what I desire and achieve the purpose for which I sent it. (Is. 55:10–11)

Has God gifted me in ways that will enable me to teach and disciple others?

Our Creator has invested many rich gifts in each of His human creatures. Each of God's human creatures can say with the psalmist, "I am fearfully and wonderfully made" (Ps. 139:14). In addition, the Scriptures tell us that God gives each member of His family one or more particular gifts—some have called these "spiritual gifts"—to be used as we serve Him for the benefit of others.

We cannot always tell where a specific, created ability or talent leaves off and a spiritual ability, worked by the Holy Spirit, begins. Nor is that dissection necessary. The natural talents and abilities given to us by God our Creator blend and mix with the spiritual gifts given us by God our Sanctifier to equip us for the most effective service possible.

On the one hand, knowing God gifts us for the ministries into which He calls us can keep us from tripping into the chasm of spiritual pride, especially when we begin to see the results God brings about through us. On the other hand, it can also keep us from leaping into the pit of discouragement when we look at the challenges of our ministry in light of our own inadequacies. Since God has gifted us, we can count on His adequacy, not on our own.

In several places, the New Testament talks about the ways God gifts His people and explains how to use the gifts we receive from Him. One gift the Holy Spirit includes in these lists is the gift of teaching.

Sometimes those who teach physics or economics or reading in a secular context are said to be "gifted teachers." God has given these people a marvelous gift, a First Article gift we might say. No one would dispute the fact that good teachers need a basic understanding of the science, math, art, or history they will teach. Good teachers read professional journals and use educational methodology based solidly on the best current research. God has allowed human beings to discover many powerful principles that help teachers understand how young minds learn and develop. He has given us such knowledge as one of His good gifts to us in His creation. How foolish we would be to ignore what psychologists and those who study human growth and development have learned!

However, as we read the biblical texts that deal with the Holy Spirit's gift of teaching, we quickly see that the New Testament writers did not have a degree from the University of Corinth in mind. We do not receive this distinctive gift of God's grace through any university or from any course of study devised by human beings. Neither can we reduce this gift to simply a natural knack, talent, or ability.

From the outset, I must admit that we are dealing here with mysteries too deep for finite human minds—my own certainly included. However, the Scriptures seem to indicate that God's Spirit takes the natural teaching skills and abilities which God has created in a given individual and enhances them, co-opts them in our Baptism as it were, for the good of His people and His kingdom.

Thus, someone gifted by God's grace with the ability to teach in His church has the ability to explain God's Word clearly and to help God's people apply it to the nitty-gritty stuff of daily life. This gift can go further still, to include the ability to see and to help others see God's fingerprints, as it were, on the entire created universe—not in an artificial way, but in a way that genuinely recognizes and glorifies the Lord of creation. An astronomy lesson can vibrate with excitement over black holes and quasars as the students come to understand that their study of these things brings glory to the God who created the highest heavens. Students in a physical education class can dance with joy at the chance to stretch and run and throw and kick to the glory of God who not only created, redeemed, and is sanctifying their spirits and souls—but also their bodies (1 Thess. 5:23).

In a way that baffles our limited human understanding, God takes the "natural" abilities He has created within us, adds the knowledge and insight we gain as we study and learn from others, and then—and this is the mysterious part, the part which the Scriptures do not seem to thoroughly explain—He adds the power of His Spirit. He takes our abilities beyond innate human talent, beyond proficiencies we can develop in ourselves.

But note this well—He does not work these abilities in us primarily for us as individuals. God gifts His people so we can use the gifts He gives us *for others:*

> Now to each one the manifestation of the Spirit is given *for the common good.* . . . You are the body of Christ, and each one of you is a part of it. And in the church God has appointed first of all apostles, second prophets, third teachers. (1 Cor. 12:7, 27–28; emphasis added)

God gives the gift of teaching because of His deep concern that His people be taught. Left to ourselves, none of us could understand God's Word. Left to our own insight and skill, none of us could adequately communicate the deep truths of God. God gives the gift of teaching because His people need teachers!

Most important, God gives this gift, as He gives all other spiritual gifts, only by His grace. He chooses whom He will call and whom He will gift for a particular kind of service. None of us receives the gift of teaching because we deserve it, because we have worked hard enough for it, or because we have met some standard of personal holiness. It comes to us purely as a gift from our King and Father:

> We who are many form one body, and each member belongs to all the others. We have different gifts, *according to the grace given us.* If a man's gift is prophesying, let him use it in proportion to his faith. If it is serving, let him serve; if it is teaching, let him teach; if it is encouraging, let him encourage. (Rom. 12:5–8; emphasis added)

This truth removes the possibility of pride. The King never calls His people into ministry or gifts them in that ministry so they can parade their privilege and position. Rather, He calls them as servants. He calls them to disciple others as they pour out their lives for Him.

When we begin to catch sight of the scope of God's call and of the responsibilities He has entrusted to us, we begin to recognize beyond doubt our personal incompetence to do what needs to be done. With Paul we ask, "Who is equal to such a task?" (2 Cor. 2:16). Then we wait for God's answer:

> Such confidence as this is ours through Christ before God. Not that we are competent in ourselves to claim anything for ourselves, but our competence comes from God. He has made us competent as ministers of a new covenant. (2 Cor. 3:4–6)

Our King calls us by grace to serve publicly for Him. Then He makes us competent, again by His grace. That's both humbling and encouraging. Luther once wrote, "When God contemplates some great work, He begins it by the hand of some poor, weak, human creature to whom He afterwards gives aid, so that the enemies who seek to obstruct it are overcome."[5]

It seems obvious that someone whom God has gifted with the ability to teach His Word will grow in the desire to study that Word and to understand the deep truths of God. Such a servant will demonstrate an increasing ability to explain God's Word to others in such a way that they understand it too. Perhaps most telling of all, someone with this gift will experience deep satisfaction in helping others put God's Word to work, in helping others apply the truths and principles of God's Word in specific, day-to-day situations. In other words, a person whom the Holy Spirit gifts as a teacher experiences great satisfaction in seeing someone else grow and mature in God's grace.

If you see these traits in yourself and if others who know you well see them, too, it may indicate that the Holy Spirit has given you the gift of teaching. It may indicate that God is calling you to serve Him in one or another aspect of public ministry as you teach and disciple others.

Keep in mind, though, that the gift of teaching, like any other of the Spirit's gifts, needs time to mature. It does not suddenly spring up in God's servants, full-grown, overnight. Jesus spent three years teaching His disciples and preparing them for their ministry. Paul spent time discipling Timothy and Titus, too, so that they in turn could disciple others. Priscilla and Aquila spent time with Apollos, teaching him to understand the Scriptures more accurately. The Holy Spirit gifts His servants and then nurtures those gifts—most often through the ministry of other believers who share those same gifts.

- *What do I enjoy doing? What do I do well?*
- *What is God saying to my heart through His Word?*
- *What do other, more mature Christians who know me say about me? Do they see gifts in me that will enable me to serve God's people, and will my mentors help me grow in these gifts?*

- *What kind of results do I see when I use the abilities God has given me?*
- *Do I experience joy as I minister even in small ways? Has God helped me to be faithful in little, and is He giving me opportunities to be faithful in more?*
- *Is God's creation and the study of it a "spiritual" thing for me?*

All these questions will help as you think about whether God is calling you into the full-time teaching ministry. In addition, you will want to consider your response to two final questions:

What do my circumstances seem to say to me?

Circumstances can sometimes help us think through God's will. For instance, we may think we hear God asking us to serve Him as a director of Christian education. But if we find it impossible to raise money for books and tuition no matter where we turn, we might want to go back to the throne room to ask our Lord whether we have heard Him clearly—both about the ministry and the timing He has in mind for that ministry.

We may think we feel God's hand on our shoulder, guiding us toward ministry as a counselor in a Christian school. But if we consistently run up against a stone wall whenever we apply to a graduate school of psychology, we may need to ask our King to clarify His call and some of the details of the service He has in mind for us.

Even if you encounter difficult circumstances, you need to keep in mind the fact that Satan often uses circumstances to dissuade and discourage God's servants. When we hit a roadblock, most often we do not immediately know whether it represents the enemy's harassment or whether it means that God has shut the door on a specific set of plans we have made. We dare not base any of our decisions, least of all decisions about ministry, strictly on our circumstances.

When we encounter obstacles, we can go to our King and ask His help in finding a way around them or over them. We may even ask for the courage to go through them. If the obstacle comes from the enemy, our King will intervene on our behalf, perhaps even in a spectacular way, sovereignly setting aside Satan's harassments. At other times, our Lord will provide the wisdom, courage, and persistence we need to slog through the morass of Satan's schemes to the high ground on the other side.

In whatever way our Lord chooses to deliver us and to put us back on the road to full-time service to His people, we can rejoice in those victories with renewed confidence and courage. Such intervention by our King for us reveals something of the depth of His commitment to the service He has in mind for us. We can be sure that our Lord will work with us to help us find a way to defeat Satan's schemes to derail our ministry.

On the other hand, if God shuts a door to ministry, we will not find a way to open it, no matter how hard we pray and struggle. If we find ourselves up against truly insurmountable circumstances, we may with confidence begin to ask God to show us an alternative door of service. And we can trust Him to walk with us through that door.

So then, after you think about your circumstances and pray about them, start out in a direction that seems right. Remember that no one can change the course of a ship that lies dead in the water. As you yield to the Lord's will for your life, you can trust Him to turn the rudder for you if He finds you off course.

A final, crucial question: What is my heart telling me?

As you ask your King about His will for you, part of the answer will very likely come as His still, small voice speaks His assurance and His challenge to your heart. If so, ask Him to increase your desire, your zeal, your commitment. You can count on your King to clarify and confirm the specific service He has in mind for you. He doesn't want His servants to wonder and guess about His will. He doesn't leave us to muddle through a maze of confusion all alone. He loves us! And He wants to make His direction for our lives plain.

A Final Touchstone

Down through the centuries, God's people have struggled to keep a proper balance between the subjective and objective evidence of the King's call. Those of us who feel God's joy and peace about serving Him in a certain way study and work to prepare for that kind of service. During that process, we continually seek the counsel of trusted and wise believers who provide encouragement and further input about the specific direction in which the Lord may be leading. This evidence of God's call is full of comfort and promise.

Still, all of us occasionally find ourselves questioning our ministry, our vocation, our call. God Himself may at times encourage us to reassess our ministry and our commitment to His service. But in such reassessment we can sometimes slip over the muddy cliff of doubt. When that happens, we may be sure that our enemy, Satan, lurks in the shadows somewhere close by. When he attacks us, when he tells us that we and our ministry amount to nothing, when he screams his lies long and loud in our ears—at times like these, we need the assurance that our King has indeed entrusted us with a distinctive work.

When the warm, settled feelings of personal confidence in our call and work disappear, we need the comfort that comes from the objective fact of our Lord's call. How does that objective call come to us?

In the same spirit of freedom and concern for quality ministry as we saw in Acts 6, God's people in local congregations today meet together with the spiritual leaders God has given them. God's people seek His will for them and for their corporate ministry in a given parish. The Lord of the church helps them identify specific areas of service He has in mind for them. As they acknowledge that need, they may decide to extend a call in the King's name, asking an individual servant of Christ to provide public leadership in that ministry.

The person who receives that call may be led by God to accept it. If so, the worker and the congregation alike can confidently rest in the knowledge that God has entrusted the worker with that particular ministry. As the worker lives in repentant faithfulness, the King will give that person the gifts needed to fulfill that ministry.

When the winds of doubt blow sharp, when the feelings of willing servanthood evaporate, when Satan lies to us about our effectiveness, when the people whom we serve forget to appreciate us—and even if they attack us—we need never throw up our hands in despair. Our King is faithful to the servants He has called. He watches over us and over the Word we speak in His name. He calls us to be faithful. Then He assumes the responsibility for producing results from our work. Please note: He assumes *all* the responsibility for those results.

Sent to Serve the King

Loved by our King. Called by our King. Gifted and empowered by our King. Sent by our King as one of His children to serve others who are also His children. What an assignment! What an inheritance!

But if we expect to disciple the children and young people our Lord entrusts to us, we ourselves must be growing in our own discipleship, in our own personal relationship with Christ. How does that happen? How do we grow in grace and faith?

The next chapter will challenge you to think through the critical process, the one and only process, that makes spiritual growth possible.

To Think About

1. Analyze Acts 6:1–7. To do so, outline the events in the sequence in which they transpired. Who did what and when? What did this exercise reveal to you about responsibility, authority, and ministry in the body of Christ as the early church saw it?
2. Read Luke 22:24–30. Why do you suppose the Twelve had this argument repeatedly? Do those in public ministry today ever repeat this debate? Explain. What do Jesus' words say to your heart as you think about the office to which Christ calls you.
3. Suppose someone asks you, "How do I know if God is calling me into public ministry in His church?" How would you help that person answer this question? What subjective evidence would you urge that person to consider? To what objective evidence could you point?
4. Imagine yourself serving a Christian congregation in some office of public ministry and imagine yourself feeling defeated in your calling because you fail to see much happening as the result of your work. What factors would you want to keep in mind as you think through this problem?

Notes

1. Luther's Works (Philadelphia: Fortress Press, 1967), 54:9.
2. See Mark 10:5ff. in which Jesus discusses divorce (a societal problem similar in

many respects) and explains God's reasons for giving laws that both allowed and regulated it.

3. An understanding of the office of the holy ministry and its relationship to other offices in Christ's church, while critically important, is beyond the scope of this book. For a more indepth discussion of this doctrine see the following:

    The Ministry: Offices, Procedures, and Nomenclature, Report of the Commission on Theology and Church Relations of The Lutheran Church—Missouri Synod, September 1981.

    Eugene F. Klug, "Augsburg V: Intent and Meaning of the Confessors on 'Ministry,' " *Concordia Journal* (January 1991):30–41.

    Samuel H. Nafzger, "The CTCR's Report on 'The Ministry,' " *Lutheran Education* (January–February 1983):132–55.

4. This episode, by the way, details the procedures God's people used in issuing what has come to be know as a "mediate call"—a call from God through His church (e.g., Stephen, Philip) as differentiated from an "immediate call," one which comes directly from God to the servant without the action of any human agency (e.g., Saul of Tarsus, Isaiah).

    A brief, but useful discussion of the distinction between the immediate and mediate call appears in Luther's commentary on Gal. 1:1. See Luther's Works, 26:17–21.

5. Thomas S. Kepler, ed., *The Table Talk of Martin Luther* (Grand Rapids: Baker Book House, 1952), 44.

CHAPTER 3

Law and Gospel—in My Life, in My Ministry

I rolled onto my side and pulled the covers up more tightly around my neck. A dim winter sun streamed in the window. The alarm clock shrilled. I reached out from under the pile of blankets just long enough to hit the snooze bar—for the third time that morning.

Sunday. I knew I had to crawl out of bed and into the shower. Within one minute. Otherwise, I would find myself walking into the worship service during the last stanza of the first hymn. I lay still. Thoughts of the past several weeks came tumbling through my mind.

So many demands. So little time. So many needs among the children in my classroom. So many meetings at church. So many parent contacts. So much energy—all of it now spent.

As the mosaic of ministry moved slowly through mind, I made a decision. I could not handle one more thing. Not this morning, anyhow. I rolled over again, hit the clock's off button, shivered, and turned up the electric blanket.

Hard as I tried, I could not drift back to sleep. My conscience refused to adjust so quickly to such aberrant behavior. It began to protest. I closed my eyes. The volume of protest rose. In self-defense, I switched on the radio and began fumbling with the dial, trying to find a Christian program with which to salve my guilt feelings.

Tuning from station to station, I landed on a one-sentence sermon I have never forgotten. "Sometimes," the preacher said, "we get so busy giving our service to God that we have no time or energy left over to give ourselves to Him."

In that instant I knew that I had heard a message directly from the King Himself, a message addressed to me. This one-sentence sermon initiated a time of self-examination, in fact, a complete reappraisal of my ministry—a reappraisal which ended, several months later, in a dramatic new direction for my ministry.

God's Priorities

The truth may surprise you as much as it surprised me that morning, but God's main concern for your life is not primarily your ministry; what concerns God most of all is *you!* You see, your King wants to spend time with you. He wants to help you get to know Him better and better. He wants to help you realize His love in deeper and more intimate ways. He wants to give you a fuller experience of worship. To put it succinctly, Jesus cares, first and foremost, about the relationship He shares with you. Our God is a personal God. As Luther once put it:

> The life of Christianity consists in its possessive pronouns. It is one thing to say, "Christ is a Savior"; it is quite another thing to say, "He is my Savior and my Lord." The devil can say the first; the true Christian alone can say the second.

Of course, the more mature your own discipleship, the more ably you will disciple those whom He entrusts to your care. Even so, the Lord is not interested in helping you grow in your own discipleship simply as a means to some other end—not even a laudable end, like your effectiveness in ministry. Often times, those whom the Holy Spirit has called into full-time public ministry find this truth either hard to believe or easy to ignore. But the Scripture is crystal clear: God gave up His Son into death for you so that He could enjoy an eternity of fellowship with you. He looks upon His relationship with you—with you personally—as a very precious and important thing.

Keeping that top priority in mind, God has laid careful plans for your personal spiritual growth. Like all good teachers, our Lord has specific goals in mind. Discipleship goals. Goals that will bring you satisfaction and joy. Goals that will bring Him glory.

God has always had the same goals for all His people; He has never kept them a secret. Scripture returns to them again and again. Psalm 78, for example, begins with our Lord's commission to godly parents, especially to fathers. Here our Lord patiently and precisely explains the crucial discipling role He wants parents to play in the lives of their children.

But as we study these verses, we quickly see that the psalmist's words also have a wider application. They summarize the goals God has for all of His people:

[The Lord] decreed statutes for Jacob
    and established the Law in Israel,
which He commanded our forefathers
    to teach their children,
so the next generation would know them,
    even the children yet to be born,
    and they in turn would tell their children.
Then they would put their trust in God
    and would not forget His deeds
    but would keep His commands.
They would not be like their forefathers—
    a stubborn and rebellious generation,
whose hearts were not loyal to God,
    whose spirits were not faithful to Him.

(Ps. 78:5–8)

Do you see the four basic goals our Lord lists in these verses? That from infancy through adulthood all of us as Christ's disciples will

1. put our trust in God;
2. remember God's deeds;
3. keep God's commands;
4. have loyal hearts, faithful toward God.

Holy Scripture details many, many of our Lord's specific objectives for us and for the students whom we disciple (e.g., confidence in our Father's forgiveness for our sins, peace and joy in our relationship with God, a regular pattern of worship with other believers, basic honesty in our relationships, love for our neighbors, respect for those in authority). But all of these specific objectives for our relationship with God and with others can be grouped under one of the four overarching goals mentioned in the psalm. Let's take a quick, closer look at each of them:

That we may put our trust in God. Christianity grounds itself in the bedrock of God's grace. First and foremost, we believe that God has reached out to us and has made it possible for us to enjoy an intimate, personal, eternal relationship with Him through the redemption Christ Jesus has won for us by His life, death, and resurrection. We Christians believe that, as the Holy Spirit graciously works within us, we come to trust God for forgiveness and for the priceless gift of eternal life.

50

But so kind and compassionate is our heavenly Father that He invites us to trust Him for even more. The New Testament word often translated as "salvation" also connotes concepts like peace, healing, wholeness. Our God cares about us as total persons. He wants us to come to Him for whatever we need. He invites us to lean on Him as we face all the troubles and struggles of daily life. Trusting His total care for us, we receive courage to face each new day.

That we may not forget God's deeds. God has rooted Christianity deep in the soil of human history. Unlike religions invented by human beings, the Christian faith affirms that God has acted and continues to act in the lives of the people who live on planet earth. God has said and done specific things at specific times in specific places. He has seen to it that specific people witnessed His deeds and recorded these deeds for us. God's sacred record, the Holy Scriptures, gives many precise details about these events:

> We did not follow cleverly invented stories when we told you about the power and coming of our Lord Jesus Christ, but we were eyewitnesses of His majesty. . . . And we have the word of the prophets made more certain, and you will do well to pay attention to it, as to a light shining in a dark place, until the day dawns and the morning star rises in your hearts. (2 Peter 1:16, 19)

As the apostle Peter here affirms, well-meaning leaders in the early Christian church did not simply create a series of religious stories to manipulate the faithful. God actually said and did the things the Scriptures report Him to have said and done. It would be difficult to overestimate the importance of this truth. The apostle Paul, for example, waves the banner of Christ's physical resurrection as he exclaims, "If Christ has not been raised, your faith is futile; you are still in your sins" (1 Cor. 15:17).

Standing firm on this historic fact, Paul dares the enemies of the cross. We can almost hear him shout the challenge: "Try to refute it, cynics! Disprove it, Satan! But you never will! For we know beyond doubt that Jesus Christ walked away from death's dungeon. The tomb is empty! And now we stand forgiven before all heaven! Come and see!"

We do not learn historic facts about God and His deeds so that we can win at some cosmic game of spiritual Trivial Pursuit. God wants His people to know His deeds because in coming to know what He has done, we come to know Him—our God, our Father, our King—better and better. God's deeds reveal His character. His deeds warn, comfort, and encourage us. They teach us to know and rely on our great God of love and power. They equip us for the spiritual battles we must fight.

That we may keep God's commands. God gave His Law as a gift of love to His enemies. He intended that His Law show sinners their need for the Savior. But once the Law has done that, and once the Holy Spirit has melted our hearts with the Gospel so that we receive from Him the gift of a new life, the Law continues to bring benefits into our lives.

God gives His Law to His children as an undeserved gift of kindness. God's Law gives specific directions as to how we can live lives of deep fulfillment, joy, and peace. God's Law also explains ways we can bring these blessings into the lives of those around us. Our Creator made us to bring glory to Him and to enjoy fellowship with Him and with one another. The Law functions, then, as a kind of "manufacturer's handbook"; it tells us how to fulfill the purposes our Maker has always intended for us.

Of course, the Law has no power to help us do the things it directs us to do. Once God has used His Law to help us set our course, the Gospel must provide the energy, the ability we need to obey God's commands. Still, the Law—rightly used—comes to us as God's gift for our good.

That we may have loyal hearts, faithful to God. The psalmist explains this point in fuller detail by reminding us of Israel's negative example down through most of the nation's history. These people lived, for the most part, in stubborn disobedience and open rebellion. Worse still, their outward sins grew like noxious weeds from the soil of disloyal hearts.

All sin, as Jesus would later tell His disciples, begins first with an attitude, an inclination toward evil that lies deep beneath the surface. All open rebellion and disobedience begins as "heart trouble":

Out of the heart come evil thoughts, murder, adultery, sexual immorality, theft, false testimony, slander. These are what make a man "unclean." (Matt. 15:19–20)

God wants each of His people to walk before Him with a contrite heart. He wants each of us to serve Him with an undivided heart. He wants each of us to present to Him a loyal, faithful heart. He eagerly looks for righteous *actions* in His people's lives, but He looks more eagerly still for righteous *attitudes*.

Faith. Facts. Actions. Attitudes. These four words sum up the areas of our Lord's concern for us as we continue to mature in Christian discipleship.

Fruitfulness or Frustration?

Henry David Thoreau once wrote, "The mass of men lead lives of quiet desperation." Sad to say, many Christians find their lives filled with a quiet frustration, if not despair. Many have, as Dwight L. Moody observed, "just enough Christianity to make them miserable." People like that know enough about Jesus to identify areas of their lives where change is needed, but they do not understand how to plug into the power of God in such a way as to make those changes possible.

All those who know Jesus Christ want to be like Him. As Paul says of us, "If anyone is in Christ, he is a new creation; the old has gone, the new has come!" (2 Cor. 5:17).

It may well be the best-kept secret of the Christian faith: Our Lord has not called us to a life of frustration. Rather, He has called us to a life of fruitfulness. He wants us to grow as His disciples to the point that, by His grace, we bear abundant fruit.

To move from frustration to fruitfulness, we must understand and consistently apply two key doctrines of Holy Scripture—Law and Gospel. Only as the Holy Spirit counsels and encourages us through His Word in this way can we begin consistent growth toward Christ-likeness. Then, and only then, will we find our own personal discipleship exciting and fulfilling. Then, and only then, will we have anything of real value to share with our students.[1]

Law and Gospel in Justification

Whether they use these terms or not, every true Christian grasps the difference between Law and Gospel for justification.

The Law, of course, thunders its thou shalts and thou shalt nots. Written in our hearts, the Law dogs our steps, demanding of us perfect thoughts, perfect words, perfect deeds. It sets a standard that no human being can attain; it requires 100 percent compliance with its regulations. The Law shouts accusations at us. It exposes each of our specific sins in wretched detail. It forces us to recognize our complete inability to resist sin's power in our own strength.

The Law goes further still. It paints a picture of God's impending judgment and of the punishment we inarguably deserve for our rebellion.

The Gospel, on the other hand, demands nothing from us. It comes to us as a kind invitation from our loving Father. Instead of demanding righteousness from us, it declares that God has already given us His righteousness because of what our dear Lord has done for us. The Gospel presents Christ as our Substitute, the one who drank the bitter wine of God's wrath to the dregs—for us.

The Gospel goes further. It promises that God gives the free gift of eternal life to all those who believe in Jesus as their personal Savior from sin. The Gospel declares us free from sin, from death, and from Satan's power. We need not, in fact we cannot, do anything to earn these benefits. They come to us without any effort or merit at all on our part. They come solely as free gifts of God's grace.

The Holy Spirit gives us faith to believe the promises of the Gospel. Thus we escape the threats of the Law. By God's grace, we become the Father's new creation. By His grace, we become His heirs, members of His family, part of His royal priesthood. And, yes, our King, our Teacher, also confers on us the title disciple.

Almost any fourth-grader, given the proper instruction, can discriminate statements of Law from statements of Gospel. It seems so simple, almost childishly so. But do not let Satan or your own flesh deceive you. In his Thesis III, Dr. Walther asserts the following:

> To distinguish properly between Law and Gospel is the most difficult and exalted skill of Christians and theologians, a skill that only the Holy Spirit teaches in the school of experience.

Walther then goes on to comment:

> Some of you may perhaps think, "What? Is that really true? . . . Can this be the most difficult skill? I have mastered it." But, my dear friend, you are badly mistaken! Bear in mind, the thesis does not

mean that the doctrine of Law and Gospel is so difficult that it could not be learned without the assistance of the Holy Spirit. It is easy, even for children. Every child can grasp this teaching; . . . it is not strong meat, but milk. . . .

But here we are speaking about its application and function. It is the practical application which is so difficult that no human being can achieve it on the basis of his own reflection. The Holy Spirit must teach it to us in the school of experience.[2]

We probably struggle little, if at all, as we think intellectually about the concepts of Law and Gospel. The slippery work begins as we apply these two doctrines, especially in the area of sanctification.

The Law's Role in Sanctification

Many Christians view their growth in sanctification as a kind of spiritual do-it-yourself project. They willingly admit they can do nothing to save themselves, but they believe that they must somehow sanctify themselves. Once they have received God's free gift of salvation, they assume they must take charge of their own sanctification, their own growth in discipleship.

Christians caught up in moralism like this often use terms like *try,* or *try hard,* or *try harder.* They set the Law in place like a ladder, grit their teeth in determination, and begin to climb, rung-by-rung, toward Christ-likeness. Immediately, the basis of their relationship with Christ slips from grace to a concern with performance. Such believers conveniently forget or ignore the fact that God's Law never says *try*; God's Law says *do.*

Believers who insist on living under the Law in this way often end up in despair. After they have fallen on the sharp rocks of the Law's demands time after time, they begin to believe that their faith is somehow faulty. They carry a tremendous load of guilt. They feel inadequate. They begin to wonder how God could possibly love them. Eventually, most give up. They conclude that Christian maturity is a mirage. They may even come to look with suspicion on anyone interested in spiritual growth.

At the other extreme lie those believers who trick themselves into believing they actually have clambered up the ladder under their own steam. They believe they have kept the Law, or the important parts of it anyway. Like the Pharisees of the New Testament, they feel slightly superior to those of us who still slog along in the swamp of temptation and who still sometimes slip into disobedience.

No matter how diligently we search, we will never find any scriptural evidence that God gave us His Law as a ladder. Rather, His Word describes it as a mirror.[3] A mirror makes it possible for us to see the smudges on our face. But no one in her right mind ever tried to wash her face with a mirror!

God's Law can point out our sin. And, the Law, like a compass, can point us in the right direction as we follow our Savior down the road of discipleship. But the Law cannot help us get rid of sin— its guilt or its power. The Law cannot give us the desire or the strength we need to pick up our feet and walk down the path of discipleship. The Law is powerless to produce the fruit of sanctification in Christ's disciples.

Only the Gospel can do that.

The Gospel's Role in Sanctification

God justifies us by grace. What a marvelous truth! But equally marvelous is this: God also sanctifies us by grace!

We will never become good by trying hard. The students who sit under our teaching will never grow in their discipleship by trying hard, either. God has already declared us good, holy, righteous. He has already made us His disciples. The Holy Spirit leads us to believe that. Then He begins the sanctifying process by which we live out the new life He has placed in our hearts.

This is not just theological double-talk or religious mumbo jumbo. It makes a tremendous difference in how we look at our relationship with God. This truth can literally revolutionize a believer's life. God wants to lift from our shoulders the crushing burden of responsibility for our own spiritual growth. If we are honest with ourselves, we know that we could never carry it anyway.

But if God does not expect us to "try hard" to obey Him, then what does He expect? How exactly does sanctification happen? How do we grow to become more like Jesus?

A Life of Repentance

The answer to that question lies in a process, the process of repentance. As with everything else in our life with God, this process centers in the cross and the relationship with God that Christ Jesus died and rose again to restore. The waters of Baptism and the covenant our God made with each of us individually there figure prominently as well. The apostle Paul writes:

> What shall we say, then? Shall we go on sinning so that grace may increase? By no means! We died to sin; how can we live in it any longer? Or don't you know that all of us who were baptized into Christ Jesus were baptized into His death? We were therefore buried with Him through Baptism into death in order that, just as Christ was raised from the dead through the glory of the Father, we too may live a new life.

> If we have been united with Him like this in His death, we will certainly also be united with Him in His resurrection. For we know that our old self was crucified with Him so that the body of sin might be done away with, that we should no longer be slaves to sin—because anyone who has died has been freed from sin. (Rom. 6:1–7)

The Process of Repentance

A Christian teacher once asked her class, "What is the first thing we must do in order to be forgiven?"

One boy's hand shot up immediately. "Sin!" he shouted.

And of course, he was perfectly correct. The process of repentance begins as the Holy Spirit uses His Law to convict us of a specific sin and to produce true contrition in our hearts.

As the apostle Paul once discussed contrition, he sought to help his readers distinguish between "godly sorrow" and "worldly sorrow."[4] As anyone with a few traffic tickets can testify, most of us regret being caught in some violation of the law. We dislike the inconvenience of going to court to pay a fine, or we find ourselves embarrassed as we face the police officer. Perhaps we fear possible future consequences (e.g., higher car insurance rates). In any case, most of us regret having our transgressions exposed, because in one way or another, we fear punishment. This is one definition of

A Life of Repentance

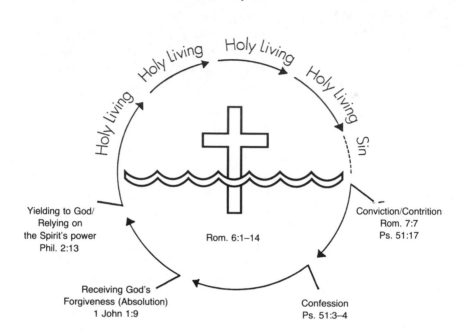

"worldly sorrow," and we, like our students, have all experienced enough of it to recognize it instantly.

Another definition of worldly sorrow involves what the Scriptures sometimes call condemnation—the feeling of despair that crashes in on us when we fear that we have used up our quota of God's grace, and, therefore, that He will refuse to forgive us for a particular offense. Probably all Christians struggle with the sense of condemnation from time to time too. We recognize it in ourselves, and Christian teachers who listen carefully to their students will almost surely discover individuals who struggle with this kind of worldly sorrow as well.

Worldly sorrow comes from Satan; it brings death. By way of contrast, Paul commends "godly sorrow." This kind of sorrow for sin leads us to the next step in God's process of repentance. Recognizing our sin and sorrowing over it, we confess it.

The word for *confess* in the Greek of the New Testament means literally "to speak together" or "to say the same thing." When we confess our sins, we simply say what God says:

- We have indeed done what His Law has forbidden.
- Our action (thought, attitude) was wrong.
- Our sin hurt God; it hurt us; it hurt other people.
- We deserve God's punishment.

When we honestly confess our sins to God in this way, we do not try to excuse ourselves. We do not try to shift the blame for our sin onto someone else's shoulders. We do not trivialize what we have done, nor do we minimize the consequences we deserve. As the apostle John wrote, "If we claim to be without sin, we deceive ourselves and the truth is not in us" (1 John 1:8).

Standing before God stripped of all self-righteousness, we hear the beautiful words of our Father's absolution:

> If we confess our sins, He is faithful and just and will forgive us our sins and purify us from all unrighteousness. (1 John 1:9)

Absolution is, for the Christian, a glorious emancipation proclamation. The Latin word from which we derive the English word *absolve* literally means "to set free; to release." Absolved from our sins, we find freedom from their guilt and shame and from the punishment we have deserved. But also—and this is critically important—we receive in God's absolution release from the power of our sins to enslave us.

That freedom comes, not as we try hard to amend our sinful lives, but as we rely on the Holy Spirit's power to "purify us from all unrighteousness." We realize that in our own strength, we cannot obey God. We acknowledge that, left to our own resources, we do not even want to obey God. And so we ask Him to work these things in us. To quote just two of many, many New Testament passages that comment on this process:

> It is God who works in you to will and to act according to His good purpose. (Phil. 2:13)

> May the God of peace, who through the blood of the eternal covenant brought back from the dead our Lord Jesus, that great Shepherd of the sheep, *equip you with everything good for doing*

His will, and may He work in us what is pleasing to Him, through Jesus Christ. (Heb. 13:20–21; emphasis added)

Contrition. Confession. Absolution. Yielding to God's Spirit. We repeat this process of repentance as often as we need it. We may, at times, find ourselves mired in a sin that we confessed only minutes before. In fact, we may find ourselves repeating the steps of the cycle a dozen times within a 10-minute period. But God will not become impatient or angry with us. He simply invites and encourages us to use the medicine He has prescribed. We can take it as often as we need it; we need not worry about overdosing.

As the Holy Spirit leads us through this process, He continually adds the surges of power we need so that, little by little, we can obey on ever-so-slightly higher a plane. By the Spirit's power, our cycle becomes a spiral headed gradually upward. Not that we will never fall back again into the same sins, but the general trend of our lives will be toward increasing Christ-likeness.

Perhaps we will not see perceptible changes from day to day, but months or years into the future, we will look back and will worship God for what He has worked in our lives. We will see that we are becoming, by God's grace, more and more like Jesus, and we will know that all the credit for our growth belongs to Him:

We, who with unveiled faces all reflect the Lord's glory, are being transformed into His likeness with ever-increasing glory, which comes from the Lord, who is the Spirit. (2 Cor. 3:18)

But perhaps all this seems too simple. Admittedly, it *is* simple, so simple that we could easily let our human pride prevent us from using the process our Lord has given us to enable us to live more fruitful, less frustrating lives of discipleship. It is simple. But it works. It is the only thing that works. And our Teacher yearns to help us use it.

No Hothouse Fruit

As much as we might wish that God had made different arrangements, He does not lead us to saving faith and then remove us from planet earth so we can grow to maturity in some kind of spiritual incubator. As most of us recognize, fruit grown in a hothouse environment often turns out small, woody, and tasteless. God wants to cultivate sweet, luscious fruit in our lives. So He leaves us in this world, tenderly nurturing and caring for us.

Even though we know this, most of us have probably found ourselves at one time or another dreaming about how fruitful we could be

- if only we lived in a more ideal environment;
- if only we had a lot less difficulty, trouble, or pain;
- if only we did not have to deal with churlish clerks and nosy neighbors;
- if only our salary was higher and our car payment lower;
- if only our spouse or our best friend took more of an interest in the things of God.

But when the Master Teacher enrolls us in His class, problems like these almost never disappear. Instead, our Lord incorporates them into the curriculum! Our Teacher finds ways—very creative ways—to use them in the course of study He has designed for us. In essence, He leads us through both "lecture" and "lab" experiences to help us learn.

The "lecture" part of our course includes all those times of spiritual input God provides for us, chiefly through the means of grace—His Word and the Sacraments. The "lab" part of our course, on the other hand, involves everything else that happens to us.[5]

As we sit, stalled in traffic; as we push a wobbly-wheeled grocery cart up and down the aisles of the supermarket; as we coach softball or chair a faculty meeting; as we kick our shoes off and turn on the television set—as we do all these things, our Lord gives us as His disciples opportunities to practice the principles He has taught us. We never work on a given "lab experience" on our own. Our Teacher always stands beside us, reminding us of His Word and offering us His encouragement and His help.

Most chemistry teachers recognize their students' need for lab time. Lab experiences challenge and deepen each student's understanding. Lab experiences also quickly reveal which students have daydreamed their way through a given lecture and which students do not fully grasp the concepts presented.

Of course, a student can walk into a chemistry lab and attempt an experiment without having read the text and without having attended a preparatory lecture. It is possible; but in most cases, foolhardy. At the very least, such a student will make a mess. At worst, the lab may explode.

We sometimes find ourselves walking into a lab experience of our own either ignorant of the wisdom from God that could help us with it, or—worse still—deliberately choosing to ignore God's wisdom.

Sometimes, in pure grace, our heavenly Father will reach down, wrap His arms around us, and keep us from blowing ourselves up. Sometimes He will stand back while we create smoke and fire and melt our flasks into puddles of glass. Then He will graciously hear our confession, forgive us, and offer to help in our mop-up operation. Sometimes, especially if we willfully ignore what our Teacher has told us, we suddenly find ourselves sitting in a pile of rubble. Even then, our gracious Teacher extends His hand to us, pulls us up, leads us through the process of repentance, and helps us pick up the pieces of our lives.

Maybe you have never thought of it in quite this way before, but we live most of our lives in God's lab. We often fail the lessons we encounter there. But we have a compassionate, forgiving Teacher. He always reaches out to rescue and help us. Even so, He wants to help us grow in our discipleship to the point that we become more confident in Him and more fruitful in our faith. That kind of growth occurs as we spend time with our Teacher each day, listening to what He has to say about our circumstances and receiving from Him the wisdom and strength we need to follow His instructions more consistently.

The Christian Classroom—Lecture and Lab

Perhaps you have heard Christian schools called "laboratories of Christian living." True enough, some well-meaning proponents of Christian education like to think of Christian schools as a kind of hothouse in which students can hide from the realities of life. But potentially, every Christian classroom serves as a place where children and young people encounter consistently helpful "lecture" and "lab" experiences as they grow in their walk with the Lord Jesus.

Each Christian teacher can set up a classroom environment in which students hear God's Word and then practice living it out all day long, each and every day of the school year. Every activity, every class period, every lunch hour can provide lab time for our students, time in which we can help the young Christians we teach understand and apply God's wisdom in practical ways. What an exciting challenge! What an incredible opportunity!

A great many teachers in Christian schools have snatched this baton and run with it. God has used the ministry of these teachers and their schools to His glory and for great good in the lives of thousands of students. These teachers differ from one another in many ways. But they share at least two critical characteristics. Productive disciplers plan their "lecture" activities carefully. They craft lessons designed to lead their students deeper into the truths of God's Word. They also work from an intentional, well-thought-out approach to the "lab" part of the school day.

The next three chapters will explore some ways teachers can implement helpful "lecture" and "lab" experiences for the students in Christian classrooms.

To Think About

1. "God's main concern for your life is not primarily your ministry; what concerns God most is *you!*" How do you react to that statement? What biblical evidence could you offer to support it? What implications do you see for your personal life and ministry?
2. What four discipleship goals did this chapter identify? Why is each important in our relationship with Jesus Christ?
3. Define the work of Law and Gospel in justification . . . in sanctification.
4. God wants his people to grow to become more and more like Jesus. If we do not become more Christlike by "trying hard," how does growth in Christ-likeness occur?
5. Define these terms as they are used in the Holy Scriptures:
   - Contrition
   - Confession
   - Absolution
   - Yielding to God's Spirit
6. What role do feelings play in the process of repentance? Even though feelings are important, why must we rely on the revealed

truths of God's Word, rather than on our feelings as we work through this process?

7. Explain the "lecture" and "lab" metaphors used in this chapter. What "lecture" experiences are important in your own personal life right now? What "lab" experiences is God using in your life?

8. How would looking at the Christian classroom through the lens of both "lecture" and "lab" stimulate teachers to think about discipling students all day long, not just during times of Bible study and classroom worship?

Notes

1. A teacher in a Christian school could scarcely do better than to read C. F. W. Walther's *The Proper Distinction between Law and Gospel* and to then reread it once each year, perhaps in October to celebrate the Reformation.

   This classic has been published in three translations. The complete translation in English was prepared by W. H. T. Dau, *The Proper Distinction between Law and Gospel* (St. Louis: Concordia Publishing House, 1929; reprinted 1986).

   A somewhat condensed and possibly more readable version is *Law and Gospel* translated by Walter Bouman (St. Louis: CPH, 1981).

   An even more condensed version is the one by Walter C. Pieper, *God's No and God's Yes: The Proper Distinction between Law and Gospel* (St. Louis: CPH, 1973).

2. Bouman, 32–33.

3. James 1:22–25.

4. 2 Cor. 7:5–16.

5. These metaphors, of course, do not imply that those who teach the faith should adopt the method of literally lecturing about the faith to their students or that hydrogen peroxide and bunsen burners will become staples of the confirmation classroom. Rather, the terms will serve as a shorthand way of referring to all the times God provides for us to intentionally put ourselves in the position to listen to Him ("lecture"—e.g., group Bible study, private devotions) and those times He gives us to practice what we have learned ("lab"—practically everything else in our lives).

CHAPTER 4

Time Together with Jesus

Hikers without a compass who must hike through a dense forest do well to set their sights on a specific, distant landmark and then walk toward it. That way, they can avoid wandering in aimless circles for hours—or even days!

As we scan the pages of the four gospels, we begin to see that our Lord Jesus never taught aimlessly. He set His sights on specific goals for His disciples, and He led them deliberately toward these goals. The writers of the New Testament give us a sense that the Teacher structured dozens of "lecture" and "lab" experiences, experiences designed to help His disciples mature spiritually.

As we disciple the students whom our Lord has entrusted to us, we—like our Lord before us—need to think carefully about both the lecture part of our teaching and the lab experiences we supervise. As we do this, we need to keep our sights set directly on our Lord's discipleship goals for us and for our students, goals He has set for all His people. The previous chapter examined four of our Lord's overarching discipleship goals for His people:

- That we may put our trust in God
- That we may remember God's deeds
- That we may keep God's commands
- That we may have attitudes pleasing to God

Faith. Facts. Actions. Attitudes. These goals help us keep our bearings as we teach. When we continually refer back to them, we more easily avoid walking in circles around the periphery of what our Lord would like to do in the minds, hearts, and lives of our students. The methods we use and the learning activities we select will take us and our students on a much more direct course toward a growing, maturing discipleship.

Preparing a Discipling Lesson Plan

As you work in a Christian classroom, some of the discipling you do will take place in formal, structured settings. For example, you will almost certainly take time each day to teach your students from the Scriptures. The plans you write for these lessons will serve as a kind of map. Your daily plan will remind you of your destination and of the specific path you hope to take to get from here to there. It will perhaps even indicate landmarks to look for along the way.

Perhaps you teach preschoolers. Or maybe confirmation students. Perhaps you have decided to lead your class in a study of the parable of the Good Samaritan. Or maybe you want your students to tackle several verses from one of Paul's epistles. Regardless, good lesson plans have similar elements. Therefore as any teacher designs a plan to lead his students into God's Word, he needs to approach that Word in a certain way; he needs to think through certain specific questions; he needs to make certain specific decisions; he needs to work through certain specific steps.

Step 1—Come Prayerfully into the King's Presence

Whenever we approach God's Word, we do so in an attitude of reverence and prayer. Preparing a lesson plan is no different. Our Lord Jesus invites us to begin, continue, and end our study of His Word with prayer; He invites us to saturate our study in prayer. Even as He does so, He holds out an incredible promise—incredible in a literal sense—for if we meditate on it for long, we will find His promise stretching our capacity to believe:

> The Counselor, the Holy Spirit, whom the Father will send in My name, will teach you all things and will remind you of everything I have said to you. (John 14:26)

Just think of it! It is as though our Redeemer-King has invited us into His throne room and has asked us to pull up a chair! He tells us that He has arranged for us to study under a private tutor, the one the Scriptures call "the Counselor," "the Spirit of truth," "the Spirit of wisdom and understanding." That is how much our Lord yearns to help us grow as we study His Word.

Our Savior promises that the Holy Spirit will teach us all things—things about Himself and what He has done on our behalf, things about His plan of salvation, things about His love for us. He wants us to grasp our place in His family. He wants us to recognize the fullness of the victory He has won for us. He wants us to understand how to wage spiritual warfare—and win! He wants to give us true wisdom and the ability to exercise that wisdom in every situation we face.

Furthermore, Jesus promises that as we learn, the Holy Spirit will bring *everything* Jesus has taught us to our remembrance. The Counselor will remind us of the things we have already learned. He will help us remember His Word so that we have His truth at our fingertips whenever we need it.

Knowing our Lord's invitation and promise, we can confidently ask His Spirit to help us as we study His Word. We can ask for deeper insight into concepts that we do not quite grasp. We can share our thoughts, our struggles, our sins, our deepest feelings with Him and ask Him to show us from His Word just exactly how He feels about them and how He would have us adjust our attitudes or actions.

It is truly incredible. Our Redeemer-King comes to us in gentle love and offers to disciple us, even as He prepares us to disciple our students.

Step 2—Apply the Text to Your Own Life

After we enter God's presence in prayer, we read the text. Perhaps you find it strange that something so obvious should appear here. But every teacher who has led a dozen different groups of students through a specific pericope sooner or later confronts the temptation to think that "I know that story."

Fleshly pride can contribute to this mistaken idea. So can a superficial understanding of Scripture. God's Word is not a threadbare recitation of historic facts; it is dynamic. It is a living tool in the hands of God's Spirit, the Spirit who wants to use His Word to mold and shape us so we become, little by little, more like our Lord Jesus. Luther once speculated:

I wonder whether Peter, Paul, Moses, and all the saints fully and thoroughly understood a single word of God so that they had nothing more to learn from it, for the understanding of God is beyond measure. To be sure, the saints understood the Word of God and could also speak about it, but their practice did not keep pace with it. Here one forever remains a learner.[1]

So as we read a specific text, we ask ourselves three simple questions:

- What does the text say?
- What does the text mean?
- What does the text mean to me?

Maybe you have seen this brief list before. It has been used by Christians in one form or another for decades. The questions probably have lasted so long because they have helped so many believers down through the years in personal and group Bible study. The questions may be simple; their answers are not always easy. The questions help us focus our thoughts in such a way as to keep us from falling into the abyss of dry intellectualism on the one hand and from launching into flights of subjective fantasy on the other.

After we read the primary text and, perhaps, any parallel accounts and cross references, we ask ourselves, "What did this story (letter, psalm, proverb) mean to the audience who first heard it?" Sometimes commentaries can help answer this question. Sometimes the answer shines clearly for us from the text itself. But we must understand the "then and there" meaning before we can adequately think about any text's "here and now" application.

We cannot lead someone to a place we ourselves refuse to go. Therefore, before we let ourselves set discipleship objectives for our students, we think about the text's meaning for our own discipleship. We ask ourselves, "What does this text mean to me?" As we think this through, we deal with questions of Law and of Gospel:[2]

- What command(s) from God lie on the text's surface or are embedded in it? Have I kept these commands? What, specifically, would God lead me to confess?
- What comfort, promise, or word of encouragement does God's Spirit reveal to me in this text?

At this point in your planning process you may become aware that your Lord wants to make some course corrections in your personal walk with Him. Before you move on, allow some time for Him to do that. Let Him lead you through the four-step process of repentance—contrition, confession, absolution, and yielding to God's Spirit. (See chapter 3.)

If you have never begun a lesson plan in this way before, by now perhaps you have begun thinking to yourself, "This will take a lot of time!"

Yes, it will. Especially at first. And time is one of a busy teacher's most precious commodities. Yet as you continue to use the process, familiarity will make it somewhat easier and less time-consuming.

Regardless, though, we need to recognize that teaching the King's kids to know Him better differs from teaching social studies or math. It helps if a math teacher enjoys his subject, but a love for math is not, strictly speaking, a prerequisite. As we seek to disciple others, however, the condition of our own hearts is absolutely critical.

More than once I have found myself stymied by a lesson that refused to go together. Upon further reflection, I became aware that the Holy Spirit wanted to put His finger on a sore spot in my own heart through the words of the text I had been studying. After I recognized that and let Him work through His lesson plan for me, the lesson plan for my students came easily and quickly.

Step 3—Prayerfully Set Objectives

Having submitted to your Teacher's work in your own life, you can move on to think about the specific discipleship objectives He may have in mind for your students. How might God want to use the text in their minds and hearts?

To answer this question, you should briefly review what the Lord has shown you in the text. Then think about what you have seen in your students on the playground or in the hallways. Think about what you have heard during previous class discussions and about what you have read on the students' test papers. Think about the Bible knowledge and the experience with God's Word that your students already have. Think about the challenges and struggles your students face. Think about the developmental stage(s) at which your students function intellectually. What are they capable of thinking about and understanding?

Then write a series of lesson objectives. Be sure to actually *write* them! The discipline will force you, among other things, to be clear and specific rather than fuzzy and too global.

As you write, keep in mind the three questions you asked yourself as you studied the text earlier. But this time ask them in reference to your students:

- What does the text say?
- What does the text mean?
- What does the text mean for my class?

Three kinds of objectives—cognitive, affective, and psychomotor—will grow from this exercise. In every lesson plan you write, you will almost certainly want one or more of each kind of objective. When your lesson ends each day, you will want your students to

- know certain specific facts or concepts (e.g., Esau sold his birthright to Jacob; *redeem* means to "buy back");
- feel certain specific things (e.g., sorrow for the sin of lying to Dad; joy in knowing that Grandma is in heaven with Jesus);
- act in certain ways (e.g., the students will show love to Mom by helping to set the table without being asked; they will resist peer pressure to use recreational drugs or to view pornographic movies).

Faith. Facts. Attitudes. Actions. We set lesson objectives with an eye toward a good balance of these four. And as we do, we remember—above all—that we teach as disciplers.

That means that we teach for repentance. We teach God's Word in such a way that the Holy Spirit can use it to bring our students to an awareness of their sins, a true and godly sorrow over them, and an honest confession of these sins to God.

Teaching as disciplers also means that we teach God's Word in such a way that our students breathe the fresh air of the freedom that comes with God's forgiveness. We want them to experience the relief and the release that comes with the heavenly Father's absolution.

As we teach, we remind our students that, along with His forgiveness, God promises to give them the power they need for sanctification, the power that will enable them to become more fully like Jesus, more fully the people He has already declared them to be in Christ.[3]

In short, the objectives we write for the lessons we plan must include both Law and Gospel. Each lesson should set up a situation in which the Savior can lead our students through the process of repentance. As we plan for that, we remember that the Gospel must remain preeminent in every class session. The Gospel is the power of God for salvation; the Gospel brings us and our students peace and the assurance of forgiveness; the Gospel energizes us to bear the fruit of sanctification. So, in any given lesson, *the Gospel must predominate.*[4]

One other brief comment about objectives before we move on. Christian teachers over the past several decades have debated about whether the objectives we write for our Bible lessons can (or should) all be measurable and observable. As some have pointed out, no one can measure spiritual realities like faith or hope. Others have pointed to the fact that faith, hope, and the rest almost always show themselves somehow in deeds. These educators have suggested that our objectives should concentrate on these "fruits of faith."

As we teach the Christian faith, we can fall off the fence on either side:

If we never submit to the discipline of setting measurable, observable objectives, we may teach in such generalities that we never know what we have accomplished. Our students' growth in both knowledge and sanctification may be stunted. Our planning can deteriorate to the point that every lesson plan, in effect, repeats the objectives of the day before, and an outside observer who checked our lesson-plan book could not tell from our objectives whether we had dealt with the account of Noah's ark or Paul's conversion.

On the other hand, if we insist on only measurable, observable objectives, our "objectives" can easily deteriorate into a simple listing of class activities (e.g., "That the students will make a model of Noah's ark"). We may also find ourselves neglecting to address the attitudinal and faith-related issues so critical to our students' personal discipleship.

Perhaps a compromise is in order. Alert to the dangers of both extremes, force yourself to write as many objectives as possible in measurable, observable terms. However, if a worthwhile objective

71

simply will not allow itself to be squeezed into that mold, include it in the lesson plan anyway.

Then check up on yourself over time. Read back over your objectives for the past few weeks. Are they clear? Do you see growth toward the goals you have prayerfully set? What specific evidence of that do you see? After all, our goal is not that we as Christian teachers learn to write ideal objectives, but that our students continue to grow, to grow luxuriantly in the ways God's Spirit would have them grow. Specific, measurable objectives are a tool He has given us to use as we cultivate the faith He has planted.

Step 4—Plan a Hook

After you have written lesson objectives and have thought through the Law/Gospel accents of a lesson, you can begin to map out a strategy for that particular class session.

As you begin each session, you will want to use some kind of "hook"—an activity, a story, a demonstration, a picture, an intriguing fact, a song, an unusual statement—something that will invite your students to join you as you walk through the lesson. This introduction will set the stage for your pupils. It will help them make the transition from the busyness of the class day into the particular Bible story or doctrinal concept you plan to address in your lesson.

If you use a published curriculum, your teachers guide may give you several lesson openings from which to choose. If you design your own lessons, or if your teachers guide does not include this feature, you will need to devise an introduction of your own.

Avoid lesson hooks designed simply to evoke a "gee whiz" response from the class. Rather, select an activity to which you can refer later on, perhaps as you make a particular lesson application. Or choose a lead-in with a direct tie to the day's Bible story.

For example, to introduce the parable of the sower you might don a large apron and have a bag of grass seed nearby. As the class period begins, you could take your group outside and demonstrate the method farmers used to plant grain in New Testament Palestine.

To begin a lesson dealing with Baptism you might present a stack of magazines to the class and give them five minutes to find pictures that show the power and usefulness of water. Post the pictures on a bulletin board as the students find them. After you have worked through the day's biblical material, return to the picture display briefly and superimpose a photo of a Baptism. This could then lead to a discussion of the source of Baptism's power—not the water itself, but God's Word.

As you develop your "hook" and the other lesson activities you will use each day, plan a way to keep track of them so you can use your best ideas over again from year to year. Discard the ones that do not work so well. Save those that do. Some teachers label a new file folder for each Bible story or each doctrinal topic they teach. They tuck ideas or even whole lesson plans into the folder and refer to these whenever they return to a particular lesson. Maybe a set of note cards would work better for you. But regardless of your method, develop a way to systematize a lesson repertoire and refine it as you go along.

Step 5—Share Your Objectives with the Learners

Someone has said, "If you don't know where you are going, you are likely to end up someplace else." We need not think about this advice for long before we see the truth in it. The truth applies to the students in our classroom too. Robert Gagne and other recognized curriculum experts agree that teachers need to share instructional objectives with learners.[5]

As we walk with our students into a specific Bible narrative, we will have already set our sights on one or more specific lesson outcomes. We cannot assume, though, that our students have any idea about the point we intend to make. Research has shown, however, that learners who understand the objectives of a specific lesson up front are much more likely to attain those objectives.

We need not take much time to share our lesson objectives, but we do need to put these objectives into words our students can readily understand. As we write the objectives for a specific lesson plan, we will probably use adult terminology, but as we share the hoped-for outcome of that lesson with our students, we will then need to simplify and perhaps condense our thoughts.

If your students can read, you might even want to write the lesson's point on the chalkboard or on a large piece of poster paper. Then you may want to take a moment to pray a short prayer with the class, inviting the Holy Spirit to enable each person in the group to learn, to remember, and to apply the lesson. Of course, the prayer needs to be phrased in developmentally appropriate words.

Step 6—Lead Your Students into the Word . . . Actively!

Lesson activities should grow directly from lesson objectives. Choose activities and experiences that will lead your students toward the specific objectives you have set. Usually, teachers plan to address their cognitive goals first. Then they move on to the affective and psychomotor goals. Obviously the three will often overlap. And, sometimes, you will want to begin with an activity aimed primarily at a particular attitude or behavior.

Regardless of your approach, at some point in the lesson, usually early on, you will want to take the class into Scripture itself. As you teach, do not just talk about God's Book; lead the students in opening and reading it. Even preschool teachers should hold a Bible open on their lap as they tell Bible stories. As Luther once remarked, "The Holy Scripture is a stream of running water, where alike the elephant may swim, and the lamb walk without losing its feet."[6]

At least by third grade, each student needs a personal study Bible. During your time together around the Scriptures, help your students understand that this is the one book in which they can (and should) definitely write. Show them how to customize their Bibles for themselves. If some student brings to class a Bible that is too fragile or too precious to mark, politely send it back home. Replace "display Bibles" the students bring with ones they can actually use for serious Bible study.

Personal notations make any study Bible infinitely more useful. For example, you might provide yellow or pink watercolor markers and help each student highlight the memory verses you assign. Choose markers that will not bleed through the pages. Students can review these verses easily, and they will be able to find their memory verses in the Bible when they want to refer to them.

Some students may want to underline different kinds of verses in different colors (e.g., red for verses that speak of God's forgiveness, yellow for verses that contain God's promises, orange for verses that give God's commands). That way, when they need the assurance of God's forgiveness or the encouragement of a specific promise, they can more easily locate the help they want. Many Christians also find such a marking system valuable when God gives them an opportunity to witness or to share God's comfort and counsel with someone else.

You will want to mark your own Bible as you study, too, and then use your personal Bible as you teach. Keep it on your desk. Use it as you lead worship. Refer to it when you counsel students or their parents. Let the students see that you yourself do what you ask of them. In short, model the attitudes and behaviors toward the Scriptures that you would like to see in your students.

As you lead your students into the Word, you will doubtless teach them many facts about the Bible stories they study. When the pupils' age and developing abilities make it appropriate, you will also help them cultivate an intellectual understanding of important doctrinal concepts and a clear grasp of the meanings of important theological terms.

But if we teach only Bible story facts and doctrinal vocabulary, we may as well teach Aesop's fables and elementary Latin! In such a course of study, the students may pick up an appreciation of morals and manners, but little real growth in Christian discipleship will result.

So as you plan each lesson, you need to think about the opportunities you will provide to help your students push beyond intellectual facts—important as facts are—to a response, a response empowered by the Holy Spirit.

What specific application does the Holy Spirit want to make in individual students' lives? How will you set up classroom activities so that your students interact with God's life-changing Word? How will you help your students understand that Word and think through its meaning for them?

The specific activities you decide to use in your classroom on any given day will depend upon many factors—your students' interests, abilities, and learning styles; the resources you have available; the time frame within which you must operate; your own interests, skills, gifts, and abilities.

In choosing learning activities, keep in mind that each student has a unique learning style. This is true in math class; it is also true as students approach God's Word. You may find that some of your students learn best by reading and writing, some by participating in group discussions, some by acting in impromptu plays, some by writing new lyrics for familiar tunes. As you teach, keep looking for clues about each student's particular learning style. Then capitalize on it.

Choose methods that will keep your students actively engaged. Keep in mind that learners of any age remember a little of what they hear. They remember more of what they see *and* hear. But most of all they remember what they *do!*

So, as often as possible, plan projects and assignments that will allow students to use more than one of their five senses. Good preschool teachers recognize the power of this teaching style and almost always build much hands-on activity into their lesson plans. But those who teach elementary, junior high, or adult learners can also capitalize on the power inherent in this approach.

To recap: As you plan lesson activities, you will need to keep in mind the learning styles, the needs, and the strengths of your students.

But even as you do this, also keep in mind the particular strengths and gifts our Lord has given you, their teacher. Then use what He has given!

Perhaps you have polished dramatic skills. Great! Dress up as Jeremiah and thunder into your sixth-grade classroom one day. Or pretend to be David. Help your first-graders make shields from round pizza boards. Then lead your army out to the "wilderness" behind the piano to hide from King Saul. Creep silently through "caves" and "deserts." Later, as you sit around the "campfire," introduce a few verses from one of the psalms David wrote while in exile.

Or perhaps you are an accomplished banjo player. Fantastic! Bring your instrument to class and teach your students to make a joyful noise in praise to our God.

In short, plan for learning activities that will mesh the needs and strengths of your students with your own specific teaching skills. The more precise this match, the more effective your lesson will be.

The ideal of active learning fits hand-in-glove with our Lord's concern for the attitudes and actions of His young disciples. The best way to shape attitudes and behaviors involves planning activities in which your students can practice the specific skills and behaviors you want them to develop.

For example, a fourth grade teacher might lead his class through a series of lessons on the ministry of the Christian church in the book of Acts. A unit like that could easily include some exercises in which the students practice specific witnessing skills in class. Then the teacher could assign some witnessing "homework" to be done outside the classroom (e.g., a discussion question like, "What does Jesus mean to you?" that students could ask family members over the weekend).

Or perhaps you would like your students to pray more systematically and unselfishly. At the beginning of each week, some teachers write the names of each of their students on individual slips of paper. The teacher then puts her own name and all the students' names into a hat. Pupils and teacher alike "draw names" and commit themselves to pray (sometimes secretly) during that week for the person whose name they drew.

A teacher in almost any elementary grade could profitably lead her class in Reformation, Thanksgiving, Christmas, or Easter caroling. The group could visit the congregation's shut-ins. Through this experience, the teacher could help her students understand and value the ministry of care for one another that God has given the members of His family, the church.

Whatever lesson activities you plan, plan for variety, for freshness. Even banjo music can lose some of its appeal after several dozen consecutive lessons based on it. We have an infinitely creative God who has given us a fascinating universe. In addition, He has given us His Word through which He has revealed many deep mysteries, especially the mystery of His grace in Jesus Christ. What a shame—really, what a sin—if our time together around that Word bores us or our students.

After you have written each plan, check it over one last time. Look back at your objectives. Will the activities you plan lead the students to attain what you hope to accomplish? Where is the Law in your lesson? Where is the Gospel? Does the Gospel predominate? If your answers do not satisfy you, tinker with your plan a bit more. And before you conclude your planning session, spend a bit more time in prayer. Commit yourself, your students, and your lesson plan to the Lord, asking Him to give the growth as you cultivate and water the faith He has planted.

Step 7—Evaluate the Lesson

After each class session, you will want to evaluate what went on. Evaluation procedures can be formal or informal. Teachers vary in the degree to which they rely on each.

You may, at times, want to use formal evaluation. For example, a confirmation teacher will often listen to his students recite the Bible verses or Catechism portions they have memorized. A teacher of middle-graders may give a true/false quiz to her students at the end of the lesson period. A preschool teacher might lead his class in a circle prayer, listening carefully to which children pray what specific petitions.

You need not—in fact, you should not—depend solely upon formal evaluation techniques as you disciple your students. You can learn much of value by watching for clues about the students' learning as you teach:

- Which students are most attentive?
- Who answers what questions?
- What is Lynn's body language saying?
- Does Ryan's frown indicate disagreement or confusion?
- Which students expressed excitement and thankfulness to God for His creation during or after our unit on the First Article?
- Did Joey's vague questions in class signal some deeper concern he is carrying?

After class, think about your students' responses, but do not limit your evaluation only to their reactions. Think, too, about yourself, your lesson plan, and your technique. All teachers can learn much by asking questions like the following:

- How comfortably can I lead my students as we roleplay the Bible stories? How might I lead more effectively next time?
- How much of the talking did I do today? Am I asking questions that lead to productive discussion?
- Did everyone have a chance to respond during class, or do I seem to call on the same five or six students who are eager to answer?

- What could I change in the classroom or in my approach that might help Kim and Donya learn our Bible memory verses more easily?
- Are my objectives realistic, given this group of students? Am I expecting too much? too little? about the right amount of cognitive, affective, and psychomotor growth?

In general, you will want to spend some time after class thinking about how your students responded, which objectives the students met, and which specific areas of discipleship still merit further attention. Consciously evaluating your students' progress will help you better identify and rejoice in what God is doing in your classroom. It will also help you zero in on your students' needs. The more accurate your diagnosis, the more precisely your future lesson plans can address these needs.

By the same token, consciously evaluating your own performance and techniques will help you identify and celebrate what God is doing in you and through you as you teach. Self-assessment will also help you modify your approach, your technique. As God directs and empowers these changes in you, you will become a more effective catalyst in the discipling process God is directing in your students' lives.

When to Abandon Your Plan

Joey raced into Mr. Nelson's classroom a full 30 minutes late. The class had finished its opening devotion and also the review activities on the Third Petition Mr. Nelson had planned. The students had already begun reciting the previous day's memory work when Joey sat down at his desk.

"Are you okay, Joey?" asked Mr. Nelson, looking up and noticing Joey's ashen face.

"We ... my mom and me had an accident on the way to take Kim to the day care center," the fifth-grader stuttered. "This guy ... he ran a red light. The police said it could have been bad, but nobody got hurt."

"Sounds like God's angels had their hands full with you this morning!" Mr. Nelson said. He smiled softly.

"Yeah," replied Joey, "It's like my mom said, we don't think about angels too much, but we're glad they're there when something like this happens."

Thus began an impromptu discussion of angels and their ministry on the behalf of God's children. Two students used a concordance to find Scripture verses that mention angels. The class then read these verses and talked about them. Some students chose to highlight one or two of these verses in their own Bibles. Several fifth-graders shared instances in which they experienced God's protection in dangerous situations.

Mr. Nelson will return to the Third Petition tomorrow. At this point, he has seized what educators have called "a teachable moment." Even though Mr. Nelson had not planned to talk about angels until the class studied "Jacob's Ladder" later in the semester, he has just seen a window for learning open before his eyes. Chances are very good that most of the students will remember today's discussion. They will know more about God's angels, and they will value the ministry of angels on behalf of God's people. Had Mr. Nelson insisted on sticking with the Third Petition today under the premise that "angels come next month," he would have passed over an excellent teaching opportunity.

As you write lesson plans, you do so intending to follow them. Over the course of a semester, you should be able to look back over your plan book and reflect upon the journey of discipleship on which the Lord has taken you and your students.

That does not mean, however, that you must follow any given lesson plan with mindless rigidity. As we began this chapter, we said that a lesson plan serves as a kind of map through the forest. As you walk through a given lesson, you and your class may come upon a path that does not appear on the map you drew up as you planned the day's lesson. God may have some delightful surprises in store for you along that unmarked pathway. Be flexible enough, bold enough, confident enough in God's leading, to step off the main highway once in a while.

If you find yourself teaching first-graders in Phoenix on a day when snow flakes begin to powder the outside of your windows, go ahead and abandon the Cain and Abel lesson plan you have prepared. Bundle the children up and take them out to enjoy the wonder of God's creation. Maybe you will invite your students to work together to write prayers or poems of thanks to Jesus later in the day. Maybe not. But seize the moment!

Sometimes a world event will loom large in the news and capture the attention of your students. Sometimes an individual student will come to class distraught by the death of a pet or by a family argument during breakfast. Often, if you take a few minutes to listen to students, to comfort them, to counsel with them, they will then be able to concentrate on the Bible lesson you have prepared. With such departures from your carefully thought-out lesson plans you are not sidestepping your discipling ministry. Sensitivity and care for students *is* your ministry!

Life in the classroom will present marvelous opportunities to help your students grow in God's grace more fully as God deepens their discipleship. At such times you can help them better understand and practice what it means to be a disciple when Grandma dies or Dad loses his job or the Pirates win the World Series or God sees to it that a tornado veers away from the school building despite everyone's worst worries.

Keeping all this in mind, though, teachers need to guard against the temptation to abandon lesson plans for trivial reasons. If you find yourself consistently diverted from the topic you planned to teach, you need to ask yourself why. Perhaps you need to write more appropriate plans and objectives. Or perhaps your students have discovered a few techniques of their own, techniques that effectively take you off course.

Feel free to seize teachable moments when they occur. But remember to go back later and pick up your original plan.

A Note of Caution—Keep Vocabulary Meaningful

The folklore of Christian education abounds with stories about children who pray, "Our Father who art in heaven, Harold be Thy name." Everyone knows that Noah's wife was "Joan of Ark." And what first-grade teacher has not chuckled when presented with a hand-lettered portrait of "Pontius the Pilot" streaking across the night sky with Mary, Joseph, and Baby Jesus on the "Flight to Egypt"?

Such misunderstandings would be more humorous if they did not hint at the confusion so many students feel when they confront even simple theological words or phrases. Students from nonchurched families will almost certainly stumble in defining words like *sin, grace,* or *forgiveness.* We probably expect this. But, perhaps surprisingly, students who regularly attend worship services, Sunday school, and Christian day school sometimes have only a shallow understanding of important words and concepts like these.

As we teach, we need to pay particular attention when our students use phrases like *Jesus died on the cross,* or *to take away our sins.*

Of course, there is nothing wrong with these phrases in and of themselves. But often times students learn them by rote and repeat them without really understanding them. They seldom reflect on what the words actually mean. If we consistently accept superficial responses like these to our questions, if we consistently ask questions that let our students get by with answers like these, chances are good that those we disciple will have only the most shallow theological understandings. They will never grasp the magnificent, life-changing truths that lie behind these phrases.

How can we lead our students beyond mere pat answers? How can we encourage class discussions that stimulate our students' growth in the understandings and attitudes Christ wants to work in all of His disciples?

First, we can analyze our questioning technique and work at asking questions that require more than a one-word answer (yes, no, Jesus).

Then, too, as we note rote responses to our questions, we can follow up by asking, "Please tell me what you mean by that." Or, "How would you explain that to someone who has never heard about Jesus?" Or, "Do you really believe that? Tell me why."

We can illustrate difficult concepts (e.g., redeem, justification, holy) by telling stories, by drawing pictures, by using diagrams, or by illustrating the idea in some other memorable way.

Finally, we can share our faith and our love for Jesus in our own words with our students, and we can encourage them to share with us in the same way.

A Word about Worship

In addition to a structured Bible lesson each day, most teachers in Christian schools plan daily worship times for their students. As you think about the specifics of classroom worship, keep in mind the general goal that lies behind all the worship activities in which God's people participate:

Every worship experience should lead the King's kids into the King's presence, there to receive His comfort, His encouragement, His forgiveness, His strength. Having received these gifts of His grace, the worshipers respond to the King's goodness by offering to Him the sacrifice of praise.

We can truly worship, of course, only as our Lord empowers us to do so. Having acknowledged that, however, we also need to recognize that certain methods usually work better than others as we seek to lead children and young people into the heavenly Father's throne room.

What methods make classroom worship a more effective discipling tool? The answers will vary somewhat, depending upon your students' ages and their previous worship experiences. Some general guidelines, though, always apply:

1. Worship designed for children and young people should never be a spectator sport. Get the worshipers involved in singing, reading, clapping, kneeling. Keep worship active.
2. Keep it brief. The appropriate length will depend on the age and average attention span of your group, but remember that you want your students to walk away glad they have had the chance to worship, not stiff or wiggly from sitting too long.
3. Avoid using worship time as a time for instruction. Teach the songs and hymns you expect to use in worship during classroom music time. Let worship truly be a time for everyone present to reflect and respond to God's presence and goodness.
4. Model the behavior you expect from the students and provide opportunities in which older students can model worship behavior for younger ones. If your school has a corporate chapel service each week, urge faculty members to let older students pair up with younger ones. Before this arrangement debuts in your school, talk with the young mentors about the modeling process and the ministry they can each have in the life of the kindergartner or second-grader with whom they share a song-sheet or hymnal.
5. Plan ways to keep worship times fresh but familiar. Too much

change simply for the sake of change will distract you and your students alike. On the other hand, you want to avoid any hymn-devotion-prayer rut too. Retain certain specific elements from day to day, from week to week, but think about ways to keep worship routines meaningful. And do not be afraid to let the students work with you to plan worship. They will grow in their own discipleship as they lead worship activities for others.

6. Finally, remember to let the Gospel predominate in your worship as well as in your lesson plans. The music you use, the devotions or worship talks you lead, the prayers and liturgies that you pray—all of these should reflect a deep understanding of God's grace to us in Christ.

Many of the worship helps prepared specifically for children fail dismally in this regard. Well-meaning adults so easily lapse into moralizing as they write children's worship talks and devotions. Yes, God does want His people to obey Him. But piling on the shoulds and musts of the Law will not bring about true sanctification. Only as we appropriately apply Law and Gospel to our own lives, and to the lives of our students, will lasting, God-pleasing changes begin to happen. Evaluate all worship helps with this filter clearly in mind.

Into the Lab

This chapter has presented in some detail the basic components of the "lecture" time you will spend with your students each day as you seek to disciple them. But, important as the daily Bible lesson time and worship time are, both of them combined will probably take up less than 45 minutes of the class day.

When our preplanned special time with Jesus ends, the day's social studies activities begin and the math worksheets appear. Does that mean that we as teachers tuck our discipling goals inside the Bible and forget about them until the next day? Certainly not.

When the "lecture" ends, "lab time" begins. We can, by God's grace, disciple our students all day long, every day. But how does that happen? How do we plan for it? How do we direct it? The next chapter will address these questions.

To Think About

1. Which lesson preparation steps seem most important to you? Why? Which steps might you be tempted to omit? Explain.
2. Why is it important to know both the Scriptures *and* your students as you write a lesson plan involving Bible study?
3. Why must teachers who want to disciple their students effectively live a life of repentance themselves?
4. The chapter states that every lesson plan must provide a Law/Gospel focus, a chance for students to identify specific sin in their lives, to confess that sin, and to receive God's forgiveness. Why is this so important?
5. Why must the Gospel predominate in every lesson?
6. Look through a Sunday school teachers guide or one written for Christian day school teachers. What kinds of objectives do you see? How would you improve the objectives? Explain any changes you would suggest.
7. Describe an experience in which a teacher (either you or one of your instructors) abandoned the day's lesson plan. What led to this change in plans? What did the students learn as a result? Was the change justified? Explain.
8. What worship experiences hold special meaning for you personally at this stage in your life? Do you remember a meaningful worship experience from your childhood? If so, describe it. What does this say to you as you think about the classroom worship opportunities you plan for your students?

Notes

1. Luther's Works (Philadelphia: Fortress Press, 1967) 54:9.
2. "If some passage is obscure I consider whether it treats of grace or of Law, whether wrath or the forgiveness of sin [is contained in it], and with which of these it agrees better. By this procedure I have often understood the most obscure passages. Either the Law or the Gospel has made them meaningful, for God divides His teaching into Law and Gospel" (Luther's Works [Philadelphia: Fortress Press, 1967] 54:42).
3. If anyone is in Christ, he is a new creation; the old has gone, the new has come! (2 Cor. 5:17).
4. See Walther's Thesis XXV in any of the translations of *The Proper Distinction between Law and Gospel* referenced in chapter 3.

5. For further discussion of this issue and a deeper discussion of the process of curriculum development itself, readers may wish to consult Robert M. Gagne, et. al., *Principles of Instructional Design,* third ed. (New York: Holt, Rinehart, and Winston, Inc., 1988).

6. Thomas S. Kepler, ed., *The Table Talk of Martin Luther* (Grand Rapids: Baker Book House, 1952), 11.

CHAPTER 5
All Day Long

The bushmen of the Kalahari will always hold a special place in my heart. I have never been to Africa and will probably never go. I had never even heard of the Kalahari Desert until I taught about it in fourth-grade social studies. Even so, the bushmen played an important role in my classroom each year for five consecutive years, as together the fourth grade and I learned about the people of the Kalahari.

The social studies series we used included a veritable smorgasbord of activities and teaching resources. Beautiful maps, evocative photo posters, brilliant filmstrips, and exciting videocassettes supplemented an attractive textbook. In addition, the teachers guide included so many intriguing ideas that the lessons almost taught themselves. In short, the series looked like every busy teacher's dream.

The fourth-grade text involved the students in a study of cultural anthropology—simplified anthropology to be sure, but heady stuff nevertheless. From the moment I saw the materials, I couldn't wait to teach the course. As I left my new classroom after the faculty's first planning day in August, I took a stack of booklets, boxes, and videocassettes back with me to my apartment. I wanted to dig in that evening.

As I studied, though, I found myself more and more concerned about the content. Not about what the materials specifically said, but about the inferences which the students would almost inevitably draw, inferences which they, in fact, were supposed to draw. Inferences so subtly woven into the fabric of the materials that teacher and students alike might not even notice. Perhaps this sounds polemic, even paranoid. But let me explain.

The course led students to examine and compare people groups from many different cultures around the world. During the year, the children would discover that people in different places find differing ways to feed, clothe, and provide shelter for themselves. People everywhere organize themselves into some kind of social structure; these structures differ from group to group, from culture to culture. People in different cultures follow differing cultural rules and expectations.

In short, human beings live in cultures that are alike in many important ways, but that differ in some ways too. These differences are neither bad nor good; they just are. On feast days, Yanamamo families of South America eat banana soup and roasted monkey meat. Some Irish Catholic families in Chicago enjoy corned beef and cabbage on St. Patrick's Day. No particular feast day menu is inherently more festive than any other.

Now, I admit that I might not necessarily relish a roasted monkey meat sandwich for lunch today, but I have no quarrel with the fact that cultures do differ and that we need to look with tolerance and respect on those whose cultures may differ from our own. As Christians, we recognize the freedom the Gospel gives us to enjoy both corned beef and banana soup as good gifts that come to us from our Creator.

But the series did not stop with a discussion of food preparation and family customs. It said, in essence, that different peoples in different cultures worship in different ways, and they worship different gods. The Naga who worships his ancestor's skulls, the bushman who worships the spirit gods in the natural world around him, and the 10-year-old in Chicago who worships Jesus Christ all have equally valid religious experiences. To say that, or worse, to subtly imply it without directly confronting and discussing the truthfulness of that premise, hacks away at the roots of the Christian faith we want to nurture in the hearts of the children and young people who sit under our teaching.

Those familiar with secular textbooks, and who have carefully analyzed them from this standpoint, recognize that this particular social studies series is, unfortunately, not unique. As Christian teachers intent on discipling the students in our classrooms, we dare not assume that the texts we use will support us in that task. We dare not even assume preprinted materials will be value-neutral.

But what then? Do we abandon textbooks from non-Christian publishers altogether? Must all teachers in Christian schools earn advanced degrees in curriculum development so that we can competently and professionally design our own materials for each class we teach? In an ideal world, perhaps. But that solution is hardly practical for most of us.

In many—perhaps most—cases, the solution lies rather in analyzing, adapting, and then using available published materials. The bushmen, for example, became an ongoing prayer project for my classes. As we studied about this people group each September, that year's fourth-grade class would pray, "Lord, send someone to the bushmen of the Kalahari to tell them about Jesus." Each January or February, months after the mechanics of long division and the subtleties of plural and possessive nouns had blown all thoughts of the Kalahari out of my mind, one or another of the children would often remember to mention the bushmen in prayer during our morning devotional times.

Christian Math?

In His Great Commission, the Lord Jesus said to His followers:

> Go and make disciples of all nations, baptizing them in the name of the Father and of the Son and of the Holy Spirit, and teaching them to obey everything I have commanded you. (Matt. 28:19–20)

If we translated the Greek verb tenses more literally, the passage might begin as follows: *Going, therefore, disciple the nations . . .* Implied in these words is the assumption that the Lord's people will indeed go, but the verb most English Bibles translate "go," is not written in imperative mood in the original Greek. The sense of our Lord's words might be better rendered, "As you go . . ." or "While you are on your way . . ."

To each of His people the Lord says, "As you go about your daily lives, as you work and play, as you eat and rest, as you engage in each of your daily activities—do it in My name. Take My power. Live as My people. And, as you go, lead others by My grace to become My disciples and to grow in their discipleship."

To us specifically as teachers in Christian schools, our Lord Jesus might say, "As you unlock your classroom door each day, as you teach math or spelling, as you play kickball or coach soccer, as you worship with your class in today's chapel service, as you do all these things—and everything else besides—disciple your students."

By our Lord's grace, we live as both His disciples and as His disciplers. We disciple our students all day long in everything we say and in everything we do. Language arts. Math. Handwriting. World history. Spelling. Each part of the curriculum has tremendous discipling potential! But potential untapped lies forever wasted.

Finding ways to integrate the Christian faith into the entire menu of each day's curriculum goes far beyond adding the words *sanctification* and *absolution* to the week's spelling list. It goes far beyond assigning the words of Eph. 2:8–9 as today's handwriting exercise.

Neither of these activities is wrong, in and of itself, but neither cuts to the heart of what it means to integrate the faith into the curriculum of the Christian school. "Christian math" is not adding two altar candles plus three altar candles to get five altar candles. But if not, then what is it? Indeed, is there really such a thing as "Christian math," "Christian language arts," or "Christian spelling"?

The Hidden Curriculum

Dr. Benson Snyder first coined this term in the early 1970s.[1] While serving as staff psychiatrist for both MIT and Wellesley College, he noted that universities in effect function with two curriculums—one open, acknowledged curriculum generally characterized by specific courses, textbooks, and assignments; the other hidden, but powerful nevertheless. The hidden curriculum included such things as the informal social structure of the university; the bases on which professors, in fact, awarded grades, regardless of their stated grading policies; class attendance rules; the regulations governing dormitory life; and so on.

Since Snyder first published his observations and articulated the effects he believed this hidden curriculum had on university students, other educational thinkers have adopted the terminology and applied it to other school settings. The term as it is commonly used today can be understood in somewhat the same sense as the pundit who has observed, "Life is what happens to you while you're waiting around for something else." We might paraphrase that to read, "The hidden curriculum is what students learn while they are waiting for class to start."

90

We might think of the hidden curriculum as including all the procedures, all the activities, all the rules, all the ways teachers approach children, and children approach one another, in the school apart from the formally recognized, planned curriculum or course of study. The hidden curriculum includes virtually all the nonplanned experiences a given child confronts in the classroom, on the playground, and even in the rest rooms and on the school bus. Teachers, obviously, control only part—and probably only a small part—of this curriculum, but it asserts inestimable influence on every student nevertheless.

What does this have to do with how we integrate the Christian faith into our daily lesson plans? Just this. Much of what we do (or fail to do) routinely as we teach math or reading forms a kind of "spiritual hidden curriculum." This curriculum can impact a student's discipleship for great good or ill.

Take math, for example. We have all known students who seem to have a natural affinity for working with numbers. They catch on to new mathematical concepts readily, and they enjoy practicing the skills we introduce. Other students' attitudes border on math phobia. They literally hate math. They find new mathematical concepts threatening at best, incomprehensible at worst.

If a teacher prepares a lesson on, say, decimals, thinking only about decimals, she will teach only decimals. But if she looks at the lesson on decimals as a lesson in math *and* as a lab experience in which she and her students can practice Christian discipleship, the lesson can truly serve as an opportunity for spiritual growth. The students' relationship with Jesus can deepen to become richer and fuller.

How might that happen? As the teacher sits at her kitchen table preparing next week's lesson plans, she notes that the unit on decimals will probably prove difficult for at least some in the class. Even as she prepares, she begins to pray for the whole class in general and for specific students in particular.

As she introduces the decimal unit in class, she might pray with her students before they even open their textbooks. She might ask them to pray specifically that the Holy Spirit will enable her to show Jesus' wisdom, love, and patience as she teaches and especially as she answers questions. Then, as she helps students one-on-one with their assignments during math study times that week, she might pray with individuals who are struggling.

Does Jesus care about fifth-graders and about whether or not they understand decimals? Of course He does! He created our world—a world of beautiful symmetry and order—for our benefit. He wants to show us the beauty He has placed in His creation for our enjoyment. Part of that beauty is mathematical! Besides that, He has invited us to come to Him with all our needs and difficulties. Young people trying to understand the intricacies of decimals for the first time often experience difficulties. They need help in understanding and manipulating new concepts.

We and our students can come together to our Creator, to our Redeemer, to our Lord, to ask His help at any time, with any difficulty—including difficulty with decimals. We can assure our students that their Lord will help them focus their attention as they study. They can trust that He will help them use the intelligence and abilities He has given them to learn how to function in our world. They can trust Him to help them discipline their minds. They can ask Him to enable them to control the nervousness, or even panic, they might feel as they approach a given mathematical concept.

A teacher who communicates this kind of powerful truth to her students has done much more than teach them how to manipulate decimal points as they multiply or divide. She has shown them that their relationship with God through Jesus Christ has tremendous value—real, serviceable, practical value—for the life they live now as well as for the life that is to come (1 Tim. 4:8).

"Teacher, I Heard What You Never Said"

Our patient kindness—Christlike, Christ-empowered kindness—coupled with our prayers for our students and our assurances of Jesus' care and compassion can go a long way toward integrating the Christian faith into the minute-by-minute life of our classroom. Our ultimate goal, of course, is not Christian spelling or Christian social studies. Our ultimate goal is not even an integrated Christian curriculum.

Rather, our goal is an integrated Christian lifestyle. We want the Holy Spirit to use our students' classroom experiences to work in their hearts the ability to live the Christian life with full integrity, integrity in the fullest sense of that word.

As we watch the world system and the people who belong to it disintegrating all around us, we want our students to see every aspect of their lives as part of an ongoing, intimate, and personal walk with their Lord Jesus. We want them to come to Him for His continual forgiveness and cleansing from sin. We want them to rejoice in His love. We want them to celebrate the new life He has given them. We want them to look forward with hope-filled hearts to the heavenly home He is preparing for them. We want them to enjoy a rich, fulfilling relationship with Christ throughout their lives, regardless of whether they face hard times or prosperity, troubles or success, failures or victories.

Curricular materials produced by secular publishers do not—and cannot—give teachers guidance about ways to foster this dynamic faith relationship with Jesus Christ in the classroom. Most curriculum developers have long ago abandoned the philosophy that lay behind the New England Primer's first lesson:

In Adam's fall
We sinned all.

For obvious legal (and fiscal) reasons, secular texts now claim neutrality about religious issues. We may argue about whether this is really so in any given case. But regardless, we as Christian teachers need to face the fact that we cannot look to published curriculum materials for direction as we think about how to nurture the Christian faith and Christian values in our classrooms.

The Fish Doesn't Know . . .

Some curricular materials directly contradict scriptural teachings. We have all seen biology texts and natural history videos that explain megaevolution in great detail and present this belief as incontrovertible fact. Some, but by no means all, values clarification materials unashamedly teach total moral relativism.

This kind of obvious frontal assault presents little danger to the teacher and children in a Christian classroom. We readily see the enemy's fingerprints all over such material. We can even use some materials like these, especially with middle and upper grade students, as we discuss non-Christian worldviews and what we as God's people can say in love to witness to those who believe such philosophies.

We confront an infinitely greater danger as we import Trojan horse curriculums into our classrooms.[2] Just as the wetness of water escapes the proverbial fish, the assumptions of the society around us often escape our notice. These beliefs often directly contradict the truths God Himself has revealed to us. Yet they crop up in reading workbooks, in language arts worksheets, in units on self-esteem or ecology, and we can so easily fail to notice. What are some of these beliefs? If you sat and thought for a few minutes, or better yet, if you listened to a few radio call-in talk shows or read two or three popular magazines, you would probably recognize many of these and come up with more of your own besides:

- Absolute truth does not exist. All truth and all morality are relative. Each person much decide for himself/herself what moral standards to follow. Sincerity of belief matters more than any one person's narrow view of "truth."
- We live in a closed universe. If God exists, He does not care about human affairs and does not intervene in human history. Events that seem to be "miracles" have some other rational, physical explanation.
- Only things we can see, touch, hear, and otherwise experience with our physical senses are real. If something cannot be measured, it does not exist or, at best, it is unimportant. Spiritual realities (God, Satan, angels, heaven, etc.) are inconsequential in the "real world."
- My body, my life are my own. I may do what I please with them.
- The idea of sin and personal human responsibility for evil is outdated. Perhaps society is to blame for individuals who have run amok, but the individuals themselves bear no responsibility for choices that cause harm to themselves and/or others.
- The human race is basically good and is improving right along as we evolve.
- Technological advances will eventually solve all human problems.
- Self-esteem is the greatest achievement to which an individual can aspire, and it could well prove the salvation of our society as well.

- Self-esteem ultimately comes from within each individual, not from any external source. Each individual needs to derive self-esteem from inside himself, quite apart from a relationship with God through Jesus Christ.
- Gender differences involve only differences in physical plumbing. Men and women are interchangeable cogs in the machinery of society, not unique creations of God designed by Him to complement and complete one another.
- God is everything or, alternatively, god is in everything. Nature is god and god is nature. God lives in the rocks and trees and lakes. God is the principle behind everything. I am god; you are god; ultimately everything that exists will merge to become part of the one, which is god. (Variations of this theme abound, but at their core all represent modified versions of Hinduism.)
- Democracy and commitment to individual rights are the highest values anyone can hold. Happiness does not come from receiving Christ's love and then in turn loving and serving others, but rather from asserting one's rights and having one's felt needs met.
- People are valuable because of what they can *do,* rather than because of who they *are* as God's created, redeemed children. Individuals who are no longer useful to society, and individuals who will never be useful, have a questionable claim on limited planetary and societal resources.

Our list could be expanded to fill more pages, but these examples should drive the point home. Each of the presuppositions listed contains a kernel of truth. That is precisely what makes them so dangerous—it makes each lie that much easier to swallow.

For example, our bodies and our lives do belong to us—at least in a broad sense. God has given them to us. Our Creator holds us accountable to care for our bodies and to invest the time and gifts He gives us as His stewards. But in a deeper sense, we know that the apostle Paul rightly asserts:

> Do you not know that your body is a temple of the Holy Spirit, who is in you, whom you have received from God? You are not your own; you were bought at a price. Therefore honor God with your body. (1 Cor. 6:19–20)

We are *not* our own. Our bodies and lives belong to Christ! Believing this, our "right" to commit suicide evaporates—even should we face a debilitating disease or a seemingly intolerable set of circumstances in our lives. Our "right" to use recreational drugs or to abuse alcohol disappears. Our "right" to let our cravings dictate our diet flies out the window. Our "right" to make money our god and to wreck our health in the process of accumulating possessions vanishes.

Each of the "truths" from our list could be examined and exploded in the same way. Whether we like it or not, whether we want to believe it or not, Christianity is countercultural. It always has been. The incorrigible tendencies of human flesh and the obstinate rebellion against God and His commands we see in the society around us force us to face the fact that, as Christians, we will always find ourselves swimming upstream against the cultural currents of our time.

For the most part, secular curriculum developers do not deliberately set out to undermine Christian values. They merely reflect their own values, the values of the society in which we all live. It should surprise no one, then, that the published curriculums we preview will always require careful scrutiny, and they may require major modifications before they can be used in the Christian classroom.

A Trojan Horse of a Different Color

Perhaps, then, teachers and students in Christian schools could best be served by using only curriculums prepared by Christian publishers. After all, what busy teacher has time to scrutinize each lesson for hidden cultural messages? If a Christian curriculum publisher has prepared a Christian social study series, for example, Christian teachers should be able to use it with confidence, right?

Perhaps. Perhaps not.

In an earlier chapter we looked at the way justification and sanctification both work in the lives of God's people—*only by the grace of our God, not by our "trying hard."* Unfortunately, many of the curriculums developed by Christian publishers during the past several decades drip with moralism. The students repeatedly confront admonitions to obey God, to love others, to act responsibly—always in their own power, never in the strength which God's Spirit supplies. While these curriculums do sometimes correctly

96

present justification, rank legalism lurks omnipresent as the texts deal with the sanctified life.

Forced to choose between culturally tainted secular materials and the moralistic religious curriculums available, which should a concerned Christian teacher, a concerned Christian faculty choose? No one can answer that question for you. It may be that some schools choose to purchase only materials produced by secular publishers. Others may use only materials developed by Christian publishers. More often, schools will probably make eclectic decisions based upon the needs of their students, the strengths and weaknesses of their teachers, and the features of a given set of materials.

But whatever curriculum a school finally selects, no Christian teacher dare set his powers of discernment on the shelf and mindlessly follow the lesson plans found in the teachers guide.

The good news is that we do not have to. We have a Teacher—the Holy Spirit will help us use materials with discernment. He will help us identify weaknesses. We can ask Him to show us ways to turn those weaknesses into strengths. Of course, we will still sometimes fail. Students will sometimes pick up misimpressions. They may even come to believe, for a time, things that are not true.

But praise God that He forgives the sins Christian teachers commit as we teach, just as He forgives all of our other failures and shortcomings. He assumes the ultimate responsibility for discipling our students. He is, after all, their Teacher too. And they are, after all, His children—just as we are. Of course that does not excuse sloppy preparation or careless teaching, but it does provide great comfort and the reassurance we need to keep coming back to our classroom, to our discipling task each day.

And the Bushmen?

Three years and some months after I left my fourth grade classroom to write and develop Christian curriculum, I attended a meeting in which the executive director for Missions Services of The Lutheran Church—Missouri Synod reported on the work of his department. He announced, among other things, that the church body had commissioned three new missionaries that month and was assigning them to work among the bushmen of the Kalahari. This was to be the first Christian missionary presence ever among that particular people group.

We serve a gracious and faithful God, a God who hears the prayers of His children.

To Think About

1. Explain the term "hidden curriculum." How can the hidden curriculum affect our classroom discipling goals for good or ill?
2. List ways Christian teachers can legitimately integrate the Christian faith into every aspect of the day. Are some ways of "integrating the faith" illegitimate? Explain.
3. What are "Trojan horse curriculums"? How would you identify them? How can Christian teachers deal with them?
4. Locate a moralistic Christian textbook. In your opinion, what makes this text moralistic? Could a Christian teacher, intent on discipling students, use this text? Defend your answer.

Notes

1. Snyder R. Benson, *The Hidden Curriculum* (New York: Alfred A. Knopf, Inc., 1970).
2. I am indebted to Dr. Jan Case, Concordia Theological Seminary, Fort Wayne, IN, who first suggested the term "Trojan horse curriculum" in reference to moralistic religion materials used in otherwise orthodox settings.

CHAPTER 6

Into the Lab—
Relationships, Discipline,
and Christian Growth

One of my college roommates, philosophizing about the prospect of never becoming rich while teaching in a Christian school, used to sigh, "Well, I've never seen a Wells Fargo truck following a hearse."

Most Christians, at least in our more sanctified moments, recognize how temporary material possessions really are. But most of us do not stop often enough to think about a more positive and important truth: Our Lord has graciously given us many truly precious possessions—our relationships. These relationships outstrip fiscal blessings by far. For one thing, they are eternal. Our relationship with our Lord and the relationships we enjoy with one another through Him will last forever.

As we spend "lab" time with our students in the Christian classroom, then, it stands to reason that we will pour much of our discipling energy into the relationships our students share with us and with one another. Even if an eternal thread did not run through Christian relationships, relationships would still play a critical role in our own lives and in the lives of our students here and now. Learning to relate to others in Christlike ways is an essential part of Christian education.

If we are not surprised at the importance of relationships, neither should we be surprised that Satan takes careful aim at the relationships in Christian classrooms. This holds true for us as teachers in our relationships with students, and with other staff members. It holds true for our students as they relate to us and to one another. Teachers who stop to analyze their discipline problems will quickly

99

see that most breaches involve not just broken rules, but also broken relationships.

As we plan a strategy to disarm our enemy, we need to think both offensively and defensively. How do we structure the relationships in our classroom so as to minimize the chinks in our collective armor? And then, when damage does occur (as it inevitably will in any Christian classroom), how can we best react so that our Lord can minimize the hurt and maximize the spiritual growth in our own hearts and in the hearts of our students?

Growing Together

The apostle Paul writes about this at some length in his letter to the Ephesians. He describes Christian unity and urges his readers to let God work a deep and unifying love in their hearts.

> He Himself [Christ] gave some to be apostles, some prophets, some evangelists, and some pastors and teachers, for the equipping of the saints for the work of ministry, for the edifying of the body of Christ, till we all come to the unity of the faith and the knowledge of the Son of God, to a perfect man, to the measure of the stature of the fullness of Christ; that we should no longer be children ... but, speaking the truth in love, may grow up in all things into Him who is the head—Christ—from whom the whole body, joined and knit together by what every joint supplies, according to the effective working by which every part does its share, causes growth of the body for the edifying of itself in love. (4:11–16 NKJV)

Paul has packed this passage with meaning. We could spill much ink in an attempt to analyze just these few verses and their implications for our classroom ministries. But let's look at just two significant thoughts.

In the first place, Christ has placed all of us together in His body, the holy Christian church, the *una sancta*. We belong together in a profound, almost mysterious way. As Dietrich Bonhoeffer once put it, "Christianity means community through Jesus Christ and in Jesus Christ. . . . We belong to one another only through and in Jesus Christ."[1]

Christianity means community! Our Lord has plans for the community He has established here on earth, for those He has placed in His body. His plans include, first and foremost, growth. We will grow "to a perfect man, to the measure of the stature of the fullness of Christ" (v. 13). The term "perfect man" here refers to maturity. Christ's body will one day be mature. As the NIV puts it, we will attain "to the whole measure of the fullness of Christ." Jesus is our head and someday, by His grace, the body will fit the head. The body will be mature, complete. We will be whole and holy—like our Lord.

But note—and this is the second important point—spiritual growth does not happen as we stalk off to the hills to commune alone with God. We grow as we live *in relationship to one another*. In the normal course of things, children's bones grow at the joints, though our bodies will, of course, repair a bone broken somewhere along its length. But when a child's arms grow longer, when her legs and fingers and toes grow longer, when she shoots up two inches in two months, that growth takes place at the joints.

Christian growth takes place that way too, and not just in childhood. All of God's people grow toward maturity at the joints—as two or more parts of the body come together, we relate to others in the community of believers. We grow up into Christ as we are "joined and knit together *by what every joint supplies.*" As in the human body, only pathological growth occurs when one of the members of Christ's body attempts to grow on its own, apart from the body, apart from Christian community.

What does all this mean for us as we walk into our Christian classrooms each day? First of all, these concepts help us set our direction. We do not adopt classroom procedures or structure our disciplinary techniques simply to prevent chaos or to achieve control. Instead, as we think about classroom relationships in general and classroom discipline in particular, we do so with a clear focus on our Lord's discipling goals for His children—growth toward maturity; growth toward Christ-likeness; growth toward the unity of His body, the church.

Significantly, the Greek word translated *joined* in verse 16 is related to our English word *harmony*. The word translated *knit together* comes from a term that means "to make a treaty." The Lord Christ wants true harmony among His people. He wants all the relationships in our school to sing with the joy of love—love for Him and for one another. He wants us to learn to live at peace. This is no uneasy truce put in place by force, but a peace actively sought and maintained as we fall all over one another in our efforts to honor and care for one another. That harmony, that peace, forms one of our most important over-arching goals as we disciple the children and young people our Lord has placed in our care.

Secondly, as we think about our classroom structures and our disciplinary techniques, we need to recognize and anticipate the opportunities for growth that occur when two or more of God's people come together. Sometimes that coming together will involve conflict. But even conflict can be exciting when we view it with Christ's eyes. When we take this perspective, we need not view disruptions in relationships as irritations, as interruptions of our ministry, or as threats to our own authority in the classroom. Instead, we can see times of conflict, and even times of sin, as windows of opportunity for growth.

A Pound of Prevention

Conflicts will inevitably occur in classroom relationships. So we as Christian teachers need not set them up so as to give our students the chance to practice conflict resolution! The suggestion that someone might actually do that may make you laugh right out loud. But before you do, you need to know that any teacher who has spent any time at all in the classroom has probably booby-trapped her own lab at one time or another without being aware of it.

We can, in effect, set up situations in our classroom which make problems almost inevitable. We can set our students (and ourselves) up for failure. On the other hand, we can create a climate in which our students will more likely experience success in their relationships with us and with one another.

That is not to say classroom relationships will ever be easy. It is not to say that sin and Satan will tuck their tail and leave forever. But more optimal conditions for harmony and peace in the classroom will allow you and your students to practice using God's power under more favorable battlefield conditions. Or, to go back to the lab analogy we have used all along, chemistry students find their experiments less likely to blow up when they can use the proper equipment, when the lab is cooled to the proper temperature, when the correct chemicals have been mixed for them in the proper proportions, and when the flasks are clean and not cracked.

Much depends on the way we handle certain basic elements of classroom management. Let's look at four critical areas.

"Teacher, Do You Love Me?"

As we disciple the students in our classrooms, our students need to know that we care about them, that we love them. Furthermore, they need to know our concern is not some kind of group policy that covers everyone who walks in the door between nine and three-thirty. Rather, they need to see that our love extends to each of them as individuals. This is critical. Each student needs to know that we treasure him, not just for what he can do, not even primarily for what he can do, but rather for who he is—a unique and precious creation of God, a redeemed and treasured member of God's family in Christ, a worthwhile person in God's eyes—and in ours.

We cannot assume that our students will know this automatically, or that their emotional radar will zero in on our love simply because they spend time in our vicinity. We need to tell them. Whether we teach first grade or junior high, we need to say those words that most of us find so hard to say, especially at first:

"I care about you."

"I love you, and Jesus loves you too."

"I'm on your side."

"You're an important person to me."

"I want to help you."

"I'm glad you're in my class."

William James once wrote, "The deepest principle of human nature is the craving to be appreciated."[2] Whether we deal with our students, with fellow faculty members, with other staff members, with people on the school board, with members of our congregation, or with the parents of our students, it is hard to overestimate the power of affirmation, and, in particular, of *agape* love.

As James observed, human beings *crave* appreciation. Students who do not achieve recognition for the positive things they do will soon achieve it in other ways. They will break rules. More importantly, they will act and speak in ways that will break relationships. They will do this because, most of the time, human beings find it less painful to be punished than to be ignored.

At times in the past, some in ministry have believed that by affirming their students they would encourage the sin of pride in their students' hearts. Yet if love and affirmation do that, most of the New Testament makes little sense. Jesus often affirmed His disciples. In one of the most extravagant statements of love ever uttered, Jesus once said to them, "As the Father has loved Me, so have I loved you" (John 15:9). How much does the Father love Jesus? That is how much Jesus said He loved His disciples—and by implication, us too!

That love, that affirmation, carried the first disciples victoriously through the bleakest times of persecution. Nearly every one of the disciples who heard Jesus utter these remarkable words on Maundy Thursday night would later go on to die for Him. The Savior's love has power! Life-transforming power!

Amazingly, Jesus wants to channel His love for His people through us. We are Christ enfleshed for our students. Jesus invites us as Christian teachers to live as a conduit, a pipeline, for His love as He pours it out into the lives of the young people He places in our classrooms! Let Him do that. Allow the Holy Spirit to keep the channel clear, to continually ream out the deposits of frustration and lovelessness that tend to accumulate in all human hearts. Let Him daily "cleanse [your heart] from all unrighteousness"—even as He has promised to do (1 John 1:9 NKJV). And then let the love—Christ's love—flow and flow and overflow in your classroom.

It would be easy to stop here, to assume that every Christian teacher in every Christian classroom can and will, of course, do this. Most teachers, after all, already like children. Otherwise, they would most likely leave the classroom.

But what about the student no teacher likes to think about? What about the student who has few social skills? What about the student who continually interrupts you or deliberately defies you? What about the student who will never, ever cooperate? Or the one who just plain smells bad because of poor personal hygiene? What about the student you find impossible to love?

All teachers sooner or later face this problem. Some of us run into it the first week of our first September in the classroom. Others of us teach for a few years before it happens. Regardless, it can shake our faith in ourselves—and sometimes even our faith that God has called us into the classroom. We seldom admit it to one another or even to ourselves, but eventually we all must confront this particular brand of lovelessness in our hearts.

What then?

To answer that, we first need to review the definition of love. Our culture likes to portray it as a syrupy feeling of affection that draws us to another person. And, of course, love most often does involve feelings. But love in the sense in which the New Testament uses it primarily means a commitment to seek the welfare of another person, to place that person's needs ahead of our own. Love in this sense is primarily a decision. The world system in which we live says, "Feel love first, then act in loving ways based on your feelings." God says, "Act in loving ways first, and feelings of affection will follow."

Realizing this makes love in the classroom (or anywhere else, for that matter) both easier and harder. It becomes easier in that it frees us from the need to pretend to ourselves that we feel affection for someone when in fact we do not. It also frees us from the need to try to drum up affection inside ourselves. We cannot sustain that kind of "love" for any length of time anyhow.

On the other hand, seeing love as a decision makes our lives more difficult. This truth grabs us by the lapels and tells us that we must assume the responsibility for our lovelessness. Any failure to love—even failure to love those students who act in the most obnoxious ways—is quite simply sin.

Yet, praise to our gracious Lord, we have a remedy for sin! As Christ's people, we know what to do with it. When we recognize the lovelessness in our lives, we can run with it to the cross. We can confess it to Jesus. We can receive His absolution and, in absolution, freedom. As our Lord forgives us, He breaks the chains of our guilt and of sin's power to keep us from obedience. His absolution pours His power into our hearts, enabling us to yield to His will.

The cycle of repentance works in this instance, just as it works to empower us to overcome any other sin. We may have to return to the cross 20 times an hour at first, but there is no condemnation in that. Our Lord always receives us. He invites us to come and to keep coming. Remember, repentance is God's medicine, a medicine on which no one can overdose.

By God's grace, we can decide to use His power to act in loving ways toward those students we thought we could never love. We can decide to use God's power to speak words of affirmation and love to them. As we decide to love—to put the other person's needs and well-being ahead of our own—God will change our hearts little by little. As we continue to act in love, sooner or later we will begin to feel compassion and concern, Christ's compassion and concern alive in us. His love alive in us. And our students will recognize that love as the real thing.

"Teacher, Will You Help Me Succeed?"

Alabama football coach Bear Bryant once said, "If anything goes bad, I did it. If anything goes semigood, we did it. If anything goes real good, you did it. That's all that it takes to get people to win football games for you."

Just as we look for ways to assure students of our love for them as individuals apart from their achievements, we also look for ways to help them experience success. As your students learn and practice specific skills, discipleship skills included, they need to know that their teacher is on their team. Just as a coach encourages, challenges, and drills his players, we also work to motivate, inspire, and challenge the young people in our classrooms.

If our students don't quite grasp a concept or don't proficiently execute a skill, perhaps we haven't yet explained or demonstrated it in just the right way. As our students learn and practice, we cheer them on. When a student understands a truth, acts in a Christlike way, or speaks words of compassion in a tough situation, we point out this victory. We congratulate her on what God has done in her. Together we thank God for His work in her heart.

In short, we teach for success, we disciple for success. We help shoulder the blame for failures. We show young disciples how to plug into Christ's power. We keep on encouraging. We fan the fire of hope. And we celebrate the victories—all kinds of victories, large and small—won by Jesus for us and shared by Him with us.

"Teacher, Where Are the Limits?"

Perhaps you have stood at one time or another on the brink of a deep chasm. Standing toe-to-toe with nothing but thin air in front of you can be frightening. A good many of us shy away from the edge of a cliff unless a guardrail bounds it. Then we feel safe enough to look out over the scenery below.

It seems obvious, but if we want a classroom atmosphere that fosters Christlike relationships, we need to let our students know where the limits are, what behaviors we expect and what behaviors we will not tolerate.

For some, the word *structure* conjures up pictures of rigidity, of Marine Corps boot camp or worse. Nothing could be further from the truth. Love sets limits. Whether human beings have always recognized it or not, God gave the Ten Commandments as a gift of love to His human creatures. Structure in a Christian classroom needs to provide reasonable limits, kindly but firmly enforced.

We need not apologize for having rules. All of God's human creatures need structure. Most children, particularly, find security in limits. Nearly all children find a lack of structure unsettling. For some, a lack of structure can feel as threatening as approaching an abyss without a guardrail.

Some teachers involve the students themselves in setting up the structures with which they will live. In many groups this works well, particularly if the teacher leads class members to phrase the guidelines positively, and if the students understand and can articulate the reasons behind the rules. (E.g., "Only one person talks at a time so that the rest of us can hear what that person is saying.")

Whether you involve the students in developing classroom rules or not, you will want to formulate the fewest number of rules possible, state them positively, and focus particular attention on behaviors that foster positive relationships.

For example, you may choose to begin the school year without a formal rule about using the classroom pencil sharpener. In some groups, an entire year can go by without a Pencil Sharpener Crisis. In other groups, you may look up from your desk during study time on the first day of school and see a ragged mob of 14 students elbowing one another aside so they can sharpen their pencils. In that case, you and/or the class may want to come up with a plan to prevent so many people from wasting so much of their study time standing in line.

Regardless of how you choose to formulate rules and procedures in your classroom, students will test the limits from time to time. They will push up against the boundaries. Whether you teach three's or college sophomores, your students (most of them probably subconsciously) want to know whether you mean what you have said. Usually this kind of testing happens during the first few weeks of school, but it can recur especially after a disruption in classroom routine, say, Christmas break or a stint with a substitute teacher.

As you think about setting up classroom structures, keep individual differences in mind. Just as our students differ in their interests, their intelligence, their emotions, and in their reactions to circumstances, they also differ in their need for structure. So do classes. Some individuals seem to need more structure. Some function best with less. Some groups of children or young people seem to need more structure. Some function best with less. Teachers can prevent many problems by adjusting to the needs of each given class.[3]

But teachers differ too. Some of us need more structure, some of us function better with less. No one management style works best for every student, for every class, or for every teacher. So as you encounter each new group of individuals, each new class, each new school year, you will find yourself experimenting. In fact, you probably *should* find yourself experimenting. This kind of adjustment is perfectly normal, acceptable, even healthy.

As you work this through, ask the Holy Spirit to help you settle on a style that meshes your needs with those of your students. Feel free to adjust your expectations and techniques as you go along, and do it without feeling guilty. In making adjustments, you are simply responding to the fact that God has created each of us as unique persons. We each relate to one another in unique ways. When those relationships seem to falter, God will give us the courage we need to say to our Lord (and perhaps to a colleague or two), "My techniques aren't working, at least they aren't working as well as I would like. Will you help me figure out how to adjust what I am doing?"

"Teacher, Are You Fair?"

We demonstrate Christ's love to our students. We celebrate their victories. We set and enforce reasonable classroom limits. As we follow these overarching principles, we will create a classroom atmosphere in which fruitful Christian relationships can thrive.

But as we act out these principles, we will sometimes find them in conflict. For example, showing Christlike love to an individual student may require that in a specific instance we set aside the letter of the law. Valid as our reasons for making an exception may be, we need to keep in mind the fact that most elementary school students care—care passionately—about "fairness." While most preschoolers have not yet developed an understanding of justice, some first-graders will occasionally express concern about it. By the time most children reach third or fourth grade, they have honed their need for "fairness" razor sharp.

We do want to act justly as we work with our students. We do want to be fair. After all, we model God's character for our students—and God is just. Students find it much easier to respect teachers who do not gut classroom rules by making frivolous or incomprehensible exceptions. We work toward making our rules, our actions, and our reactions as consistent as possible.

Yet all human beings act inconsistently at times. Teachers are no exception. Our tolerance for noise in the classroom, for example, will likely be lower if we have a headache. It may be higher if our favorite team has just won the World Series.

Ways to Prevent Discipline Problems

- Prepare each lesson and activity thoroughly.

- Use variety in lesson presentation and techniques. Choose activities that will interest and challenge your students.

- Have necessary lesson materials at hand when you begin.

- Establish and enforce classroom limits kindly but firmly.

- Structure each situation for success and reward it; help the students feel good about their progress.

- Comment favorably on positive behavior.

- Maintain the distinction between teacher and student; expect to be "in charge."

So then, we have rules. But we sometimes make exceptions. We treat all students alike. But we sometimes must treat a particular student or a small group of students differently. Most students who seem most bothered by exceptions to the rules will respond favorably if you take the time to sit down with them one-on-one to explain your actions as clearly and simply as possible, in keeping with bounds of professional confidentiality. While that is true, no teacher should ever place himself in the position of debating classroom rules and disciplinary techniques with students.

Be aware that sometimes, though, students who seem unduly bothered by "unfairness" have other things troubling them. Those students whose parents are sailing toward the rocky coast of divorce, for example, often struggle with a lack of security. Perhaps the limits at home have all but disappeared, either because the parents feel guilty and are trying to "make it up" to the child by relaxing the household rules, or because the parents have no time or energy left over to enforce previously observed limits.

Any situation at home that leads a young disciple to feel insecure can make classroom limits that much more important to him or her. Concern for these students leads us to help them, if possible, to understand and accept changes in procedures or inconsistencies in classroom expectations.

Of course, even if our students should fail to understand or accept the explanations we give them, we must do what we believe best for each student. God holds us as teachers accountable for what happens in our classroom. He has given us the responsibility of discipling our students. Along with that responsibility, we have received the authority to decide how we can best accomplish the tasks that He, through our congregation, has called us to do. In some cases we may need to remind an individual student or even an entire class of that fact. Sometimes, we need to remind ourselves too.

An Ideal Setting

If we could orchestrate activities in our classroom so completely that disharmony was squelched before it arose, what a joy teaching would be! Preventing relationship problems is important. Nevertheless, we will never prevent them all. And, as we said as we began this chapter, dysfunctional relationships need not signal defeat or disaster for us. Rather, our Lord will help us use classroom relationship problems as windows of opportunity. Conflicts will allow us and our students to explore important principles of discipleship—principles that usually cannot be taught or learned in any other way.

Chapter 7 will focus on ways to do that.

To Think About

1. Describe a time you found your membership in the body of Christ especially meaningful. How do we grow spiritually in relationships in ways that we cannot grow by ourselves?
2. Have you ever known anyone who decided to practice "Lone Ranger" Christianity? Have you ever been tempted to have a "just me and Jesus" faith yourself? What can lead a Christian to make that kind of decision? Why is it spiritually pathological?
3. Describe a Christian classroom set up for failure in relationships. Contrast this with one set up for success.

Notes

1. Dietrich Bonhoeffer. *Life Together* (San Francisco: Harper and Row [now HarperCollins], 1954), 21.
2. Quoted by Kenneth Erickson in *The Power of Praise* (St. Louis: Concordia Publishing House, 1984), 13.
3. For an interesting exploration of this and several other aspects of human behavior based on the Briggs-Meyer model of personality theory, see Ruth M. Ward's *Self-Esteem: Gift from God* (Grand Rapids: Baker Book House, 1984).

CHAPTER 7

When the Lab Blows Up

Mr. Roberts had never seen a parent so angry. He had served as principal at Grace for nearly two years, but never had words ricocheted off the walls of his office with such energy. After a heated discussion—no, argument—that lasted more than 30 minutes, Gary Schmidt stormed out the office door. As he left, he shot back over his shoulder, "I thought this was a Christian school. I guess my son and I can both see what a joke that is!"

The myth persists. Otherwise reasonable Christians seem to lose sight of the obvious truth in the heat of specific crises:

- Satan works in Christian schools too.
- The students and teachers in Christian schools struggle with their flesh, just as do believers in any other setting.
- No Christian school sits under a Plexiglas bubble, sealed against the evils and temptations of the world system around us.

In short, Christian people in Christian schools face temptation and fall into sin. As Luther once wrote, "We daily sin much and indeed deserve nothing but punishment."[1] What applies to Christ's people in general terms applies also to those who work and study in Christian schools.

Sooner or later as we live, play, and work together in Christian schools, the lab will blow up. When that happens, individuals will be hurt; sin always results in damage to the offender and often to those caught in the crossfire. As the last chapter pointed out, teachers who stop to analyze their discipline problems will discover that most breaches involve not just broken rules but also broken relationships.

A group of third grade girls form a club, the main goal of which is to exclude Rhonda and Elicia.

Kim comes to kindergarten pouting. By nine, she has broken all of Tiffany's crayons, slapped Russell twice, and bitten Terrance.

Brandon walks into the classroom 15 minutes after school has started. He throws himself into his chair and proceeds to pick up his desk, one of the free-standing kind. To the astonishment of everyone in the room, he calmly dumps its contents—books, pencils, papers, glue, scissors, and all—onto the floor and then guffaws.

Vincent strikes out during the sixth grade recess softball game. He grimaces with anger, charges the pitcher's mound, and comes within a hair's breadth of walloping Jeremy with the bat as all the infield players rush to stop the fight.

Sometimes a test tube pops. Other times, classroom relationships explode with such force that the roof threatens to collapse. Big problems and little ones. Minor infractions and full-blown rebellion. Each brings with it the potential for great damage and destruction. Each also presents an opportunity for growth in Christian discipleship in the lives of all those involved. Much depends upon how we as disciplers deal with the individuals who find themselves sitting in the twisted wreckage following an explosion.

Beginning teachers, especially, find themselves thinking about discipline a lot. Will I be able to control my class? Will the students respect me? What do I do when someone challenges my authority or refuses to do what I have asked them to do?

These questions and related ones run through the minds not just of beginning teachers but of almost everyone who meets a new class for the first time. Hundreds of books zero in on ways to maintain classroom discipline. Each spring seems to germinate a new crop of theories; each autumn seems to burgeon with a bumper crop of new techniques.

Teachers in Christian schools need have no quarrel with the development of new theories and disciplinary techniques. God has given us the science of psychology as one of His good gifts to us in the creation. We can learn much from many of the experts who have written in this field. Yet we must view any theory of discipline, any technique of classroom control through the lens of our discipleship goals.

We can indeed import into the Christian classroom some of the methods about which we read. We can modify other methods so that they better meet our discipling goals. But we must wholly reject some methods because they will short-circuit the discipling task our

Lord Jesus has given us. As in the selection of curriculum materials, we must be selective. We must make informed choices.

But how do we evaluate the classroom management techniques we read about? What criteria form the basis for that evaluation? What general principles must remain at the core of whatever particular techniques we might adopt?

Law and Gospel: The Cycle of Repentance Revisited

As teachers in Christian schools, we recognize broken rules and broken relationships as more than mere breaches in decorum or social *faux pas*. They constitute sin. If we accept that premise, then we must agree that sin and grace must frame any discussion of Christian discipline.

Law and Gospel form the skeleton on which we hang each Bible lesson we teach. But Law and Gospel permeate our classroom the rest of the day too. Law and Gospel provide the foundation on which we build and maintain classroom relationships. Law and Gospel point out the path we need to take whenever hurts, needs, conflicts, and problems arise.

Far more than pious-sounding theory, Law and Gospel provide practical help as we and our students grow together in Christian discipleship from day to day, from hour to hour. We and our students need to grow always deeper in what we know about these basic truths. We and our students also need to grow always more skillful in applying them. Personally. Consistently.

When teachers act and react with sin and grace, Law and Gospel clearly in mind, when teachers lead their students into a developmentally appropriate understanding of these principles, such teachers will have at hand the essential discipling tools they need when problems arise.

If, however, teachers ignore or neglect these truths from day to day, they will reach for the tools they need during times of crisis— and will come up empty-handed. Few students of any age are mature enough to sit through a thorough explanation of God's judgment on sin and His remedy for it while they are in the throes of the emotions that accompany the brokenness sin brings. But if our students have already begun to grasp the meaning and importance of

Law and Gospel in an atmosphere conducive to thoughtfulness and reflection, a brief review during times of difficulty will enable them to plug into the healing and strength God offers them.

The cycle of repentance first introduced in chapter 3 could be taught to almost any child old enough to attend school. Of course, wise teachers would simplify the terms for younger students. Wise teachers would give many concrete examples to illustrate the cycle and how it works. Wise teachers would ask students to create real-life examples of their own. A wise Christian teacher concerned about discipling his students would doubtless want to testify about the meaning and value of this process in his own personal life as well.

But regardless of the specific ways we might modify the content to make it developmentally appropriate and personally meaningful for our students, one of the first lessons of the first day of each school year should involve reviewing these concepts and deepening our students' understanding and appreciation of them.

Whether or not a teacher chooses to use the specific diagram included in this book is immaterial. Nevertheless, all Christians need to understand the purposes for which God has given His people the gifts of contrition, confession, absolution, and power through the life-changing work of the Holy Spirit.

Luther urged believers to practice the process of repentance daily. He framed his admonition as an invitation to daily remember our Baptism. How appropriate! For without an understanding of the process of repentance, young people will view Baptism either as a sweet—but meaningless—ritual or as a kind of magic spell. They will find themselves held in bondage by certain sins. They will find their witness ineffective. They will live with a defeatist attitude. Or they will stand God's Law on its head. In pride, they will look down on others, even as they convince themselves that they have somehow earned God's love by living up to His standards.

Both we and our students need a firm grasp of Law and Gospel, sin and grace. We need to review these concepts with one another often. Then when we need their power, power put there by our heavenly Father for us, we will be able to appropriate it. The principles can be taught. In fact, we can teach them best as we study Scripture with our students each day.

We can also use our formal time with Jesus each day to teach our students to recognize some of the excuses all Christians use at times to avoid accountability for our sins and repentance:

1. *Denial* ("I didn't do it.")
2. *Comparison* ("He did it too." "She did it first." "They did it twice.")
3. *Rationalization* ("It's not so bad." "Why can't we?")
4. *Blame-shifting* ("She made me do it." "You don't know what they did to me.")

Many students in a fourth-grade class I once taught used these excuses, and variations on them, with extraordinary adeptness. Exasperated one morning, I set aside the religion lesson I had planned to teach. Instead, the children and I worked our way through a list of excuses like the one above. Because our discussion was not tied to a specific incident, the students seemed to feel free from the need to be defensive.

We talked through several examples—somewhat zany examples as I remember. I struggled to keep the conversation light; we stayed away from any scenario even remotely resembling recent classroom incidents. I used some examples from my own childhood. We laughed a lot. Nevertheless, most of our laughter was the laughter of recognition. We all saw ourselves.

I remember the classroom getting quieter as we went along. At points, the discussion became quite intense. We talked about the ways adults—teachers, too—sometimes use the same excuses, perhaps couching them in different language, but trying to avoid responsibility and repentance in the same way youngsters do. We talked about God's alternative to excuses—repentance. Then, one by one, the children began to share their own examples. God's Spirit touched each of our hearts in a special way that morning.

In the days that followed, applying the principles of sin and grace became much easier with that particular class. I would still sometimes catch students red-handed, only to hear them exclaim, "I didn't do it!"

But at that point I would respond, "And I'll just bet she (he) did it first." Almost always, the student and I would both grin, and the student would say—most times genuinely—"I'm sorry, Miss Fryar." We had become allies, partners with one another, intent on helping one another grow in Christ-likeness.

Guidance, Discipleship, Discipline

If we approach disciplinary problems as discipling opportunities, we will begin to see our task as one of guidance. We do not shoot from the hip, taking purely punitive actions. Rather, we want to help our students by God's grace identify the right path, get up on it, and stay there. How can that happen? Once an infraction has occurred, once rules and relationships have been broken, what do we do? What steps can we take so that God's Spirit can bring about the repentance and restoration He so yearns to see—for His glory and for our good?

First of all, we need to find out whether or not a student knew God's will in the specific circumstance and chose to ignore it, or whether the student did not fully distinguish right from wrong. This may sound like a principle that applies only as we work with younger children, but that is not always so.

A teenager who had been in my second-grade class several years earlier ran into trouble with the law during her first year of high school. Picked up for shoplifting, the girl (we'll call her Sandy Smith) was remanded by the court to a juvenile parole officer. The court required Mrs. Smith to accompany Sandy on her visits to the parole office.

Mrs. Smith shared some of the initial meeting with me. "For the first 30 minutes I was confused," she said, "Then the officer sent Sandy out of the room and talked with me alone. I asked her about her interview with Sandy. She told me that she had chosen her questions carefully to find out if Sandy knew that stealing was wrong. She says that lots of the kids who come through the court system today have never learned basic things like 'Thou shalt not steal!' "

Even in a Christian school, even with students who have known Christ all their lives, discipling as we discipline may first of all involve finding out whether or not an offender has read and understood the signposts along God's path. Does the first-grader know that God wants pupils to obey those in authority (e.g., teachers)? Does the eighth-grader understand what the Scriptures have to say about the issue of pornography?

Law for the Sake of the Gospel

Today, probably more than ever before, discipline often begins with teaching. Suppose a student in our classroom has broken a com-

117

mandment of which he was unaware, or suppose a student has unknowingly hurt someone. As we enter into conversation with that student, we will certainly want to give attention to clarifying the issue, modeling Jesus' patience and kindness even as we do that. We remember that ignorance of God's Law does not excuse sin, and we keep one goal in mind—contrition and confession.

In other cases, students will know that they have sinned before we say a word. In cases like this as well, we have a single goal—contrition and confession.

When the Law has done its work, when a student has allowed God's Spirit to work repentance, we will immediately remind the student of the forgiveness of sins Jesus won for us at Calvary. We may want to pray together with the student, thanking the Savior for His forgiveness. If others have been hurt by a student's sin, we will offer to help the offender patch up broken relationships. In all but the most unusual circumstances, this will close the case.

The waters get deeper, though, when we confront a student who knows right from wrong, who has sinned and knows that to be the case, but who is not contrite. In situations like these, we have no choice but a firm application of God's Law. We do not do our students a favor by creating excuses for them. We do not do our students a favor by letting sin slide by while we look in the other direction. Neither do we do students a favor by treating sinful attitudes or actions as infractions of human rules. Any time we ignore or downplay sin, we also rob our students of the Gospel's power to free them from sin's guilt and sin's bondage.

Walther quotes Luther:

> That is what my Antinomians, too, are doing today, who are teaching beautifully and (as I cannot but think) with real sincerity about Christ's grace, about the forgiveness of sin and whatever else can be said about the doctrine of redemption. But they flee as if it were the very devil the consequence that they should tell the people about the third article, of sanctification, that is, of the new life in Christ. They think one should not frighten or trouble the people, but rather always preach comfortingly about grace and the forgiveness of sins in Christ, and under no circumstances use these or similar words, "Listen! You want to be a Christian and at the same time remain an adulterer, a whoremonger, a drunken swine, arrogant, covetous, a usurer, envious, vindictive, malicious,

etc.!'" Instead they say, "Listen! Though you are an adulterer, a whoremonger, a miser, or other kind of sinner, if you but believe, you are saved, and you need not fear the Law. Christ has fulfilled it all!'"

Then Walther himself continues:

For God's sake, therefore, beware! When you are about to preach the Gospel, be sure to put it in such a way that you will not make sinners secure and thus become a preacher and preserver of sin. Of course we must preach Christ as the Victor over sin, death, devil, and hell, but we must also say to the people, "You must repent, and then the Holy Spirit will come with His grace and comfort, enlighten, and sanctify you."

... If a preacher speaks only of faith and is silent about the Law, he leads his hearers to the dreadful state where they think they no longer need repentance, so that finally they are beyond help.[2]

While Walther wrote to pastors, we as teachers must apply Law and Gospel in our classrooms with an eye toward the same goal toward which Luther and Walther point—repentance. Even as we counsel with students who have sinned, our hearts cry out to God, asking Him to give His gift of repentance.

We speak Law so that we can speak Gospel. We clearly define the sin or sins involved. We identify God's attitude toward those sins. We specify what God demands of His people when they sin—sorrow over the sin, confession without excuses, and a desire to turn from sin toward obedience. We also remind the student that God wants to give these gifts. God will work within us the desire and the ability to obey Him, but we must let Him do that. We must give up our excuses. We must stop trying to justify ourselves.

If a student hardens his heart and refuses to admit his guilt, we have no choice but to speak more Law.[3] We may do this with our actions as well as in our words. For example, students who have been fighting on the playground and who refuse to admit their sin to one another and ask for forgiveness may need to sit on the sidelines during playground time until such confession is forthcoming. Students who disrupt classroom worship and who respond disrespectfully to your admonition, may need to review the meaning of the Third and Fourth Commandments in some way. We impose such penalties with one goal in mind—helping the student see the seriousness of sin and the need for repentance.

In the face of rebellion—a pattern of disobedience and impenitence—a teacher may decide to refer a student to the principal or, in some schools, to the pastor. In essence, this tactic involves no more or no less than the principles our Savior gave to His church in Matthew 18.

A teacher who has decided that this step is necessary should, whenever possible, discuss the issue with the principal or pastor beforehand rather than showing up on the office threshold with an offending student in hand. The teacher will want to share pertinent history and details beforehand too. Teacher and principal (pastor) can pray with one another, for one another, and for the student. Then, when the opportunity arises, the called workers involved can sit down together with the student to work through the issue.

As we work with young people in disciplinary situations, we must always separate the sinner from his or her sin. During the course of our conversation we might even use words like, "I care about you. I love you. But I cannot let you behave in this way. Your sin is hurting you. It is hurting others in this class (school). It cannot continue." Jesus' care and compassion must shine out through our words and actions. Our Savior always loves sinners, no matter how mired in a particular sin we may be. As the apostle Paul writes, "God demonstrates His own love for us in this: While we were still sinners, Christ died for us" (Rom. 5:8).

That's the wonder of the Gospel. That's the power of the Gospel to draw us to our Savior. Seeing the awfulness of our sin, we can throw ourselves into the arms of our heavenly Father, the Father who has been yearning for our return.

That's the point to which we want to lead our students—to the Father's waiting arms. That's the Good News of absolution we can share with our students when they have been led by the Holy Spirit to confess their sins.

If you analyze the process you have just read about, you will discover that it is not new. In fact, many in the church down through the ages have considered a part of this practice a sacrament—confession and absolution. Our Redeemer-King has given us the privilege of sharing the crown jewels of His kingdom with our brothers and sisters—our students: Forgiveness. Freedom. Peace. Power.

Bonhoeffer comments:

Anybody who lives beneath the Cross and who has discerned in the Cross of Jesus the utter wickedness of all men and of his own heart will find there is no sin that can ever be alien to him ... Looking at the Cross of Jesus, he knows the human heart. He knows how utterly lost it is in sin and weakness, how it goes astray in the ways of sin, and he also knows that it is accepted in grace and mercy. Only the brother under the cross can hear a confession.[4]

Only a sinner who stands beneath the cross can rightly hear the confession of a brother or sister. That applies whether the confession we hear comes from one who is 8 or 80. We stand together on level ground beneath the cross of Jesus. We share with our students the same grace that so comforts our own hearts. We need not, we dare not, apply that grace stingily to our students or to ourselves. But we need always, by God's grace, to apply it in humility and Christlike love.

Truth and Consequences

Does God's forgiveness preclude consequences for sin? No. Someone who robs a bank may confess that sin and receive complete absolution from God for it. However, that person will end up in court and, quite possibly, in jail for the crime.

In the Christian classroom, students who have received God's forgiveness may still face consequences resulting from their actions. To pose an obvious example, someone who damages property would in most cases be asked to repair or replace it.

In less obvious cases, too, certain sins bring with them unpleasant consequences. A student who cheats on a math test may receive an F, may have to take the test over again at a time convenient for the teacher, or both. A student who fails to do a homework assignment may have to complete it the next evening or over the weekend. Most often, the principle of logical consequences applies.

Even then, we need to take special care that our students understand the reasons behind the consequences they face, because Satan will always tempt them to think that they are somehow paying for or making up for their sin as they bear its consequences. We cannot allow our students to fall for Satan's lie that the forgiveness

Christ announces to us through one another is conditional or ephemeral, having no take-it-to-the-bank value in "real life."

Unless we take exquisite care to explain this to students and unless we keep on reminding them of it, the distinction will be lost on them. The peace and joy that come from knowing God's forgiveness will quickly tarnish.[5]

Restoring Relationships

As this chapter has noted repeatedly, broken rules almost always result in broken relationships. As believers live, work, and play together, we will sometimes irritate or provoke one another. We will sometimes wound one another's feelings. At the same time we know that in Christ's kingdom, relationships matter. We might argue that they matter most of all. After all, Jesus lived, died, and rose again to restore our relationship with God and our relationships with each other.

Each believer's discipleship has two dimensions, a vertical relationship with God and a horizontal relationship with those around us. Depicted visually, these two dimensions form a cross. Imagine the crossbeams locked in place in relation to one another. That being true, when one beam is knocked off kilter, the other will at once also be skewed.

This is why as we help a young person to a restored relationship with God, we will also help that student to a restored relationship with anyone who has been hurt by the student's sin. We smooth the road along which both must travel toward restoration.

How can we do this? Many times the offender needs only to ask those she has hurt for forgiveness. Sometimes we might suggest that she write a note of apology. Sometimes we may need to help everyone involved understand and take part in a process of restitution. Always, though, we need to stick with the offender through the process to make sure that heartfelt confession is made and forgiveness is both extended and received by the individuals involved.

As the disciples in our classroom grow in their ability to use God's wisdom and power to work through relationship problems on their own, we need to inch our way out of the process. A growing ability to settle conflict God's way signals growth in discipleship.

We look for this signal. We nurture and encourage independent use of these skills.

At the same time, we keep in mind the risks. We pray God for the wisdom not to abandon students who still need guidance. We walk a fine line. We want to give our students freedom to fail, yet we do not want to doom them to failure. We set up situations that will allow students to practice interpersonal skills, but we avoid throwing young disciples into waters where their inexperience or spiritual immaturity will drown them.

What Is the *Real* Problem Here?

We cannot leave the topic of discipling as we discipline without a short discussion about situations that seem like disciplinary problems but in reality involve much more.

For example, certain allergies or other physical problems can cause hyperactivity or aggression. Certain types of epileptic seizures can cause a child to "phase out." Most times the child will show few outward signs to betray what is happening. During a relatively minor seizure like this, the child may simply appear to be day-dreaming, but she will be unaware of what is going on around her. A student caught in a seizure like this may, legitimately, not know about the math page you just assigned or the social studies project you explained this morning. Some children take medications with side effects that will similarly alter their ability to think, to stay awake, or to concentrate in class.

Sometimes students act in unacceptable and sinful ways, but extenuating circumstances lie at the core of the misbehavior. All human beings find it harder to cope with life's demands when confronted with unusual stresses and strains. Many children today bear burdens far heavier than they can comfortably carry.

Some children growing up in dysfunctional families, for example, may feel great pressure to perform, to be the best, to succeed. In this way the child hopes to minimize strains within the family. Such a child often blames himself for family problems. He thinks, "If I were a better student (athlete, son, brother, etc.), my parents wouldn't have to drink (do drugs, divorce, etc.)." Many times, a student caught in a family system like this will excel in anything he

123

tries. But given the right set of circumstances, his internalized anger can explode like a powder keg.

Other children, filling a different role in a dysfunctional family system, will act out their anger and frustration nearly nonstop. Such children live in a war zone of their own making, at odds with everyone around them.

When we confront classroom behavior that seems to stem from a dysfunctional family life, we need to address the student's specific, offending behaviors directly. However, helping the student find ways to deal appropriately with the family problem must be an equally important priority for the Christian teacher.

Most classroom teachers do not have the kind of training nor the time needed to counsel families through serious problems. But God can use us as channels of His concern and as tools through which He can direct families who need help to the professionals who can help them.

Child abuse, parental neglect, drug abuse, health problems, an impending family divorce—the children and young people in our classrooms may face many overwhelming challenges. Lest we punish someone already being victimized by a deeper problem, we need to listen, to listen with our heart as well as with our intellect. As we disciple troubled students, we need to consult with parents and with one another on the school faculty.

When it is possible, teachers, principal, pastor, and parents need to form a team that works and prays together. As we commit each situation to our Lord in prayer and as we do some detective work, we will find doctors, clinics, counselors, social workers, and other people who can help our students and their families live more comfortably with themselves. In doing so, we will remove some of the barriers that keep individual students from growth in their discipleship—in their relationship with the Lord Jesus and with one another. Chapters 9 and 10 discuss this concept in more detail.

Debris, Discipleship, and Our Own Emotions

Eight-year-old Taylor did not come back from the playground after lunch. When his teacher asked about him, another third-grader reported, "He went home. He didn't have his spelling done." Taylor lived more than two miles from school.

Put yourself into this teacher's nightmare. What feelings run through your mind and heart? Fear? Anger? Worry over Taylor's safety? After an initial rush of emotion, you would almost certainly report the incident to the principal, call Taylor's parents, and then pray your way through the afternoon.

As the minutes and hours slipped by, you might question your relationship with Taylor in particular and with your class in general. Why might a third-grader want to walk two miles to his home rather than tell you that he had not done his homework? How could you have inspired such fear in the heart of an eight-year-old?

> Later on in the afternoon Shaun, Taylor's best friend, came to the teacher. "Taylor's mom and dad had a big fight this morning," Shaun said quietly. "He told me he thinks his dad might set the house on fire. He's really scared for his mom. I think that's why he went home."

Put yourself back into this teacher's nightmare. What feelings hammer at you now?

Before you could deal effectively with Taylor, before you could meet productively with Taylor's mother or dad, you would almost certainly need to deal with your own emotions. No teacher or principal would have the luxury of time to work through all his or her personal issues before an initial meeting with Taylor's family, but to attempt to guide Taylor or his parents further down the path of their own discipleship without recognizing the impact this incident is having upon your own discipleship would, without doubt, compromise your effectiveness as a discipler.

As the seams of our society continue to unravel, as families— even Christian families—find the stresses of life ripping through the fabric of relationships, teachers find themselves dealing with serious problems in the lives of their students. Whether we confront a first-grader violating a playground safety rule or an eighth-grader sharing amphetamines with classmates, we need to be aware of how each incident affects us, how it impacts our own emotions, our own relationship with God and with the student(s) involved. Taking time out—even a brief time out—to think and pray gives the Holy Spirit an opportunity to work self-control and wisdom in our hearts.

In most cases a teacher can legitimately say to a student, "I am too angry (upset, sad, confused) to discuss this right now. We will talk about it later today after I have thought and prayed." For the most part, students will respect this kind of statement, and some will learn to emulate the behavior. A teacher who consistently follows this practice will almost always come back to the problem better equipped to minister to her students in a Christlike way. She will be much more likely to speak words that will bring repentance and healing rather than further damage.

Taking even a brief time out can also help us think through the needs of the individual student or students involved in a given circumstance. We can ask ourselves questions such as the following:

- Has this behavior happened in the past? Under what circumstances?
- How mature in the faith is the student involved? Does she intellectually understand the concepts of sin, grace, and repentance, or will we need to review them?
- At what level does this student reason about questions of morality and sanctification? What does that say about the content of the conversation we need to have with one another?

"I'd Like to Get to Know You"

We need to know our students well if we are to use disciplinary situations as discipling opportunities. In fact, we need to know our students well if we are to disciple them in any situation. The next two chapters will focus on knowing your students.

Chapter 8 will focus on what some prominent researchers in the field have concluded about how children and young people think, reason, feel, and make decisions, especially about moral questions and spiritual realities.

Chapter 9, then, will suggest exercises you can do, records you can keep, and methods you can adopt that will help you get to know the individual disciples that occupy the chairs in your classroom from 9:00 to 3:39 each day.

To Think About

1. What does it mean to "speak Law for the sake of the Gospel"?
2. When does a Christian teacher need to apply Law in a disciplinary situation? When do we need to apply Gospel?

3. What factors can make the decision about whether to apply Law or Gospel difficult? In those instances, how can we decide which to use?

4. Suppose a student breaks a rule or fractures a relationship. If that student confesses the sin and asks for forgiveness, should a teacher in a Christian school punish the student? Explain.

5. What is the difference between logical consequences and punishment? Why is this distinction important in a classroom based on Law/Gospel principles?

6. Describe a time in your own life, or in the life of someone you have known, in which a problem that appeared on the surface to be a disciplinary problem really masked a deeper difficulty. How can we decide whether the "presenting problem" is the real problem?

7. Describe a time someone shared the Gospel with you in a particularly meaningful way. What made it so meaningful? What does this say to you about the methods you might use as you share the Good News of forgiveness with a penitent student?

Notes

1. Martin Luther, Explanation of the Fifth Petition. *The Small Catechism* (St. Louis: Concordia Publishing House, 1986).

2. C. F. W. Walther, *Law and Gospel,* trans. Herbert Bouman (St. Louis: Concordia Publishing House, 1981), 72–73.

3. We must take care as we determine the attitude of a given student in a particular disciplinary situation. Tears, for example, are not necessarily a sign of contrition; nor does contrition necessarily require tears. Many times children confronted with their sin will cry, and their tears are an outward indication of true inward sorrow for the wrong they have done. On the other hand, some children have learned to manipulate adults with their tears. Many students will, no doubt, experience deep, heartfelt contrition without demonstrating their sorrow outwardly. As we disciple our students in disciplinary situations, it's important to know them as individuals and to pray for the Holy Spirit's wisdom so that we will apply Law when necessary and Gospel when repentance has occurred. See Walther's Thesis VIII.

4. Dietrich Bonhoeffer, *Life Together* (New York: Harper and Row, 1954), 118.

5. Some have found Luther's distinction between the "kingdom of the right" and the "kingdom of the left" helpful as they have thought about discipline in the Christian classroom. If teachers see themselves as disciplers, and if they apply Law and Gospel when each is appropriate, they will find themselves most often exercising authority in the kingdom of the right. In fact, Luther's distinction

seems to apply more appropriately to Christians who teach in public or private schools rather than in Christian schools. However, even in the Christian school, teachers and principals may find themselves exercising authority in the kingdom of the left from time to time.

Helpful references include the following:

Albert G. Huegli, *Church and State under God* (St. Louis: Concordia Publishing House, 1964).

"To the Christian Nobility of the German Nation Concerning the Reform of the Christian Estate," Luther's Works, 44 (Philadelphia: Fortress Press, 1966).

"Temporal Authority: To What Extent Should It Be Obeyed," Luther's Works, 45 (Philadelphia: Fortress Press, 1962).

CHAPTER 8

Getting to Know Your Students— Developmentally

Imagine a free-standing scaffold set up around a gigantic block of marble. Imagine a world-famous artist using this scaffold as a place on which to stand as she sculpts the marble. Now suppose that you drive past the artist's work site each day. Imagine that at first the scaffolding looks quite simple—not many platforms, not many ropes, not many upright supports.

Then one morning, as you drive past, you notice that the old scaffolding has suddenly collapsed. Overnight a new, more intricate one has risen in its place. Day by day you watch the sculptor continue her work from this new structure until one day you pass by the work site and notice that the second scaffolding has collapsed. A third and even more complex maze of wood and metal has appeared in its place. Meanwhile, the sculptor continues her task, hardly seeming to notice the new scaffold from which she works.

Stages of Mental Growth—Universal, Discrete, Invariant, Sequential

While not a perfect analogy, this metaphor illustrates the way many developmental psychologists believe children and young people experience mental growth.[1] Jean Piaget, a Swiss psychologist and biologist, pioneered the theories of human development that take this view.

As Piaget studied the intellectual processes of children, he discovered that children think and reason differently than adults. Not only the *content* of their thinking differs from that of adults, the very *structure* of their reasoning processes differs as well. Adults do not respond to their environment differently than children do simply because adults have more facts at their command, but primarily because adults differ from children in the ways they mentally manipulate the facts they have acquired. It is as though we stand in a different place and see reality from a different perspective.

From what we now know, it appears that as a child sculpts her view of reality, she experiences not one but several radical changes in the structures of her thought. Piaget found that, unlike the usually smooth, upward curve of prepubescent physical growth, structural changes in the mental processes of children do not occur gradually over a period of months or years, but rather, quite rapidly and dramatically. The child's mental scaffold periodically collapses, as it were, and a new one rises to take its place.

Piaget identified and described six distinct levels or stages of intellectual growth. He theorized that these stages are

- *universal*—all human beings of all cultural, racial, and economic backgrounds pass through each of these stages in the process of maturing;
- *discrete*—a child never works from two scaffolds at the same time;
- *invariant*—no individual can skip a stage;
- *sequential*—individuals do not regress to earlier stages; a complex scaffold will not be replaced by a simpler one.

A Look at Why and How

Piaget's research has withstood scrutiny by dozens of researchers who have followed him. But why—and how—does this kind of mental growth occur?

Each of Piaget's stages of intellectual growth represents a way of thinking about the world and about how it works. Each stage is, as it were, a platform on which the child stands as she manipulates her experiences, as she shapes her thoughts, as she works at making sense out of the physical world. In the process of everyday living, each child collects more and more data, more and more facts about the physical world around her. She hangs this data, these facts and observations, on the scaffold of her understanding.

But sooner or later she begins to notice discrepancies between her understanding of reality and the data she has collected. She will live with some inconsistency for a while, but eventually the weight of evidence pulls the old scaffold down. Then a new one rises in its place. This new scaffold accommodates the facts the child has accumulated, the observations she has made. The new structure of thought makes possible a coherent, internally consistent worldview. But after a while, just as before, the child begins to find the new thought-structure inadequate. The scaffolding must once again collapse, while a still more complex structure arises in its place.

Developmentalists seldom focus much attention on the content of a child's thinking. Rather, they concern themselves with the child's reasoning process, with the structural characteristics of the child's thought patterns, with the explanations the child gives for having come to the conclusions she has reached.

Piaget, trained as a biologist, theorized a genetic component of mental growth. But Piaget and the developmentalists who followed him also affirmed the crucial role of social interaction in stimulating intellectual growth and development.

Piaget worked primarily with the logical reasoning abilities of children, with their mental growth and development. He focused most of his research on the ways children and young people conceptualize objects, space, time, and actions.

But he did preliminary work also in the areas of spiritual and moral development. His early exploration of these topics has led others to extend his work, asking questions important to those who teach the Christian faith, those who disciple children in that faith. For example, how do children make sense out of social relationships, customs, and conventions? How do children reason morally and make moral choices? How do children think about God and about other spiritual concepts?

Those who followed Piaget have tackled these issues. Lawrence Kohlberg, in particular, has written extensively about the moral reasoning of children. James Fowler has worked with faith development, focusing primarily on how individuals, children as well as adults, find meaning in their lives.[2] James Rest, Robert Kegan, and Robert Selman, along with Kohlberg and Fowler, have all explored the development of social perspective in children. David Elkind's work has overlapped all of these areas. He, more than the others, has stressed the spiritual development of children.

131

Kohlberg and most of the developmental psychologists who followed him in studying the development of moral reasoning ability conducted their research much as Piaget did—presenting specific situations to individual children and concentrating primarily on the *reasoning* that lay behind each individual's responses to each situation. These researchers could not present a series of physical experiments to their subjects as did Piaget in studying intellectual reasoning ability (e.g., beakers of various sizes filled with liquid, clay manipulated into various shapes). Rather, Kohlberg used a series of stories or "moral dilemmas" as his jumping-off point.

Perhaps the most famous of Kohlberg's dilemmas is the story of Heinz. It tells of a woman in Europe who is dying of cancer. The doctors believe that a certain drug might save her life, but the druggist decides to charge the woman's husband, Heinz, 10 times what the drug costs him to make. Heinz does not have the money to pay for the drug. He borrows half of what he needs and offers that to the druggist, who stubbornly refuses to sell it for that price. Desperate, Heinz breaks into the drug store and steals the drug.

The researchers on Kohlberg's team worked this way: they would present a moral dilemma like the story of Heinz to a given child. They would then ask the child whether the protagonist's actions were right or wrong, and, most important, why. After hundreds and even thousands of responses had been collected and analyzed, Kohlberg and his associates began to see patterns develop in the answers their subjects gave. The researchers categorized the data and arranged them in a hierarchy based on their analysis of the maturity of the reasoning the children used to arrive at their solution to the dilemma. How well-developed was a particular child's concept of justice? That question figured most prominently in Kohlberg's mind as he formulated his stages and categorized individual responses.

If you teach in a Christian school, or if you hope to do that sometime in the future, some critical questions have probably begun to pop into your mind. For example:

- Are Kohlberg's theories right? Does moral, social, or even spiritual growth take place in the same kinds of stages Piaget defined as he studied intellectual reasoning ability?
- Or do children grow socially, morally, and spiritually much as

they grow physically (before adolescence)—in almost imperceptible, incremental steps?

- Do the observations of experts like Piaget, Kohlberg, Elkind, and the others give us any clues about effective methodology as we carry out the discipling process in Jesus' name in the Christian classroom?
- How might the massive amount of data collected by secular researchers and the insights they have gained help us become more skilled as disciplers?

What the Developmentalists Say

Before we can explore those questions, we first must have at least a rudimentary understanding of the specific conclusions to which developmental psychologists have come. The paragraphs that follow contain a summary of key concepts and theories that have gained wide acceptance over the past two decades or so. The descriptions you will read describe children from about ages 3 through 13. These summaries are by no means complete. Rather, they contain enough specific information to illustrate the almost cataclysmic shifts in thought patterns children and young people seem to experience during early childhood and through the years of elementary and junior high school. The summaries detail information researchers have gathered and the ways they have organized and interpreted their data to help explain social, moral, and spiritual development.[3]

These summaries have been culled and compiled from the work of developmental theorists like Piaget, Elkind, Fowler, and Kohlberg. Rather than describing the conclusions of each researcher individually, I have chosen to lay their conclusions side by side in an effort to give the reader a glimpse into the overall thought structure a particular child may be using at any given point in his or her development. As you read, you should note that Piaget, Elkind, Fowler, and Kohlberg each propose slightly different, overlapping age brackets for each stage, while each of Piaget's stages encompasses a slightly wider age-range than that used by the other theoreticians.

Early Childhood—Ages 3 to 8

Piaget termed early childhood the *preoperational* stage. Children at this point in their intellectual development do not reason logically.

133

Furthermore, they are unconcerned with, and even unaware of, adult logic. Rather, they accept appearances as reality. For example, if the water in a short, wide flask is poured into a tall, narrow beaker, a preoperational child will assert that the tall beaker has more water than did the short flask. When asked to explain, the child will say something like, "It's taller."

Piaget studied this and similar behavior extensively, because he believed that it provided him with a unique window into the thought processes of the young child. He soon discovered that children at the preoperational stage believe that the amount, weight, or volume of any substance can vary according to the shape it assumes or the container in which it rests. Preoperational children do not yet grasp a fundamental principle—the conservation of matter.

Preoperational children also have difficulty separating fantasy from reality. A seven-year-old watching a movie with his family may interrupt a dozen times to ask, "Daddy, is that real? Daddy, did that really happen?" Related to this is the magical thinking common to preoperational children. In their view, gingerbread men can indeed hop out of the oven and run down the road. The tooth fairy truly does put quarters under your pillow.

David Elkind has also noted what he terms *phenomenalistic causality* in children at this developmental stage. In this phrase, Elkind refers to the strong tendency in young children to believe that events that happen together cause one another. If a frightened child hugs a teddy bear until her fear dissipates, she will likely believe the teddy bear can protect her in other fear-provoking situations.[4]

Preoperational children also tend to be animistic. They credit inanimate objects with being capable of thoughts and feelings. A four-year-old encountered a battery-operated vibrating pillow for the first time at her grandma's house. She picked it up. The pillow, activated by her touch, began to hum. Her eyes grew round as she threw the pillow into a corner and whispered in genuine fright, "It's alive!"

Children at this stage focus on one striking dimension or feature of an object to the exclusion of other features. A four-year-old visited her aunt who lived in St. Louis. The aunt took the child to the McDonald's restaurant located on a floating steamboat replica, permanently anchored along the Mississippi riverfront. "Look, Cari, we're on a boat!" Cari's aunt exclaimed.

"It's not a boat," replied Cari. "It's McDonald's."

No amount of arguing could convince Cari, a very bright little girl, that the restaurant could be *both* a boat *and* a McDonald's restaurant at the same time.

In addition to all this, three- and four-year-olds are usually not yet able to form mental pictures of past experiences. For example, having been to the zoo the week before, younger preoperational children will be unable to remember elephants and giraffes or imitate their actions. But by age 8, this ability is fairly well formed.

Four- to eight-year-olds retain the egocentricity they have had since birth. They see themselves as the center of the universe; the world and everything in it revolves around them. They are unreflective, unable to project themselves into the circumstances of others.

Adding up all these facets of a young child's thought process, we can see that young children structure their world quite narrowly. This goes a long way toward explaining why young children often give magical, erroneous, or partial explanations for phenomena they observe.

As we think about the social awareness and growth of young children, few of us would be surprised that they experience the family as their primal group. Unless significant adults go out of their way to make a racial, religious, ethnic, or class grouping important, young children will not personally identify themselves as having particular loyalty or attachment to these kinds of groups.

As preoperational children think about moral questions, they decide that actions are "good" or "bad" because of the physical consequences each of those actions brings. For example, a six-year-old might reason, "Climbing the fire escape of my apartment building is bad, because Mom will spank me if I do it." Children at this stage will often control their own behavior or that of others by using the words, "You'll get into trouble."

Additionally, a four-year-old will likely assign guilt in any given circumstance in proportion to the amount of damage that has been done. Piaget and the researchers who followed him explored this aspect of the young child's social and moral reasoning by posing scenarios something like this:

A child opens the kitchen door, not knowing a tray of glasses sits on the counter behind it. The door hits the tray and many glasses fall to the floor and break. Another child becomes angry at Mom, picks up a glass and throws it down. The glass breaks. Who deserves to be punished most? Preoperational children will respond to a question like this by saying that the child who broke the most glasses deserves the most punishment.

For children at this developmental stage, authority comes primarily from physical size, power, or symbols. If I am bigger than you or older than you, then I have the right to make you do what I want you to do. Parents of young children often discover their oldest child taking charge of the younger ones. If, for some reason, the oldest sibling is gone for the day, almost invariably the next oldest child steps in to fill the shoes of leader.

To illustrate the important link between symbols and authority, one need only point to the awe young children feel toward the pastor of their congregation, especially if he wears liturgical vestments. In fact, it is not at all unusual for a three-year-old to confuse the pastor with Jesus Christ Himself!

Elementary Children—Ages 6 to 11

As children enter Piaget's stage of *concrete operations* (which usually begins somewhere between age 5 and age 8), they begin to adopt adult logic in their thought processes, although they still think quite concretely. For example, they can work with the concept of addition or multiplication, but they will understand it best if they can manipulate toothpicks or colored metric rods as they work through a page of math problems.

Thus metaphors like "Jesus is the light" or "Jesus is the door" will be lost on both preoperational children and children at the stage of concrete operations. As you might guess, many of Scripture's parables will likewise have little meaning for lower or middle elementary grade children, because these children cannot yet grasp the symbols involved in parables and the meanings behind those symbols. This is also the reason many elaborate object lessons developed by adults for use in children's sermons so often fail to make the point that the well-meaning, but misguided, adults intend.

Toward the end of this stage, children develop the ability to readily classify objects and to take into account more than one characteristic at a time as they do so (e.g., this restaurant can be both a McDonald's restaurant and a boat at the same time; people from Kansas, California, and Texas are all citizens of the United States).

As the cognitive abilities of elementary students mature, they also develop the ability to analyze series of events and identify both cause and effect. (E.g., Because Jesus died for me, God forgives my sins.)

While Piaget grouped children from about age 6 through 11 in one stage (concrete operations), Kohlberg divided this group into two stages.

Kohlberg's stage 2 includes most children ages 6, 7, and 8. As these children reason about the thinking of others, Kohlberg posits, they believe others are as egocentric as they themselves. However, children at this developmental stage are aware that others see things differently than they themselves do. Kohlberg also asserts that at about this point, children begin to obey in order to win rewards and approval rather than to avoid punishment as they did earlier.

As Kohlberg documented (and as most elementary school teachers can verify), children at the stage of concrete operations place a premium on "fairness," a concept preoperational thinkers have not yet discovered. From about age 6 on, elementary school children can and will consider the needs and demands of others to be valid, but they expect reciprocity in their relationships. They tend to treat others as others treat them, operating within a system of strict justice. As Kohlberg's research has shown, most six-, seven-, and eight-year-olds reason that people should pay back good for good and evil for evil. They see society as useful because it prevents evil and harm, punishing offenders and rewarding good behavior.

Stage 3 in Kohlberg's scheme of moral development overlaps the upper end of Piaget's stage of concrete operations (ages 9, 10, and 11). According to Kohlberg, a child at this stage develops the ability to identify with an ethnic, racial, or religious group or with a certain social class. In fact, a child's self-image can become quite thoroughly intertwined with this new-found group identification. Powerful personal stereotypes can develop.

A 10-year-old, the son of a Christian mother and a non-Christian father, visited the library in his Christian school for the first time. His teacher, realizing the child was new to the school and wanting to get to know him better, took this chance to chat with him. The student asked for help in selecting a book, so the teacher guided him to the shelf that housed the Bible story book collection. Pulling out a colorful possibility, the teacher showed it to the youngster. "I don't want *that* one!" the student exclaimed. "It's for girls."

We need not be surprised that, given their newly developed ability to identify with a group and the influence strong group identification brings with it, children at this stage assume a moral stance that conforms to that considered acceptable by that group with which they most strongly identify. Children at this stage may justify their behaviors by saying things like the following:

- "Christians don't . . ."
- "My people always . . ."
- "Americans think . . ."
- "The guys on my team say . . ."

While often identifying strongly with a specific group's values and norms, children at this stage do have the ability to imagine themselves in another person's situation. They can experience genuine empathy and concern for another person, but usually this empathy is limited to those closest to the child (family, friends, neighbors) and perhaps to an approved group of less-fortunate people.

Older elementary school children have the ability to form stable friendships based on genuine affection. They see society as made up of small groups (e.g., friends and family). For children at Kohlberg's stage 3, authority rests with trusted adults or older siblings.

At this stage, children reason on a different level about moral as well as social behavior. Most notably, they have developed a moral perspective that allows them to take a person's intentions into account as they judge between right and wrong.

A baseball pitcher who beans a batter on purpose will be condemned by most 10-year-old teammates as bad or wrong, even if the ball caused no physical damage. On the other hand, a pitcher who accidentally hits a batter with the ball will not be thought of in this way, even if the ball bruises the batter or breaks her arm.

Attitudes truly matter to children at this stage of development. The plea "I didn't mean to do it" will often take a 10- or 11-year-old offender off the hook in the eyes of his peers.

Junior High—Ages 11 to 16

Piaget discovered that the ability to think abstractly can begin as early as age 11. He termed this stage of intellectual development the stage of *formal operations.* Subsequent research has shown that some young people do not develop the ability to think abstractly until late adolescence; some individuals pass into adulthood never having developed this ability. These persons are not able to manipulate symbols and complex ideas apart from specific, concrete pictures, stories, or examples.

A person capable of formal operations can think through ideas without having to look at or manipulate the physical objects about which he is thinking. He can imagine a situation, hypothesize possibilities in a systematic way, and evaluate each possibility in turn. In short, someone capable of formal operations can think about his thinking.

Kohlberg posits that further growth in moral thinking is made possible when an individual becomes capable of formal operations. Kohlberg considers the moral thinking of children at both stage 3 (summarized above) and stage 4 (made possible by increased mental flexibility) "conventional." He uses this label because a person at this point in his or her moral development is acutely atuned to social conventions—to the expectations and judgments of others—and usually bows to them. Right and wrong are defined according to the specific norms and laws of one's society; the letter of the law carries more weight than the spirit behind it. Social concepts like duty, loyalty, and sincerity regulate behavior and play a major role in evaluating truth and in appraising the values of others.

Someone at Kohlberg's stage 4 has developed the ability to fully project himself into the situation of another person. Those using the kind of reasoning Kohlberg defines as stage 4 will often base decisions on this question: What will *they* think? Such a person will derive his values primarily from his interactions with others and from their opinions. He has not yet critically examined and systematized those values; he has not yet made them his own. His beliefs are sincerely held, but largely unexamined. He sees these values and beliefs as quite self-evident.

Fowler writes that such a person also takes his spiritual life—his faith—at face value, intellectualizing very little about it. He is

139

much more concerned about living out that faith in the community and integrating his faith into all the areas of his life, rather than troubling himself about intellectual inconsistencies within his belief system. Consequently, such a person will experience few religious doubts and will expend little mental energy in trying to resolve deep doctrinal problems. The statement "I just accept it on faith" concisely expresses this individual's viewpoint.

A young person or adult at this developmental stage tends to look to social institutions to legitimize an individual's authority (e.g., "The church sent this pastor to us, so we should listen to him"). People at this stage also look for qualities in their leaders that evoke trust. Quite often these qualities are outward ones (e.g., appearance, traditional ways of doing things).

Beyond Stereotypes

Despite all the research, despite all the publicity developmental theories have attracted within the educational community, teachers, pastors, and parents are still often tempted to approach children as simply miniature versions of themselves.[5] Piaget, Kohlberg, and the rest have exposed the fallacy inherent in educational methodology that ignores the developmental needs and characteristics of the children and young people whom we disciple.

The research shows quite convincingly that children reason differently than adults. Knowing this can help us deal more appropriately with the questions our students raise and with the relationship and faith problems they share with us. Knowing that children approach intellectual ideas, moral questions, and spiritual concepts differently than we adults can also help us plan more appropriate, more effective Bible lessons.[6]

Overwhelming research documents the folly of teaching children as though they possess the reasoning abilities of adults. Yet we commit an equally gross error if we post a chart outlining developmental characteristics next to our desk and proceed to write lessons plans designed to fit the hypothetical child described by our favorite researcher. No competent theorist, in fact, suggests pigeonholing children in this way.

Knowing the broad outlines of developmental theory and keeping in mind typical, age-related patterns of thought, we work at

Age 4

1. Views prayer as "talking to God"
2. Recognizes the Bible as "God's Book"
3. Distinguishes make-believe from reality and associates Bible stories with reality
4. Exhibits a simple, deep faith in Jesus

Age 5

1. Visualizes Jesus as a person
2. Recognizes the Bible as a special book that tells how God wants people to live
3. Enjoys "church" activities (singing, learning, praying)
4. Feels secure in God's love and care
5. Thinks in literal, factual, and concrete terms
6. Enjoys repetition and humor

Ages 6 and 7

1. Have a vague understanding of God because they do not think in abstract terms
2. Can understand that God is our heavenly Father; that God gives us everything; that Jesus is God's Son; that Jesus loves each one of us; that Jesus died on the cross for each one of us
3. Feel they do no wrong and thus lack true repentance
4. See only the wrongs of others
5. Find unconditional love hard to accept
6. Show complete trust in their heavenly Father
7. Consider actions as wrong only if caught or punished
8. Apply the letter of the Law rather than the spirit of the Law
9. Favor severe punishment to "pay back" for the wrong
10. Show curiosity about death, dying, and heaven

Ages 8 and 9

1. Have internalized their concept of God and can share their faith quite readily
2. Are able to study the Bible chronologically
3. Enjoy learning about heroes of the Bible
4. Are better able to understand the church's role in world missions
5. See God at work in the every day world
6. Are generally able to tell someone who has hurt them their wrong rather than tattling to the teacher
7. Pray readily for others
8. Continue to derive satisfaction from helping others
9. Are growing in ability to carry on deep discussions about God and their Christian faith
10. Are building moral standards that will help them make difficult decisions

Ages 10 and 11

1. Are capable of deep religious feeling
2. Seek a powerful influence in their lives (look for models, heroes)
3. Have a questioning nature in religious matters
4. Have developed a conscience
5. See God as more rational and less vindictive than earlier
6. See Jesus as God's Son, but don't really know what this means
7. See goodness and badness in everyone, but see it quantitatively
8. Accept the Bible as true because God gives it authority
9. Expect immediate answers to prayer
10. Pray in a less egocentric and materialistic way than primary children

Ages 12 and 13

1. Are able to understand concepts of increased complexity
2. Contemplate the mysteries of the Christian faith
3. Wonder about and try to resolve questions about attributes of God, concept of the Trinity, the virgin birth
4. Marvel at the awesomeness of the creation of which they are a part and wonder within themselves what the Maker's special plan is for them
5. Are able to see the hand of God at work in history and in the world around them
6. Can understand the redemptive work of Jesus Christ more fully and also can appreciate it in a deeper and more personal way

Adapted from *Teachers Interaction,* copyright © 1990 Concordia Publishing House.

discovering the unique learning needs, strengths, and weaknesses of individual students. We work at making ourselves aware of possible blind spots in their thinking—"blind spots," of course, from our developmental point of view. We use insights the theorists have gained to plan more appropriate lessons and to lead class discussions in more fruitful directions.

Helpful as it is, however, developmental theory has its limitations. For one thing, the discipline as it is currently configured deals almost exclusively with reasoning ability. It speaks to the way children *reason* about moral decisions, the way children *reason* about spiritual realities, the way children *reason* about social relationships. While most theorists would deny it, the theories, taken to their logical conclusion, would lead us to believe that only those persons with the highest level of intellectual reasoning ability can attain the most mature levels of morality or faith!

Developmental theory, dealing as it does with the moral or spiritual reasoning abilities of children, ignores many other aspects of their spiritual and moral growth. As one critic of the theories has noted:

> Children experience before they know and know before they conceptualize. As we grow older and try to understand, we substitute thought for feeling. In doing so, we lose much. The intellect may inform, but it is the imagination that comforts. The imagination outstrips language.... some experiences are beyond explanation, especially by children who have neither the vocabulary nor the security to express what they feel.[7]

We need to keep in mind that children are much more like adults in their emotional lives than in their intellectual lives. We can enter a child's world to experience what that child experiences much more easily if we enter through the doorway of emotion rather than the doorway of the intellect. Unfortunately, we as adults often tend to ignore emotion or to downplay its significance.

As we disciple children, we often reach out to help them at times when they find themselves in a red-hot furnace of anger. We offer them comfort when they find themselves in a fog of confusion or sadness. We celebrate with them times of flag-snapping, exuberant joy given to them by their heavenly Father. At all of these times of intense emotion, God the Holy Spirit flings wide for us windows of opportunity to share our faith and to support our students in living out its implications.

This leads us to perhaps the most serious limitation Christian teachers will find in applying the stage theories of moral and faith development. All the mainstream researchers, with the exception of David Elkind, write from a secular orientation. Their theories, quite naturally then, do not allow for the supernatural power the Holy Spirit channels into His sanctifying process.

As the Scriptures make clear, faith simply is not in its essence a thing of the intellect. It is primarily a *relationship* between the living God and each of His children. This relationship comes to us as a gift from Him. Faith is something the Holy Spirit works in individual hearts. The New Testament makes it clear that young children, even infants, can experience this relationship.[8]

We find the inside-out world of the spirit filled with paradoxes, not the least significant being one that our Lord Jesus shared with His disciples:

> He called a little child and had him stand among them. And He said, "I tell you the truth, unless you change and become like little children, you will never enter the kingdom of heaven. Therefore, whoever humbles himself like this child is the greatest in the kingdom of heaven." (Matt. 18:2–4)

Jesus did not use this three-dimensional object lesson to disparage intellectual acumen. Instead, He used these words to point His followers to true spiritual maturity—total reliance on the heavenly Father and His forgiving grace rather than on their own personal merit and importance.

As we have seen, those who study moral development almost of necessity limit themselves to a study of moral reasoning ability. But a highly developed ability to reason one's way through knotty moral problems does not necessarily translate into consistently moral behavior.

The Lord Jesus folded up His towel after He finished washing His disciples' feet on the night before He died. As He did so, He spoke with His followers about true greatness and about servanthood. He had just shown them His heart—His servant-heart—in action. Then He explained what He had done. His explanation ends with these words: "Now that you *know* these things, you will be

145

blessed if you *do* them" (John 13:17, italics added). Knowing and reasoning, loving and serving—these are often quite different things.

More significant still to us in our role as disciplers is the fact that outwardly moral actions, in and of themselves, do not conclusively tell us anything about someone's personal relationship with Christ. Jesus once warned, "Many will say on that day, 'Lord, Lord, did we not prophesy in Your name, and in Your name drive out demons and perform many miracles?' Then I will tell them plainly, 'I never knew you. Away from Me, you evildoers!' " (Matt. 7:22–23).

Some very morally principled people will find themselves excluded from the kingdom of heaven on the day Jesus comes again. Why? Because they continued to resist God's efforts to draw them into relationship with Himself through Jesus Christ. Jesus will say to them in grief, "I never knew you"—that despite their public morality.

Fowler, while often seeming to write from a universalist rather than from a Christian point of view, nevertheless recognizes and comments on this gap in developmental theory in a helpful way. He writes:

> Most often faith is understood as belief in certain propositional, doctrinal formulations that in some essential and static way are supposed to "contain" truth.... [But] truth is *lived*; it is a pattern of being in relation to others and to God. In this light, doctrines and creeds come to be seen as playing a different though still crucial role. Rather than being the repositories of truth, like treasure chests to be honored and assented to, they become guides for the construction of contemporary ways of *seeing and being.*[9]

In his explanation of the First Petition of the Lord's Prayer, Luther summarizes the relationship between correct doctrine and moral living a bit more simply:

> How is God's name kept holy? ... When the Word of God is taught in its truth and purity, and we, as the children of God, also lead holy lives according to it. Help us to do this, dear Father in heaven! But anyone who teaches or lives contrary to God's Word profanes the name of God among us. Protect us from this, heavenly Father![10]

A four-year-old came to his teacher to ask, "Is Jesus real? Or is He magic?"

The boy's teacher launched into a discussion of the difference between miracles and magic. After listening patiently for a few minutes, the boy responded, "I don't know about all this stuff. All I know is that God gave me Jesus to die on the cross to take all my sins away. And when I die, I'm going to be in heaven with Him. That's all I know."

For now and for eternity, those are the truths that God wants all people to know and believe. Perhaps this student is intellectually capable of grasping the difference between magic and miracles, perhaps not. But this child knows Jesus as Savior—for now and for eternity.

That is our ultimate purpose as we disciple students. We want to touch our children's hearts, not just their heads; we want to help young people experience a deeper personal relationship with Jesus Christ, a relationship that will, of course, then show itself in outwardly righteous actions.

Having said all this, though, we dare not deny the importance of the head, of the intellect. We do need to help our students reason their way through the moral dilemmas they confront in their everyday lives. We need to help them verbalize the reasons that lie behind their decisions and their actions. We need to help them "always be prepared to give an answer to everyone who asks [them] to give the reason for the hope that [they] have" (1 Peter 3:15). But moral reasoning ability, like mere intellectual knowledge of the Scriptures, can never be the measuring stick by which we assess either a child's faith or her level of sanctification.

Robert Coles, the noted child psychiatrist, tells a moving story about his experiences with a first grader during the early days of the civil rights movement in the '60s. The girl, Ruby, experienced horrendous treatment at the hands of adults as she participated in the first phase of school desegregation in New Orleans. One day Coles' wife, a teacher herself, handed her husband a typewritten note describing the situation as she saw it:

> For over six months we've been watching a little Negro girl face possible assault, if not death, every morning and every afternoon. We've heard the obscenities the men and women shout at her, and we wonder how she can take it, day after day. She does, though. She goes even further: she forgives her tormentors; she prays for them.

Analyzing the experience, Coles remarks:

Kohlberg found that in response to certain stories he presented, with implied choices possible to the protagonists, children (and adults) sort themselves out in various ways. Soon those responses are made into "stages," and we are all deciding that *life* follows (scientific) art, so to speak. That is to say, we are all rushing to the conclusion that children can only learn certain things at such-and-such an age, or that their moral reasoning has to follow one or another (fixed, steplike) sequence.

Children may well move along a given scale of performance with respect to intellectual and moral tests, but life awaits their affirming actions, and thank God, sometimes those actions do indeed come.

Reprinted with permission from the July/August issue of *Learning81* copyright © 1981 Springhouse Corporation, 1111 Bethlehem Pike, Springhouse, PA 19477. All rights reserved.

Know Your Students

Ultimately that is the message developmental psychologists have to share with us. And it is an important message, a crucial message in fact. We must know our students, know them as individuals. As we disciple the children or young people our Lord has placed in our classrooms, we can assume that

- each student is in a different place along the road in his or her personal walk with Jesus Christ;
- each student is at a different place in his or her ability to think through and reason about moral decisions and spiritual questions;
- each student has different personal needs and hurts;
- each student has different strengths of character and hopes for the future given by God Himself;
- each student has a different learning style and unique intellectual potential.

Because this is so, a teacher who assumes that each student in a particular first-grade classroom reasons and acts at Kohlberg's moral stage 1 or who believes that all the students in a given seventh-grade classroom will reason and act at Kohlberg's moral stage 3 will without any doubt miss opportunities to nurture his students' relationship with Jesus Christ.

Christian teachers will often find the insights of developmental psychologists helpful, a good gift from the Creator who allows His creatures to explore the richness of His creation. At the same time, we cannot overlook our need to get to know individual students. Where do they struggle with understanding the Christian faith? With applying it? For what hurts do they need Christ's comfort? With what sins do they need to be lovingly, but firmly confronted? With what causes for celebration has God gifted them, and how can we join and encourage them in that celebration?

We leave this chapter with one final question. Since teachers in Christian schools need to know their students as individuals in order to effectively disciple them, how can that best happen? How can we come to understand the individuals to whom we minister? The next two chapters will provide some practical hints about getting to know our students and their families, too.

To Think About

1. Explain the stage theory of human development psychologists have proposed to describe intellectual growth in children.
2. Developmental psychologists posit that the stages of mental growth are *universal, discrete, invariant,* and *sequential.* What do each of these terms mean?
3. Make a chart that summarizes the main stages through which developmental psychologists theorize all children pass on their way to intellectual maturity. Include the names for each stage suggested by the major researchers (e.g., "concrete operations"). Also include characteristics of each stage and examples of the kinds of reasoning children at each stage use.
4. Critique from a Christian perspective the "stage theory" as it applies to children's spiritual development. What can Christian educators learn from the theorists? What limitations do the theories have?

Notes

1. To the best of my knowledge, James Fowler was the first to utilize this scaffolding metaphor. He applied it to a discussion of the development of faith in

Stages of Faith: The Psychology of Human Development and the Quest for Meaning (San Francisco: Harper and Row Publishers, 1981). See page 293.

I have elaborated on his analogy, extending it for the purposes of this discussion to encompass intellectual growth and growth in moral and spiritual reasoning abilities as these are defined by mainstream developmental psychologists.

2. In most of his written work, Fowler uses the term *faith* to refer to the source from which any individual derives life's ultimate meaning. Defined in this way, "faith" may or may not involve the individual's relationship with God. However, Fowler does comment that while faith is not always religious, it is meant to be. Human beings, he asserts, were created for faith and with the capacity to develop faith.

   Fowler distinguishes between faith and belief. For him, belief is intellectual assent to a series of theological propositions. Faith runs deeper than belief but should be congruent with it. Faith involves trust in and loyalty to centers of value (that from which we derive meaning, purpose, and worth in our lives), images of power (our ways of accepting and living with threats and limitations), and a master story (our source of hope and purpose).

3. A full explanation of developmental theory lies beyond the scope of this book. Texts that detail the research done by Piaget, Kohlberg, Fowler, and others abound. Besides books and articles written by the researchers themselves, the reader may wish to consult *Developmental Journey: A Guide to the Development of Logical and Moral Reasoning and Social Perspective* by Mary M. Wilcox (Nashville: Abingdon, 1979). The chart included in the back of the Wilcox text is particularly helpful. Even though Wilcox wrote more than a decade ago, her text contains clear, concise summaries of the basic theories of developmental psychology. She also attempts to analyze these from a Judeo-Christian perspective. I find her observations helpful.

   The reader should also note that both Kohlberg and Fowler extend their theories into a description of more mature stages of moral and faith development, stages that both theorists believe are attainable only in adulthood. They posit that this is so, at least in part, because the necessary cognitive reasoning abilities do not exist until the individual has matured intellectually. For the purposes of the present text, a discussion of the stages of adult faith and moral development would be extraneous. Interested readers may wish to refer to the Wilcox text referenced above or to two other works worthy of special note by those involved in teaching the Christian faith:

   James W. Fowler, *Stages of Faith* (New York: Harper and Row, 1981).

   Craig Dykstra and Sharon Parks, eds. *Faith Development and Fowler* (Birmingham: Religious Education Press, 1986).

   An excellent critique of the theories proposed by Fowler and Kohlberg appeared in the *Concordia Theological Journal* (October 1991) pp. 419–39. Entitled "Sanctification and Moral Development," the article deals in depth with various theological issues beyond the scope of this textbook. The author, Joel A. Brondos, has made a significant, well-thought-out contribution to a discussion of this topic from a grace-based, Christian perspective.

4. David Elkind, *A Sympathetic Understanding of the Child: Birth to Sixteen* (Boston: Allyn and Bacon, Inc., 1974), 43.

5. The reader interested in exploring the concept of childhood itself, as well as

the developmental theories of David Elkind, may want to begin by reading two books by him:

All Grown Up and No Place to Go: Teenagers in Crisis (Reading, MA: Addison-Wesley Publishing Company, 1984).

Miseducation: Preschoolers at Risk (New York: Alfred A. Knopf, 1987).

Elkind contends that today's society is in the process of so completely blurring the distinctions between childhood and adulthood that children and teens are forced to take on adult roles more and more prematurely, thus causing damage to individuals and to the very fabric of our society itself, damage that may well prove irreparable. The alert reader will find many implications for Christian education and for good, basic educational practice in either of these books.

6. Readers interested in more specifics about ways in which children's intellectual reasoning abilities affect their ability to understand theological concepts should consult *God Concepts in Children: A Clue to Faith Development* by Dr. Lawrence E. Sohn (River Forest, IL: Lutheran Education Association Monograph Series, vol. 12, nos. 2/3). The implications Dr. Sohn lists in this monograph will give all Christian teachers much food for thought.

   The chart listing some important spiritual characteristics of children that appears in this chapter was taken from an article by Dr. Sohn that appeared in September 1990 *Teachers Interaction,* pages 6–7. Dr. Sohn credits the various volumes of *Integrating the Faith,* ed. Carl Moser and Arnold Schmidt (St. Louis: Concordia Publishing House, 1986).

7. Elaine Ward, "The Place of Imagination and Feelings in the Faith Development of Children," *Church Teachers,* September/October 1989. Used with permission by HarperCollins Publishers.

8. The angel Gabriel predicted that John the Baptizer would be "filled with the Holy Spirit from his mother's womb" (Luke 1:15; compare v. 44). At least in this one case, God touched an unborn infant with saving faith as God set him apart for the ministry he would later perform. Other New Testament texts deal convincingly and in more specific detail with the capacity of young children for a deep relationship with God through Christ. See, for example, Matt. 18:6 and 2 Tim. 3:15.

9. Fowler, 295. The emphases are Fowler's.

10. Martin Luther. *The Small Catechism* (St. Louis: Concordia Publishing House, 1986).

CHAPTER 9

Getting to Know Your Students—Individually

Our Lord Jesus knows human beings through and through. In his gospel, the apostle John tells us of a time early in Jesus' ministry when many people had seen "the miraculous signs He was doing and believed in His name." John then goes on to observe, "But Jesus would not entrust Himself to them, for He knew all men. He did not need man's testimony about man, for He knew what was in a man" (John 2:23–25). Jesus knew human nature in general and, as true God, He also probed the thoughts and motives of individual hearts. He read people perfectly.

Even so, the Scriptures indicate that most often Jesus chose to lay aside His divine omniscience. Our Lord learned, for example, to know His 12 disciples in the same way we learn to know other people. Jesus spent time with the Twelve. He talked and ate with them. He joked with them. He went fishing with them. He took them along with Him to parties. He answered their questions while He walked long, dusty miles with them. In short, Jesus built a relationship with each of His disciples brick by brick, experience by experience.

As we disciple the young people in our classrooms today, we rely on the same processes that our Lord Jesus used. We take into account the general knowledge we have gained about the developmental characteristics experts attribute to the second or fifth or seventh graders we teach. But even more importantly, we devote time to the process of building a relationship with each of our students. We take time to get to know them individually.

Time—The Coin of the Realm

Many teachers keep a memory box or a memory file. On days when it seems that this year's fourth grade never will understand the difference between latitude and longitude, on mornings after a particularly difficult parent conference, at times when it seems that any career—any career at all—would be infinitely more rewarding than teaching, a memory box can help restore a healthy perspective. It can serve as a reminder of our Lord's call and of His past faithfulness in accomplishing His will through us, imperfect servants though we may be.

One teacher shared his memory box with me one rainy Saturday afternoon. As we looked through the photos of the teams he had coached and the young people he had taught, we came upon a stack of notes—some from parents, most from students. My friend smiled as he picked up a wrinkled sheet of blue paper from the stack. "This is one of my favorites," he remarked as he handed it to me. I glanced at the date. The note was eight years old.

"Thanks for taking so much of your time this year to teach Robert to play chess," the note read. "You'll never know how much it meant to him."

After I had skimmed the note, my friend told me a little about Robert. Dad had left Mom when Robert was three. A few years later, Mom remarried and moved to another state with her new husband. She left Robert in the care of his grandmother. Robert's grandfather had died before Robert was even born. The young man's grandmother did a good job of parenting him, but she couldn't satisfy one of his deepest longings: Robert needed a role model. In answer to his grandmother's prayers, the Lord Jesus gave Robert a teacher, a teacher who became both a big brother and a friend.

We live in a culture that places a high premium on efficiency, on productivity, on accomplishing as much as possible in as little time as necessary. Teachers today must often answer to parents and to school board members who expect their children to know more and more and to learn it at an earlier age. In such an atmosphere, time spent teaching a lonely 10-year-old to play chess makes little sense.

Yet we need to remember that society's expectations often collide head-on with the needs of our students to grow as Christ's disciples. If we give in to the pressures of the moment, we can easily find the relationships in our classroom taking a back seat to ventures that at the time seem more valuable:

- Rereading our lesson plans one more time before the bell rings to signal the beginning of the first class of the morning
- Explaining one more math concept this afternoon, even though we had originally planned to teach it tomorrow
- Drilling the week's Bible memory verse a few more times before the class period ends
- Reviewing once more the basketball handling skills we taught during team practice this afternoon

Now, of course, a good teacher wants to have his plans for the day clearly in mind as class begins. Good teachers make every moment count as they teach math or memory work. Winning coaches realize the importance of drill and practice. But we need to strike a balance. As a wise man once observed, it's so easy to let what's urgent crowd out what's important. In the Christian classroom, as in the Christian life, we dare not let *doing, accomplishing, completing,* and *achieving* displace *relating, loving, caring,* and *listening.*

Learning and achieving are important as well as urgent. But relationships are important too. Eternally important. Even as we deal with the urgent things that fill each day, we need to ask our Lord for the grace that will enable us to take the time we need to strengthen the relationships He has taught us to value so highly.

Children understand at an early age how much time means to adults. By investing the golden coins of time in our students, we affirm them. We say this to them:

- "You matter to me (and to Jesus)."
- "I see your potential, and I'm willing to spend some of my most precious resource to help you grow toward fulfilling that potential."
- "I care about you. In fact, I love you."

As we take time to build relationships, we make it possible for our students to see Jesus in us. We share ourselves with our students, and in doing so, we model for them what it means to live as a man of God, as a woman of God. Both now and later on, they will find comfort in following the instructions God gave His people through the writer to the Hebrews:

Remember your leaders, who spoke the word of God to you.

Consider the outcome of their way of life and imitate their faith. (13:7)

The truths we teach about the Christian faith have much more credibility when our students see us living out those truths in our relationships with them—both collectively and individually. It's hard to overestimate the power of our example as we model Christlikeness for our students, especially as we take time to show concern for them as individuals.

Then, too, as the Holy Spirit enables us to develop relationships of love and respect with individual students, we earn the right, so to speak, to correct and counsel them. Someone once observed, "You can't drive a 10-ton truck over a footbridge." The bridge of love that the Spirit of God erects between two believers must be strong enough to carry the freight that passes between them.

True enough, God's Word remains God's Word no matter who speaks it. True enough, God has a right to expect His people to obey His commands regardless of the messenger He chooses to use to speak those commands. Sometimes we will follow the godly counsel we receive from a Christian we have just met. Sometimes we will accept a fresh truth or a word of correction from a believer we barely know. But usually a bridge of trust makes it easier for us to hear and receive another person's message as God's Word to us. The heavier the truth, the sturdier the bridge must usually be.

How it must have stung Simon Peter when, after expressing concern for Jesus' safety, he heard the Lord's words: "Get behind Me, Satan! You are a stumbling block to Me; you do not have in mind the things of God, but the things of men" (Matt. 16:23). Yet Peter was able to receive this rebuke and to learn from it. He did not abandon his discipleship, and never again did he try to dissuade Christ from following the path to the cross.

Why did Jesus' reprimand not crush Peter? We can only speculate, but we do know from the Scriptures that Jesus had built a strong bridge of trust between Himself and His followers. Like the other disciples, Peter knew Jesus loved and cared for him—for him personally. The bridge between our Lord and Peter was apparently strong enough to carry the heaviest word of Law without collapsing.

As we disciple our students, we will need to confront them, at times, with their sin. If we have taken time to build bridges of love

155

Ways to Build Relationships with Your Students

Because all teachers differ, each of us develops our own particular style as we cultivate relationships with students. Here are some ideas/examples of intentional relationship-building activities that some teachers have found workable. Perhaps they will trigger additional ideas for you.

- As the school year begins, take time to get to know your students as individuals and give the students time to get to know each other. If your students can read and write, design a survey. Ask about their favorite foods, sports, hobbies, movies. Find out about their pets, their heroes, their dreams for the future. Read this information, and then keep it and refer to it from time to time as the year passes.

- Prepare each day's lesson plans and complete other paper work *before* the students arrive each day. Remember, the class day begins when the first student walks into the classroom. Be there each morning for your students. You will find that many students need a listening ear as they arrive in the classroom.

- Notice and compliment new shoes, new haircuts, friendly smiles, helpful attitudes and actions.

- Teach your students games you enjoy and play with them.

- Eat lunch with your class and spend time on the playground with them—even if you're not required to do so.

- Stop to chat with your students when you meet them at church, in the grocery store, or on the street.

- Share some of your personal interests with the students. Show them pictures of your family. Talk about your pets. Tell them about the bicycle race in which you will compete this weekend. Don't be afraid to let them see you as a real person.

- Occasionally attend YMCA basketball games, youth league soccer events, piano recitals, or gymnastics exhibitions in which your students participate. Cheer them on.

- Invite your students to share prayer requests with you and make it possible for them to do this in a confidential, nonthreatening way. For example, you might encourage them to talk with you one-on-one or to leave a note on your desk if they have prayer needs that are personal. Then be sure to keep their confidences!

in our relationships, our students will more readily submit to our words of correction in repentance rather than choosing to rebel.

The Holy Spirit strengthens bridges between us believers as we share our faith with one another, as we pray with and for one another, and as we get to know one another as friends. The bridges of mutual love and respect between Christians are seldom erected overnight. They are never built primarily by human effort.

The night before Jesus died, He prayed that all His people might grow into the kind of love and unity we have been thinking about:

> "My prayer is not for them [the apostles] alone. I pray also for those who will believe in Me through their message, that all of them may be one, Father, just as You are in Me and I am in You. May they also be in Us so that the world may believe that You have sent Me. ... I have made You known to them, and will continue to make You known in order that the love You have for Me may be in them and that I Myself may be in them" (John 17:20–21, 26).

This kind of love and unity come to us as gifts from God as we take the time to share our lives of Christ-centered hope and faith with one another.

Three Keys to Building Relationships— Listen! Listen! Listen!

We want our students to experience Christ's love in and through us. We want them to open their lives to us in such a way that we can minister to them and disciple them meaningfully. Before this can happen, we need to know our students' individual concerns, their joys, their hurts. Taking time for our students is a necessary, but not sufficient, condition for opening the doors of communication far enough to allow significant ministry to take place.

As we spend time with our students, we need to listen to them. We need to listen with practiced skill, and we need to listen with our heart as well as with our intellect.

> Cassandra shuffled into the classroom on Wednesday morning with her head down. Mr. Hendricks watched as the usually bouncy second grader eased herself into her chair, folded her arms across her chest, and sat frowning at the chalkboard.

157

"What's up, Cassandra?" the teacher asked from across the classroom.

"Nuthin'," scowled Cassandra.

"It looks like something to me. What's happened?" probed Mr. Hendricks.

Cassandra only went on scowling. Mr. Hendricks shrugged and went on grading papers.

Suppose you just saw this incident played out on videotape. And suppose that at this point you could rewind the tape and replay it to give Mr. Hendricks a second chance. What might you hope to see him do differently?

Try this scenario:

Cassandra shuffled into the classroom on Wednesday morning, her head down. Mr. Hendricks looked up to see the usually bouncy second grader wander to her chair, fold her arms across her chest, and sit down to frown at the chalkboard.

The teacher put down his pen, walked over to Cassandra, and sat down in the chair beside hers. "Hi," he said in a quiet tone. Then he waited. Silence. After a few moments, he tried again. "You're awfully quiet this morning. It looks like you must be feeling pretty down today."

Silence. The teacher waited again.

Tears filled Cassandra's eyes. After a while she sniffed, "Doughnut's dead."

For the next few minutes, Mr. Hendricks listened as Cassandra told him stories about her pet rabbit, about the fun they'd had together during the three years Doughnut had belonged to Cassandra, and about the cold, lifeless body Cassandra had found in the rabbit hutch when she went out to feed Doughnut the evening before.

As the conversation ended, Mr. Hendricks said, "I'm really sorry about Doughnut, Cassandra. And I'm sorry that you're feeling so sad. Could I pray for you?"

"Yes," whispered Cassandra.

Mr. Hendricks put his hand on Cassandra's as he prayed a simple prayer asking Jesus to give Cassandra comfort and peace. Then he gently squeezed her shoulder, smiled at her, and stood up to call the class to attention as the school day began.

In both scenarios, Cassandra's teacher was alert to a change in her normal behavior. In both instances, the teacher cared about Cassandra and sincerely wanted to help. In both instances, Mr. Hendricks was willing to spend time with Cassandra.

But in the second scenario, Mr. Hendricks enabled Cassandra to share her hurt. He created an atmosphere in which he could minister to her. As the second scenario ended, Cassandra's mind and heart were much more ready to listen and to learn, whether that learning involved the Second Article of the Apostles' Creed or the rules of subtraction.

What made the difference? The teacher listened in a more skillful, therapeutic way.

It's easy to assume that everyone is born knowing how to listen. After all, we have been listening to other people since early childhood. How many esoteric skills could listening involve? Yet, as experts in human behavior have analyzed communication styles, they have been able to identify several specific behaviors that enable people—especially people who hurt—to share their thoughts and feelings more easily and more fully. As the researchers worked, they also discovered that the listener need not always be a trained mental health professional. Often just the act of sharing a painful situation with a compassionate person who knows how to listen can be therapeutic—healing—in and of itself.

What specific listening techniques help people express themselves?

Skillful listeners communicate acceptance nonverbally. Before Mr. Hendricks said a word to Cassandra in the second scenario, his nonverbal behavior spoke volumes. He put aside the project on which he was working. He walked over to sit beside his student's desk. He brought himself down to her eye-level. Later, as he prayed for her, he put his hand on hers. He touched her shoulder and smiled at her as he got up to leave.

The people to whom we minister will know whether or not they have our undivided attention. Eye contact is vital as are simple gestures of warmth—a smile, a touch. All these help establish trust. An occasional nod lets the other person know we are hearing them, and a nonjudgmental "uh huh" will often provide the encouragement someone needs to continue talking, even about a difficult or painful situation.

Skillful listeners remember that silence is golden. As Mr. Hendricks ministered to Cassandra, he allowed times of silence to punctuate their conversation. The pauses gave Cassandra time to collect her thoughts and feelings. Sometimes, especially when someone is inexperienced in the ministry of listening, silence that lasts more than 10 seconds can feel quite awkward, and silence that lasts 60 seconds provokes agony!

But we need to remind ourselves that God's Spirit can and often does use times of silence to do great things. Silence will often accomplish what words cannot. The people to whom we minister need time to sort out their thoughts. Times of silence can allow them to discover feelings and motives of which they were previously unaware. Then, too, sometimes the other person simply needs time to cry or to reestablish emotional control before going on.

As you wait through periods of silence, remember that silence is not a sign of failure. You need not feel compelled to leap into the conversation with both feet to fill the void. Pray silently and let the Holy Spirit do His work in you and in the person to whom you are listening.

Skillful listeners sometimes paraphrase what's been said. If the conversation seems to be stuck, you may want to restate the speaker's last thought in your own words. Take care not to alter the facts. Keep your paraphrase brief. Often a brief summary of what's just been said will let the speaker know you have been listening and that you have understood. Reassured of this, the speaker will often feel free to continue.

Skillful listeners reflect the speaker's feelings and let the speaker respond. In the first version of his encounter with Cassandra, Mr. Hendricks asked two direct questions: *"What's up, Cassandra?"* and *"What's happened?"* Questions like these will usually dead-end a conversation with someone who is hurting.

On the other hand, in the second scenario, Mr. Hendricks reflected Cassandra's feelings and in doing so invited her to share her need when he said, *"You're awfully quiet this morning. It looks like you must be feeling pretty down today."*

Statements that reflect feelings can initiate conversation. They can also take a conversation a step or two deeper into intimacy and trust. As you decide how to talk about the other person's feelings, note the speaker's body language and tone of voice as well as his words. For instance, if the speaker knots a fist or raises the volume of his voice, you might respond, "You feel angry about that." Or if the speaker's eyes fill with tears, you could remark, "When you think about that, you feel really hurt."

Keep in mind that as you reflect feelings back to another person, you will sometimes miss the mark. In that case, the speaker will probably correct you—"I'm not really angry, just so very frustrated."

Sometimes, though, your comment will point out an emotion of which the speaker is unaware. In that case, the person will probably pause to think, and the self-awareness you have nurtured will often provide clues helpful to the speaker.

You may be right on target, or you may misread the speaker. Either way, your words have shown that you care enough to listen intently. And you will have helped the speaker think through her response to the situation under discussion.

Skillful listeners clarify the speaker's feelings. Good listeners reflect the speaker's feelings. They also clarify those feelings. In the conversation between Cassandra and her teacher, for example, Mr. Hendricks might listen as the second grader tells about finding Doughnut dead in the rabbit hutch. After a time of silence, the conversation might go like this:

Mr. Hendricks: You must have felt sad.

Cassandra (nodding): And a little scared too.

Mr. Hendricks (reflecting her feelings): Sad *and* scared.

Cassandra nods again then is silent as her eyes begin to tear.

Mr. Hendricks (clarifying): You're sad because you'll really miss Doughnut and finding him the way you did was a bad surprise.

Cassandra: I never saw someone I love dead before.

Notice how in clarifying Cassandra's feelings, Mr. Hendricks enabled her to identify more clearly why she felt afraid when she found Doughnut's body. Her words clue her teacher in to the fact that this is probably Cassandra's first significant experience with death—a valuable hint to the direction God may want to lead the conversation.

Skillful listeners trust the Holy Spirit to do His work. Because we care, we may often find ourselves tempted to offer our students or their parents quick fixes, instant and (in our mind, at least) fail-proof cures. But we need to remember that when we try to fix another person's pain, we usurp a role that belongs rightly to God—and to Him alone.

We also run the risk of seeming to hand a Band-Aid to a patient who needs a tourniquet. However well-intentioned we may be, the other person may perceive our advice-giving behavior as minimizing the seriousness of his problem or discounting the depth of his pain. Few things will destroy trust more quickly.

On the other hand, the person may take our advice and do what we have suggested. If our cure doesn't work, the person may blame us for the problems that our "solution" creates. And even if our recommendations do work, God's purposes may have been thwarted anyway, because the person will not have been challenged to grow in her own problem-solving skills, prayer life, or reliance on the Lord.

All this does not mean that we sit silently by while someone we love hurts herself through her own sin. It does not mean that we fail to speak words of Law and of Gospel. It does mean, however, that we use the Lord's wisdom to speak to the hurting person at appropriate times. We listen long and hard before we speak, and we ask our Lord for guidance before we do so. We allow the Holy Spirit to build a bridge of trust between us and our brother or sister in Christ. We speak the truth, but we speak it in love (Eph. 4:15). And we make sure we have correctly diagnosed the disease before we unsheathe the scalpel of the Law or apply the healing salve of the Gospel.

In his book, *Christian Caregiving—A Way of Life,* Kenneth Haugk makes a helpful distinction between what he calls care-giving and cure-giving. He points out that God wants to use His people as channels through which He can pour His love into the lives of others, especially those who hurt. Yet, Haugk reminds his readers, while God has made Christians responsible for giving care to people in pain, He has reserved for Himself the responsibility for bringing about a cure.[1]

Remembering this distinction can relieve some of the pressure we might put on ourselves to produce results in the lives of those we touch. Our Lord alone is strong enough and wise enough to carry the burden of responsibility for changing others in the ways they need to be changed. He alone deserves the glory for the changes His Spirit brings about. He has chosen to honor us by letting us share in the process of care and in the joy of worshiping Him for His cure-giving work. When we remember that, we will find His yoke truly easy and His burden light (Matt. 11:30).

Skillful listeners look for ways to cultivate their skills. No one develops good listening skills by accident. Neither do we develop them overnight. Many books have been written and many courses developed to help caregivers cultivate the skills summarized in the paragraphs above.

Simple as the skills may seem, almost everyone feels awkward using them at first. As you practice with your friends or students, you may find that you tangle yourself up in the techniques at times, maybe to the point you fault the methods for getting in the way of ministry. Then, as you become more practiced, you may begin to feel a manipulative sense of power as you discover just how well the techniques do indeed work! You may find yourself surprised at the fact that people will share their thoughts and feelings with you in a deeper way than you have ever before experienced.

Keep in mind that the awkward feelings will dissipate as you become more skilled. In fact, after a while these listening skills may become so much a part of your normal way of communicating that you hardly notice when you are using them. Until they become that much a part of you, though, it will help to review and practice them regularly, perhaps with someone in your family, perhaps with another person on your faculty.

A local community college may offer a course in communication skills. People in many different professions—nursing, education, law, psychology—all use the same basic listening skills to function successfully in their given fields. If you have a chance, take such a class. If one is not available, read as many books as you can and do the exercises they contain.[2]

It is almost impossible to state it too strongly: *Good listening skills are indispensable for anyone involved in interpersonal Christian ministry.*

Christian Schools: Therapeutic Communities

David Elkind has observed that as schools move into the 21st century, they must become, more and more, therapeutic communities. What a fantastic description of the Christian school! The word *therapeutic* comes to us from the Greek word *therapeuō*. This word in secular Greek meant "to serve" and also "to care for the sick," "to treat," "to heal." The New Testament uses the term almost exclusively to refer to Jesus' healing ministry.[3]

As the sin and trouble around us continue to rip the fabric of our society, those of us who have been trained as educators many times find ourselves cast in the role of therapist, of counselor, as well as that of teacher. Most good teachers see this as a fact of life. We care, care deeply, about the hurts of our students and their families. Still in all, at times the shoe pinches. We recognize our lack of expertise—or, at least, we should.

Few teachers have been trained as professional therapists. While some Christian schools have arranged for the services of a social worker or child psychologist, many more—especially elementary schools—have not. No matter how skillfully a teacher uses good listening techniques and no matter how much a teacher cares about his students and their families, chances are good that one or several students in any given classroom (and their families as well) need much more help than the classroom teacher can give.

To guide these students and their families to the help they need, teachers first must recognize their limitations. Intimidating? Perhaps at first. But keep in mind that no one expects any professional to have expertise in someone else's field. The true professional knows what he knows and knows what he does not know; he knows when he can help and he knows when to refer.

But how do educators find trustworthy professionals to whom they can refer families? Before teachers ask parents to think about getting help with a given problem, they need to discuss the issue first with the principal. Often in the Christian school, the staff can look to the pastor for guidance, especially if the problem is a family problem. As shepherd of the congregation, the pastor may wish to counsel with the family himself. If he does not feel competent or comfortable in dealing with a specific problem, he may suggest one or more Christian clinical psychologists to whom he refers people.

Then, too, he may be familiar with various other community resources and with the level of expertise with which community agencies operate.

Often times, community counseling agencies produce brochures or offer evening or weekend seminars, open to the public, on various topics—alcoholism, drug abuse, depression, parenting adolescents, divorce recovery for families. Sometimes a community-based agency will even be willing to present an in-service program on an appropriate topic for a given faculty or parent-teacher league meeting. Through avenues like these, teachers can familiarize themselves with the kinds of help available to young people and their families.

After teachers in a given school have had some exposure to a specific agency or program, the faculty needs to discuss a few basic questions to evaluate what they have heard, seen, and now feel:

What credentials does this person or agency have? Are these appropriate for our purposes?

Has someone whom we know and respect used the services of this person or agency? What does our source say about the experience?

How comfortable do we as a faculty feel with this agency or person? with their overall approach? with their knowledge and expertise?

Do the people involved in this agency or program appear to understand our approach to Christian education? Does it seem that their ideals would run at cross-purposes with ours, or could we support one another?

How much would it cost a family or individual who chose to use this resource? Are there alternative charges or sources of funding for those who cannot afford the regular fees?

Would the professionals in this agency or program (given a partial waver of confidentiality from the parent) be willing to work with the classroom teacher(s) involved, sharing hints for best helping students with whom the agency staff is working?

Would we as individuals feel comfortable using this agency or person if we ourselves had a problem?

Perhaps in an ideal world, Christian schools would work exclusively with other Christian agencies. But for one reason or another, that is not always possible and, as many pastors and teachers in Christian schools will testify, neither is it always necessary. In some cases, we can safely refer our students and their families to professionals who are not Christians themselves, though a thoroughly competent Christian counselor is always preferable. In any case, we would never refer a child or family to someone with values, techniques, or a life-view that would tear down the Christian faith, either blatantly or subtly.

Whether or not the therapist is a believer, both the pastor and the teacher(s) involved need to continue to support the family after a referral has been made. We can ask occasionally how things are going. While we want to avoid a circumstance in which the counselee pits one professional against another, thus sabotaging the therapy, we do want to remind the family of our ongoing concern for them in Jesus' name and of our continuing prayers for each member of their family.

One last, important thing to remember: Many times, counselors today prefer to work with the whole family rather than simply targeting one family member for therapy. From many points of view, this approach makes sense. If a child in a particular family hurts for any reason, that entire family hurts. If an adult in a family system hurts, chances are very good that the children hurt too.

If a given therapist does propose to work only with the child in a specific situation, it becomes even more critical that we remember that therapy with children requires specific training, skills, and competencies. The school and the family should question the therapist about her qualifications and experience in working with children; everyone involved should feel confident about the answers they receive before therapy begins.

Ice Cream and Lemonade

Here we come!
Where're you from?
Reykjavík!
What's your trade?
Ice cream and lemonade!
Show us some, if you're not afraid!

So goes the old game. But on many school grounds today, half or more of the players would have their own, real-to-life answer to that all-important first question. Our students come to us from China, from Haiti, from Guatemala, from Yugoslavia, from Vietnam, from Saudi Arabia, from Mexico, from Portugal, from Ethiopia—from everywhere on the globe.

Families from different cultures have different values and customs. For decades teachers have known that a child's culture profoundly influences what happens for that child in the classroom. In past decades, though, many teachers assumed that they needed to acquaint themselves with only the most obvious external cultural details (e.g., holiday observations and ethnic recipes). A piñata hung in the classroom at Christmas time and stir-fry vegetables cooked up to celebrate Chinese New Year sometimes became the multicultural "program" in these classrooms.

But if we intend to minister as effectively as our Lord Jesus intends for us to minister, we need to know much more about the cultural currents that run deep beneath the surface, deep within the core of the personal identity of each individual in our classroom. We need to ask ourselves questions like these:

- What are the root values of this student's culture? What is the ultimate meaning of life and its purpose?
- How important is family and extended family to the members of this student's primary cultural group? How important is education? work? "getting ahead"? (Indeed, what does "getting ahead" mean in this cultural group?)
- What is the value of money to individuals in this student's world? How and when is it earned? spent? saved?
- How do family members in this cultural group relate to one another? What responsibilities and privileges do children have? young people? parents? uncles and aunts? grandparents?
- How does this student's family view authority? How do most people in this student's culture relate to authority figures?
- What are appropriate gender roles for males and females in this student's culture? How are family members expected to fulfill the various roles they have in the family?
- What priority do members of this student's cultural group tend to assign to work? to leisure?

- How is time perceived and used, valued and spent by most people in this student's cultural group?

The answers to these and a hundred more questions about the basic framework of family living will guide the teacher in the Christian school as she endeavors to touch individual lives with the Gospel in deeper and deeper ways. Ask any missionary who has served on another continent. Culture matters! It matters especially as we think about ways to communicate God's love in Jesus Christ, and it matters as we help our Christian brothers and sisters become more and more like Jesus in their relationships. Knowing the cultural backgrounds of the students we teach is not just a public-relations nicety, it is essential for effective ministry.[4]

As we look for answers to questions about our students' cultural heritage, we can talk with other teachers who have more multicultural experience than we. Books, magazines, tapes, and the seminars often offered at teachers conferences can help us grasp the basic background knowledge we need. Then, too, of course, we could always do something quite radical—we could ask our students and the members of their families. Most times, they would happily let us listen to and learn from them.[5]

Out of the Classroom—into the Home

For the teacher in the Christian school, ministry cannot stop at the classroom door. Because of the compassion Christ Himself has put into our hearts, we care too much about our students to ignore the ministry to families into which our Lord leads us. If our students matter, then their families matter too. As we learn to know our students better and better, we will learn to know their families better and better as well, and as we do that, we will be better equipped to minister to them.

How can that happen? How can our ministry with families have more impact? How might God use us as teachers to touch families— not just for now, but for eternity? The next chapter will explore those questions.

To Think About

1. Why is it so essential to the discipling task that teachers know their students as individuals as well as knowing developmental theory in general?

2. What things can get in the way of knowing our students as individuals?
3. What techniques enable teachers to listen—truly listen—to their students? Give an example of each.
4. Experiment with the listening techniques explained in this chapter. Without telling the speaker you are doing so, make a concentrated effort to use effective listening techniques. Practice with two or three different people. What did you discover about the techniques? about yourself?
5. In what kinds of situations would Christian teachers find themselves referring families to outside professionals or agencies for help? What criteria would the faculty and staff of a Christian school want to keep in mind as they evaluate the professionals to whom they may decide to refer families?
6. Why is it critical from a discipling perspective for teachers to understand a given student's ethnic background and culture? How might Christian teachers familiarize themselves with cultural differences among their students?

Notes

1. Kenneth C. Haugk, *Christian Caregiving—A Way of Life* (Minneapolis: Augsburg Publishing House, 1984).
2. Some books I have found that are useful in learning basic listening skills include the following:

   Thomas Gordon, *Parent Effectiveness Training* (New York: Peter H. Wyden Publisher, 1970).

   Thomas Gordon, *Teacher Effectiveness Training* (New York: Peter H. Wyden Publisher, 1974).

   Earl Gaulke, *You Can Have a Family Where Everybody Wins* (St. Louis: Concordia Publishing House, 1975).

   Although these three were written two decades ago, the insights and examples they provide are, in my opinion, still helpful. Dr. Gaulke's book erects a biblical framework for the ideas Dr. Gordon presents in his work.

   A somewhat more recent and eminently readable book for teachers and parents is the following:

   Adele Faber and Elaine Mazlish, *How to Talk So Kids Will Listen and Listen So Kids Will Talk* (New York: Avon Books, 1982).
3. Gerhard Kittel and Gerhard Friedrich, eds., *Theological Dictionary of the New Testament,* abridged ed. (Grand Rapids: Eerdmans Publishing Company, 1985), 331–32.

4. Few teachers will find it noteworthy or surprising that the predominant culture of North America has become more and more secular and permissive in recent decades. What may be both noteworthy and surprising, however, is how much the cultures of other people-groups have to offer the majority of North Americans as we think about more positive ways to view reality and to treat one another in our families and in society.

Many students from other cultures come to us with deeply held, positive values that have been largely lost to the majority of North Americans. If we stop to examine these values, we soon find that many of them are remarkably biblical and were at one time not so long ago a part of the heritage Canadians and citizens of the United States took for granted.

What fertile ground for classroom projects and discussions!

5. Classroom teachers may find these texts helpful as they think through their ministry in a multicultural classroom setting:

Christine I. Bennett, *Comprehensive Multicultural Education: Theory and Practice,* Second Edition (Needham Heights, MS: Allyn and Bacon, 1990).

Daphne Brown, *Mother Tongue to English: The Young Child in the Multicultural School* (London: Cambridge University Press, 1979).

Racardo Garcia, *Teachers in a Pluralistic Society: Concepts, Models, Strategies,* Second Edition (New York: Harper and Row, 1990).

Gordon Allport, *The Nature of Prejudice* (New York: Doubleday, 1954).

CHAPTER 10

Family Matters

Mom squirmed in the chair next to the teacher's desk during the parent conference, self-consciously twisting a pink Kleenex tissue. "I know I haven't . . . I mean, our church attendance hasn't been very good this quarter. I know I should take Ricky to Sunday school more often . . ."

Her voice trailed off into silence. The teacher waited.

"You see, Jack lost his job in November." She paused to gulp for air. "And then . . . after Christmas . . . well, he left us. He hasn't come back. I . . . I don't guess he will. I work as many hours as I can get, but it hardly, well . . . it barely—just barely—covers the rent and groceries." She paused again, taking deep breaths, trying to pull together the courage to go on.

"There's . . . you see, there's nothing left over. I . . . I haven't had anything to give Ricky to put in the collection at Sunday school. That's why . . . that's why I haven't let him go, and it's (clearing her throat) . . . it's why I haven't been in church either. I'm so embarrassed. Can you understand that? I'm just so very embarrassed. I . . . I shouldn't come without . . . without something to give."

Implausible? Hardly. Much as we might want to believe that a tragic misunderstanding like this could not happen in a family whose child attends a Christian school, those who have worked with school families for long have almost surely participated in parent conferences very much like it.

Even after people have held membership in the church for years, even after they have heard the precious Gospel proclaimed thousands of times, some still see God as a stern judge who demands that we jump through the many hoops He has erected and who then takes great delight when we fall flat on our faces.[1]

This particular mom and many, many people like her, dread coming before their Lord empty-handed. They, as we also do at times, trick themselves into thinking that they must somehow appease Him—if not with money, then with good deeds or pure motives or a life dedicated to serving others. With clever lies like these, Satan too often succeeds in sucking the sweetness from the Gospel and leaving a dry husk in its place. This mom hurts; she hurts because it always hurts to live under the Law.

She also hurts because marital desertion hurts. She hurts because she feels the bite of real financial need. She faces loneliness and the responsibility of caring for her children as a single parent.

This mom does hurt, but she is not unique in her hurt. Many parents and other caregivers whom we will meet as we minister to families share personal, spiritual, financial, and relational dilemmas similar to hers. Some face challenges even far more serious. Someplace along the line, almost all will ask themselves the question that hurting people through the centuries have always asked: "Where is God when it hurts?"

At times when families hurt, for whatever reason, our Lord gives us as Christian teachers the privilege of being Jesus in their lives. Our Redeemer-King sometimes sends us into the lives of school families as His ambassadors. He allows us to demonstrate His compassion and share with them His love—His compassion and love for the whole person, for the whole family.

Few of us in this culture customarily think of others in terms of wholeness. Instead, we have learned to compartmentalize people and their needs. So we conceptualize a quality we term "spiritual health" and think of it in isolation, as though we could split it off from, say, physical health. Or we analyze the "social dimension" of someone's life as though it had an existence all its own, quite apart from the person's emotions or intellect.

While at times this kind of categorization may help us analyze specific problems, it is at heart subscriptural. It fails to take into account the dynamic integrity—the integratedness—our Creator has built into His human creatures. The New Testament shows Jesus ministering to people with this concept of integrity in sharp focus.

Jesus cared for people in the totality of their being. He knew that our human relationships can and do affect our relationship with God. He knew that when we allow guilt or fear to sour our relationship with Him, our muscles can and do knot up in pain; our bodies can and do surrender to sickness. Jesus knew the Old Testament concept of *shalom*—peace with God, harmony with others, health, security, contentedness. In short, *shalom* translates "total well-being."

Jesus knew the concept because He came to earth to bring the reality. He came to bring wholeness into lives shattered, fragmented, and splintered by sin. He came to heal the *disintegration* in our lives, the disruption of integrity caused by sin.[2]

As we care for people in His name, we too care for them as whole beings, recognizing that their spiritual needs often inextricably intertwine with financial needs, health concerns, emotional problems, and difficulties in relationships.

Sometimes the people to whom we minister know the Lord Jesus intimately and trust His saving grace exclusively. They know who they are and whose they are as the children of God. Nevertheless, they—like us—sometimes struggle with failure. They—like us—wrestle with the power of sin, perhaps at times with sin that seems for the moment invincible. They—like us—sometimes carry burdens of guilt, of worry, of self-contempt. Jesus calls us to minister to them and to let them minister to us as we follow His Spirit's directive that we "encourage one another and build each other up" (1 Thess. 5:11).

Sometimes the parents to whom we minister have never known the Lord Jesus, and they know that they do not know Him. They have as little interest in spiritual things as a dead man has in the luncheon served after his funeral. Apathy on their part need not surprise us. Nor should we find ourselves surprised if they display open hostility. The Scripture plainly teaches that unbelievers are dead—spiritually dead. The Word also tells us they are enemies of God. As we work with school families, we will sometimes find ourselves interacting with unbelievers like these. Jesus calls us to minister to them in times of joy and in times of difficulty. As we do so, we hold out to them the Word of life (Phil. 2:16).

Sometimes the parents to whom we minister consider themselves Christians, but base their right standing before God on their own merit. Wide-eyed and matter-of-factly, they say to themselves (and perhaps to us), "I go to church." Or "I was married in this church." Or "I teach Sunday school." Or "I've cooked the scrambled eggs for the men's club sausage supper every year since 1981." Or

"My neighbors think highly of me." Or "I do my best. God should be satisfied."

These people would almost certainly find an unvarnished explanation of the truth insulting, but Scripture declares them to be just as spiritually dead as those who have rejected outright the Savior and His work for them. They have indeed done so, we know, by choosing to rely on something they are doing or have done instead of depending totally on the finished work Jesus Christ did on their behalf.

As we work with school families, we will sometimes find ourselves interacting with people like these who grossly misunderstand and, in essence, reject the Gospel. They will thus find little comfort or power in it during times of stress. Our Lord Jesus may call us to minister to people like these too. If so, we do it taking special care to divide correctly the Word of truth (2 Tim. 2:15), so that Law and Gospel have the effects the Lord intends them to have—repentance and faith.

Different situations and problems. Different attitudes. Different levels of spiritual maturity. One assignment: Go and make disciples.

The Families We Touch

Christie left the teaching ministry less than 10 months after the first day in her new school. Words could not express the depth of the disappointment she felt as she finished her first—and last—year. She had thought that the school in which she taught would be very much like the Christian school she herself attended as a youngster.

Instead, more than half her students came from nonchurch families. Sixty percent of the students lived with a single parent, one lived with grandparents, and still another with an aunt. Several parents punctuated every conversation with profanity; three or four parents had even sworn at her on occasion. At Christmastime one student's mother, then separated from her husband for two weeks, had moved in with Stan, the student's soccer league coach. One student cried during study time every Tuesday afternoon—the day she had set aside to write to her father, imprisoned in another state for armed assault and rape.

"And this was all in a respectable, middle-class neighborhood, a middle-class school," Christie declared. "I chose to teach in a

174

Christian school even though I knew the salary and benefits would be lower. I just didn't think I could handle all the hassles that public school teachers face. But look! Maybe it's a little better than Hamilton Junior High down the street. But not much. And it's getting worse everyday. As long as the principal and congregation insist that we take in all these non-Christian families, this school is going to have trouble."

Perhaps those who serve in Christian schools do not stop often enough to analyze their role, but it has changed dramatically during the past decade, and it continues to change. In the past some Christian schools may have served as enclaves, as sanctuaries that protected church-member students (and teachers, too, for that matter) from the fury of sin outside. Today, though, Christian schools have become mission fields, and those who teach there have become front-line missionaries—front-line missionaries in the full sense of that term.[3]

Each family that comes to us brings a bundle of needs. No school and church staff can meet all these needs. But above all, we pray that the Lord Jesus would use us as His tools so that by His grace He may meet their deepest need—the need to know Him as their Savior, to know Him in a personal, life-changing way.

People in crisis tend to be open to change. They tend to feel very keenly the spiritual vacuum in their lives. People in crisis who do not know Jesus tend to be more open to the Gospel. Sometimes our Lord will use a crisis as a window through which the Gospel message can shine—lighting up the dark corners of the heart, exposing sin and the need for the Savior, scattering the excuses, and penetrating the chill of previous indifference.

Because we have daily contact with our students, we will often recognize problems in a family long before someone in the church office does. Because we have many opportunities to interact with school families, parents will often mention problems and needs to us first. Because families note the care we show their children, they will sometimes come to us for care themselves.

Like Christie, we may feel overwhelmed by some of the hurts and the problems people face. Yet these hurts and problems should not surprise us. The families of students in Christian schools today share (and probably have always shared) the pain of the society around them, a society slowly buckling under the weight of its own disregard for the will and law of God. Nevertheless, we need never sit beside the proverbial rivers of Babylon, our hearts awash in discouragement, for the same potent Word that has always armed God's soldiers for spiritual conquest will also empower us.

As we think about the enormity of what God proposes to do, we can also find comfort in the fact that we work with a team. The classroom teacher shoulders part of the responsibility; the school principal another part; the evangelism board and evangelism calling committee another. Ideally, the parish pastor(s) coordinates and oversees the effort, even as before God he holds ultimate responsibility for the entire ministry of the parish. We thank God for these partners He has given us in the Gospel!

And we also thank Him for our own Baptism. We thank Him for the call that He Himself has placed on our lives. We thank Him for the servanthood we share with the Lord Jesus, our Brother. We thank Him for these things because we realize that if we approach the challenges relying on any power except the power of God, we will fail. If we attempt this ministry for any reason other than the commission we have received from our King, we will fail. If we begin without first remembering the servant's heart our Lord has given us and then asking Him to continually renew that heart-attitude within us, we will fail. We will likely hurt others—and ourselves too—along the way.

We dare not (and we need not) see ourselves in service to others apart from the love and power that God has promised to pour through us. He will give us the compassion we need as we show His care to those who hurt. He will give us the skill we need as we use the scalpel of the Law. He will give us the words we need as we speak the forgiveness and peace of His Gospel to guilty hearts. He will give us the wisdom we need as we listen and counsel. Our students' families will see Jesus *in* us as Jesus works *through* us.

Pray! Pray! Pray!

As we minister in the Lord's name, we need the help only He can give. He has invited us to ask for it and has modeled for us the practice of prayer in His own ministry. We need our Lord's direction, protection, and guidance, especially when we assault the kingdom of darkness head-on.

Jesus addressed this need specifically in Matthew 18. This chapter, of course, includes what have come to be known as His instructions on church discipline. While the words do speak to that procedure, they apply equally well to times when individual believers have relationship problems with one another.

To conclude the section, our Lord gives His church the authority to forgive and retain sins. Then He adds this promise:

> "I tell you that if two of you on earth agree about anything you ask for, it will be done for you by My Father in heaven. For where two or three come together in My name, there am I with them" (vv. 19–20).

How interesting that the Lord Jesus attaches this promise to His directives about dealing with conflict in His family! Why might He have done that, and what does it mean for teachers as we minister to students' families?

Teachers sometimes are called to bring reconciliation into sticky situations. We sometimes initiate potentially explosive conversations in an effort to bring healing to relationships. We sometimes reach out to families with offers to help, not knowing how family members will respond. We sometimes confront people with their sin, and we sometimes make use of the opportunity to share the Good News of forgiveness through Christ, again uncertain of what response we may receive. Especially at times like these, we can remember Jesus' promise to hear and answer corporate prayer—and then make use of the power He has made available to us.

Some Christian school faculties get together for a brief devotion each day before school begins. They read a section of Scripture and pray specific prayers for themselves, for their students, and for school families. Other faculties draw names for prayer partners as each school year begins. The partners share personal and classroom prayer needs with one another. They support one another in prayer, encourage one another in the Lord's willingness to hear and answer prayer, and rejoice together when those answers come. Some teachers choose a prayer partner on their own, asking that person to intercede for them and with them.

Whatever structure we adopt, we find encouragement in the words of the apostle James, our brother in the faith—"The prayer of a righteous man is powerful and effective" (5:16b). Recognizing our righteousness in Jesus and the tasks to which He Himself has called us, we seek His face in prayer and wrap our minds in His Word before we begin ministry in any situation, asking Him to purify our motives and clarify His will.

Listen! Listen! Listen!

If the Holy Spirit has convinced us that He would like to send us as His representatives to the families of the students we teach, we will intentionally look for ways to serve. We will find opportunities to carry out the Great Commission. Often God will open up avenues for witnessing to parents in the same way He leads us to find opportunities to witness to our students—as we listen.

The listening skills described briefly in the last chapter work as well with adults as they do with children and young people. Let's recap.

Skillful listeners communicate acceptance nonverbally. We give people our undivided attention, maintain good eye-contact, and make appropriate use of nods, touches, and smiles.

Skillful listeners remember that silence is golden. We ignore our own anxiety when the conversation momentarily lapses, remembering that silence will allow the other person time to sort out thoughts and feelings. We pray during these times of silence, asking the Holy Spirit for His wisdom and asking Him to do the healing work He alone can do.

Skillful listeners paraphrase the thoughts of the other person. We help the speaker to go on by restating in our own words what he has said, taking care to do this with accuracy.

Skillful listeners reflect and clarify the feelings that the other person has expressed. We help the speaker to recognize and express deeper feelings by naming the emotion(s) we think he is communicating and then inviting him to react to our observations.

Skillful listeners trust the Holy Spirit to do His work. We speak the truth to a situation, always—by God's grace—speaking it in love (Eph. 4:15). We see ourselves as channels through whom the Holy Spirit wants to pour love from His vast reservoir of compassion. Yet we remember that God has reserved for Himself the responsibility for bringing about a solution in other people's lives. We cannot "fix" their problems, nor should we try.

Skillful listeners look for ways to cultivate their skills
listening, and we continue to read books and take cou
to help us hone the listening skills we need to be effective
witness to our Lord Jesus. It is nearly impossible to state it too
strongly: *Good listening skills are indispensable for anyone involved
in interpersonal Christian ministry.*

Open the Door—Wide!

Most Christian schools prop open the door to effective parent-
teacher communication in several different ways. In addition, each
individual teacher in a given school will adopt a personal communication style, perhaps with unique elements. Whatever methods
we adopt, the fundamental principles of effective communication
do not change—we need to make ourselves accessible, and school
families need to see us as accessible.

Some schools require teachers to conduct home visits before
school begins. (See appendix A for a sample format.) Most have at
least one and perhaps as many as four to six individual parent-
teacher conferences each year. Many send a school newsletter home
once a week or once a month. Often schools schedule monthly
parent-teacher league meetings, giving both parents and teachers
an opportunity to touch base on a regular and somewhat informal
basis.

In addition to these routines, you may want to think about adopt-
ing one or more of these practices:

- Jean Pickering makes it a point to phone each student's family
  during the first two weeks of school. She says something like,
  "I'm so happy (Roger) is in my class. I believe that our Lord Jesus
  is going to give us a good year. I'm calling in case you have any
  questions." She closes the brief conversation by assuring the family of her prayers for them and asking them to pray for her. Then
  she tells the family how to reach her by phone at home and at
  school and encourages them to call any time they have questions
  or problems.
- Steven Hughes practices what he calls "ministry by wandering
  around." He stations himself in the hallway or out on the sidewalk
  as the students leave the building each day. He arrives at church

15 minutes early for meetings and worship services, and he hardly ever leaves without spending 10 or 15 minutes chatting with someone after an activity has concluded. He sits in the bleachers with parents during basketball and volleyball games.

"It's amazing what can happen when people know you'll be around," Steven says. "Lots of times parents will pop their head inside my door and ask how the gerbils are doing. Before you know it, they've shared some problem from work or home. It has given me many chances to share Jesus' love with families in the past 10 years."

- Kelly Schroeder says, "I work to catch my third-graders being good. Then I phone the child's home to share what I've seen. Quite often, I'll call when someone has volunteered to lead devotions or when someone has done a particularly good job on a difficult memory work passage. Or I'll call if I spot a student sharing or going out of her way to be helpful. At first it seems to unnerve parents—I guess they're used to having the school phone with bad news. But it opens the door to positive communication. I choose my comments carefully to reinforce the fact that this is a *Christian* school and that Jesus' love is what we're all about."
- Mike Trainer helps his sixth-graders produce a classroom newspaper. Written by the students themselves and distributed each Friday, the paper includes articles and drawings that tell what has gone on in the classroom that week. The article about the Scripture study the class has done that week always receives a prominent spot on page one.
- Marge Hamner sends a letter home with her preschoolers at the end of every unit in her religion class. The letter explains the Bible story or topic the class has studied and gives family members hints on simple projects and activities they can do at home to review and reinforce the spiritual concepts the children have learned at school. Many parents report that they began meal-time prayers in their family as a result of their child's witness and the suggestions in Marge's letters. (See appendix B for sample letters.)
- Rosalind Meyer uses part of the time during parent-teacher conferences to discuss each child's spiritual development with the family member(s) who come to the conference. She eases into the topic by noting the information on the grade card about

church and Sunday school attendance. She goes on to talk about the growth in Bible knowledge she has seen. Then she shares an incident or two that reveals something about the student's expressions of faith in words or actions. She gives the parent an opportunity to share concerns or insights. She always closes each conference with a prayer asking the Lord to nurture the child and the child's family through His Word.

Available Resources

When we make ourselves available as channels for the Lord's love, when we pray and prepare ourselves for witnessing, when we consistently use the listening skills we have honed, our Lord will lead families to us. Most will come because they recognize a need in themselves or in their family. Some will come because of a crisis in their lives. Regardless of the need they perceive, in coming they open the door of witness through which we can step, confident in Christ—not in ourselves.

Families face so many different kinds of challenges that no one individual can possibly provide all the kinds of help that any specific situation might demand. Because this is so, teachers need to work closely with the principal, with the pastor, and with other appropriate congregational leaders in maintaining a catalog of available resources:

- The parish itself can usually provide some kinds of help (e.g., social ministry money to pay the gas bill for an unemployed parent; pastoral counseling for a couple with marital conflict).
- Individuals in the parish may be willing to provide some kinds of help (e.g., a lawyer might do some *pro bono* work to plead a bankruptcy case for a single parent in financial need; a group of senior adults might set up a rotating schedule for after-school child care so that a young mother can spend time with her husband who lies in the hospital with cancer).
- The church staff may have researched community resources which they feel comfortable recommending to school member families (e.g., an Al-Anon group for individuals struggling with the issues of family alcoholism; a clinical psychologist with expertise in dealing with severe depression).

Teachers need to know what resources are available and how to access them. Most pastors and/or principals will have guidelines faculty members should follow in suggesting a given resource to someone. If you do not know the procedure, ask before you make a referral.

Despite Our Best Efforts . . .

Sometimes parents share their needs with us. Sometimes we spot learning problems, social problems, physical problems, emotional problems, or spiritual problems in the lives of our students, and we share these with the student's family.

In some cases, as we discuss a specific problem with family members, everyone will agree. The teacher or pastor or principal or parent will suggest a course of action. Everyone will assent to it and the family will follow through. God will bring help and, eventually, healing to the situation. That kind of resolution can bring a deep sense of satisfaction to everyone involved. We look back on it later as the high point of the week. Or of the year! We thank God for the ministry He has given us to one another and for the solution He has provided through one another.

Sometimes, though, parents will resist help. In a moment of utter despair or weakness, they may share a need with us. They may even pour out our hearts to us. We, of course, listen with all the skill we have, interceding as we do. During the conversation, we witness to the person, sharing God's grace for them in Jesus. Our Lord may even give us a chance to present the Gospel to them in some detail. Then, perhaps, we suggest a source of further help. Maybe we ask them to make an appointment to talk with the pastor. Maybe we offer to go with them to talk with the staff of a drug abuse clinic.

Regardless of our conscientious efforts as we go along in some situations, we may feel the other person begin to pull back and resist the process. Sometimes we sense it happening almost at once. At other times, it may occur only after several days or weeks. Some parents resist contact with the classroom teacher—period! On the other hand, some will listen politely to our request for a conference, set up an appointment, and then never keep it. Some will keep the appointment we have made with them, but then never follow through on the promises they make to seek the outside help we suggest. What can we do when we meet family resistance?

First, we need to remember that a parent who resists our help usually does so because he or she feels threatened in some way. Something at the visceral level inside the parent may say, "I don't want contact with the school." The roots of this may wind all the way down to the dark, half-remembered experiences the parent had with a teacher in childhood. Often people will blame themselves or condemn themselves as "bad parents" if their child needs help. In most cases, such self-condemnation makes no logical sense. Still, it can paralyze the family's resolve to face the reality of the moment.

As professionals and as those called by our Lord Jesus to serve others, we need to remind ourselves of the many reasons that may lie behind parental resistance, and we need to look beyond the personal affront we may at first feel. If, relying on God's grace, we can drop our own urge to keep up appearances or to stroke our own ego, our Lord can still use us in the situation to do real ministry.

Regardless of a parent's initial negative reaction, we will want to keep on trying. If the year slips by without a response, perhaps next year's teacher can build on the foundation we have laid. It is often a mistake to think that our words have had no effect. Sometimes months or years will go by before a parent admits, "My child has a problem," or "My family has a problem," or "I have a problem." If we will admit that we ourselves are sometimes unwilling to ask for help from God or from others, we will deal more patiently with parents who struggle with that same issue.

As we approach parents about a problem that involves their child, we do it prayerfully. We speak to God about a situation before we speak to the individual human beings involved. When we do approach family members, we take care to do that as disarmingly as possible. We describe the problem and its consequences as we see them, but with nonthreatening language, "owning" our personal feelings about the situation by sending mostly "I messages":

- I'm concerned that John probably had a bad day today. I'm worried about him because he seems to be having a hard time with the other boys. I wonder if he's mentioned anything to you?"
- I'm quite upset with John because he didn't have his math done

today. It's the third time this week, and I was wondering whether or not he's shared this with you at home.

- I'm worried about John because lately he seems to daydream in class a lot. All students do this sometimes, but it kind of looks to me as though John has something on his mind. I wondered whether you might be able to help me figure it out.

Sometimes teachers find themselves tempted to think that a parent does not care about his or her child. That is almost never true. Deep down, parents do care. Very, very seldom does a parent deliberately set out to harm a child. The vast majority of parents want to be good parents. If they fail, most often they fail because they just do not know what to do or because they have never learned the necessary parenting skills.

Many parents have a hard time expressing their love or demonstrating their concern in meaningful ways. Some parents actually cannot show care. A mom addicted to cocaine will let her baby starve while she leaves the apartment in search of more of the drug. A dad who spends 24 hours a day in an alcoholic fog has neither the clarity of thought nor the emotional resources to nurture his child in any significant way. A mom who herself was abused as a child may hate herself too much to show love to her child.

People who stagger under burdens like these can learn to parent. They can develop the skills they need to nurture their children. But before this can happen, they need to receive much care and nurture themselves. Sometimes teachers who see their students in situations like these can do little to change the circumstances in which the children live. That does not mean we should avoid the issue. We may need to go to our principal or to our pastor. We may need to confront the parent. We may even need to call the police or the child welfare agency.

But finally, in some cases, we may need to reconcile ourselves to supporting the student rather than working with the family. We may need to help the student understand that mom or dad cannot provide the support we (and God) would like the student to have at home. We may need to help the student find appropriate sources of nurture and care outside the home. At such times, we thank God for His family of faith and for making us part of a caring community.

"We're All in This Together"

To be most effective, ministry with families demands a team effort. Many aspects of ministry in Christian schools work best if teachers, principal, pastor(s), board members, and other church staff people work together. Chapter 11 will talk about team ministry and how teachers can help foster team spirit in their school.

To Think About

1. What scriptural evidence can you cite to show that our Lord cares about people as whole beings, not simply about their faith-life?
2. Why do you suppose people often listen more carefully and with more interest to someone's Christian witness during a time of personal crisis? Do we care for families in crisis as a means to an end—so we can witness to them? or for some other reason? Explain.
3. What part does prayer play in our discipling ministry to families?
4. Review the listening techniques listed in this chapter. Does listening to adults differ from listening to children? Explain.
5. What practical suggestions from this chapter for making yourself available for family ministry seem workable to you? What other possibilities suggest themselves?
6. Why might teachers be reluctant to make home visits? What advantages can a home visit give Christian teachers in their discipling ministry?
7. For what reasons might a family resist a teacher's suggestions or offers of help? What can (should) we do then?

Notes

1. While God has not given teachers in His church the same responsibilities He has given pastors, nevertheless I find it instructive to eavesdrop on C. F. W. Walther as he counsels young pastors who are about to assume the duties of their first parish. Walther talks about the various spiritual states in which the pastor will likely find his members. Then he goes on to address the attitudes pastors need to have as they approach their holy work. Teachers who reflect on the opportunities God may give us to witness to parents will likely find Dr. Walther's comments insightful as well:

The newly called pastor must approach his parish with a seriousness equal to his joy. He must resolve: "I want to do everything possible so that every soul entrusted to me will be saved." Hence, when he discovers that most of his members—as often seems to be the case—are still blind and dead and unconverted, he must not allow that to irritate or discourage him, but rather drive him to the ardent desire: "I want to rouse them all from their spiritual death and through God's means of grace turn them into live Christians. I will not let the devil stop me, but approach the task in faith."

Or perhaps he discovers that some members of his new parish are living in open shame and vice. Let him not despair but rather think: "I have a potent Word, and by means of it I will try to free these slaves of sin." Or he notices that his congregation is still on a very low level of spiritual understanding, of knowing what the Gospel is all about. Then let him resolve: "I will cheerfully go to work and patiently and diligently instruct these poor, ignorant people, so they will see the light."

Or if he notes with great joy that most of his members are mature, experienced, believing, active Christians, with only a few who appear to be unconverted, let him resolve: "Very well, I must attempt, first of all, to bring the unconverted to Christ." At the same time, of course, he must resolve to give the well-grounded members the strong food they need.

(From *Law and Gospel,* trans. Herbert Bouman, [St. Louis: Concordia Publishing House, 1981], 109–110. All rights reserved.)

2. See, for example, the relationship between guilt, physical illness, problems in social relationships, and depression as expressed by David in Psalm 38. Interested readers may also want to study Rev. 22:1–5, John's description of the kingdom of God after it has come to all of God's people in all its fullness, the brokenness of sin gone forever.

3. A full discussion of ways we might witness to parents, what a full-blown Gospel presentation might sound like, and the ways to determine the content of the witness a Christian teacher might give lie beyond the scope of this chapter.

Everyone working in Christian schools should work through the video program *A Vision for Witness,* prepared by the Board for Evangelism Services and the Board for Parish Services of the Lutheran Church—Missouri Synod. Faculties could profitably spend a day or more before school begins each year reviewing and discussing the concepts presented in this program.

In addition, *Teacher Witness Workshops,* produced by the two boards mentioned above, provide valuable input and skill practice for teachers who would like to hone their witnessing skills. For further information contact either of the two boards; both are located at 1333 S. Kirkwood Road, St. Louis, Missouri 63122-7295.

CHAPTER 11

The Brothers and Sisters with Whom I Work

The waters of the Bourbois River boiled angrily. Our canoe careened from shoreline to shoreline, striking the boulders that lurked beneath the water. We lurched downstream this way for most of the morning.

My friend and I, green to the ways of the river, spent much of our time ducking to avoid being clotheslined by the branches that overhung the channel. We expended much of our energy bemoaning the fact that we had not postponed our trip a few days to allow the river, now swollen by last weekend's rains, to calm down. We poured the rest of our effort into paddling—albeit unskillfully—away from the massive rocks that dotted the river bed.

Around noon, we began to relax and to congratulate ourselves that the thuds we had encountered with such great regularity in the beginning were now jarring us much less often. I began to paddle with more assurance, looking downstream to check for future hazards and feeling a little like Mark Twain himself.

Just then my friend cleared her throat. "Excuse me," she said, "But your end of the canoe is sinking!"

Teamwork

We hear the cliche often—"We are all in this together." Cliches usually become cliches because everyone recognizes the nuggets of truth embedded in them. Especially as we work with others on a staff-team to serve Christ and His people, we share the same canoe. We paddle and float together, or we flounder and sink together.

Make no mistake. We do not build staff unity. God the Holy Spirit does it. Jesus clearly taught that He wants His people to live and work together in love, the love His Spirit is maturing in our hearts. We have a part in this sanctification process too:

- We draw on the grace He makes available to pray for oneness in purpose.
- We draw on the grace He gives to confess, as necessary, the sins of pride—especially, sins of professional pride—that keep us from helping and encouraging one another.
- We draw on the grace He gives to throw competition and ego overboard.
- We take risks; we invest time; we make ourselves vulnerable— all by grace.

The agony and the ecstasy of team ministry! Sometimes a staff grows into something extraordinary and beautiful. God's grace has been at work. Sometimes the sense of teamwork dries up and staff members want to give up. Even then, God's healing grace is still available. We need only ask Him for it.

From a practical standpoint, we have no option but to minister as a team. When individuals add hours of effort to the week or month, the benefits—at best—can increase only arithmetically; an hour's worth of input results in an hour's worth of benefit (or so).

But something marvelous, almost miraculous, happens as a staff teams up to work on a specific challenge. As they combine the gifts and abilities God has given to individual members, the benefits increase geometrically; an hour's worth of group input produces multiplied results—for the staff itself as well as for students and school families.

Even if this were not true, our Lord seldom makes team ministry an option:

- Jesus sent out the Seventy two-by-two (Luke 10:1).
- After Barnabas had ministered in Antioch for a while, he went to Tarsus to enlist the help of Paul (Acts 11:25ff).
- When the early church commissioned the first traveling missionaries, it followed the Holy Spirit's instructions to send Paul and Barnabas together (Acts 13:1ff).
- Later on, Paul traveled with John Mark, with Luke, and with Silas. Others came and went in Paul's entourage, but hardly ever did Paul find himself alone.

Even in the Old Testament, God put people in ministry together:

- The great prophet Elijah needed a friend, and the gracious Lord gave him one—Elisha, his companion and subsequent successor (1 Kings 19:16ff).
- Shadrach, Meshach, Abednego, and Daniel faced the first lonely months of Babylonian captivity together; Shadrach, Meshach, and Abednego walked into the fiery furnace together.
- About the time the prophet Jeremiah began to call Judah to repentance, young King Josiah decreed national reforms as well. Only after Josiah died did Jeremiah go on to minister alone.

Even our Lord Jesus took a team approach to ministry. He chose the Twelve. He often called Peter, James, and John to His side as He battled with the enemy during His earthly ministry. These three even accompanied Him through the gates of Gethsemane itself. Some may argue that Jesus invited them so they could witness this part of His passion. That may be true.

But I believe a strong case can also be made for the idea that Jesus needed them. As true God, of course, He needed no one. But He was also a human being. The Limitless One chose to limit Himself. As He descended into His ultimate, agonizing service for us, He reached out for the companionship of those with whom He had ministered during the previous three years. He reached out for their encouragement and love.

They failed Him that night, of course. But their failure does not destroy the principle: God gives His people to one another as partners in the Gospel. If our Lord Jesus Himself saw the need for the support and service of others, how much more obvious our own need![1]

Of course, loving like that, letting ourselves need one another like that, can spawn uneasiness in our hearts. Even so, C. S. Lewis once defined the alternative:

> To love at all is to be vulnerable. Love anything, and your heart will certainly be wrung and possibly be broken. If you want to make sure of keeping it intact, you must give your heart to no one, not even to an animal. Wrap it carefully round with hobbies and little luxuries; avoid all entanglements; lock it up safe in the casket or coffin of your selfishness. But in that casket—safe, dark, motionless, airless—it will change. It will not be broken; it will become unbreakable, impenetrable, irredeemable ... The only

place outside Heaven where you can be perfectly safe from all the dangers and perturbations of love is Hell.[2]

Has God really left us an option? To love at all is to be vulnerable. To minister at all means to take that risk. To serve effectively, to witness effectively, we must risk loving also those whom God has called to serve with us. Staff unity and team ministry demand the risk of vulnerability. And risk we must, obedient to our Lord's call. Risk we can, relying on our Lord's own forgiving love for us.

God calls us into ministry and, most times, asks us to serve Him with others whom He has likewise called. If that is so, then we need to ask ourselves what can we do, under God's blessing, to foster effective team relationships. Most fifth-graders who have had any experience at all with team sports could come up with a credible answer to that question. We would need to expand and apply their observations to the congregational ministry team, of course, but many of us who serve on staff teams could learn much by listening to our students. What would they tell us? What advice could they give?

Remember, You're on a Team!

A fifth-grader might explain this concept in words like these: "You want as many stars for your team as you can get. But if one or two players—even star players—hog the ball, the team probably won't win and everybody will go home mad. Some teammates aren't superstars. They may fumble and trip over their own feet at times. You may feel like yelling at them, but the team will do better if you help and encourage one another instead. Remember, everybody will fumble once in a while."

In a Christian school, the staff team includes everyone with ministry responsibilities for the school—the teachers, of course, and the pastor—the principal—the teachers' helpers—members of the school board (and also the school secretary and the custodian, if you have one). All the people on the school ministry team will have strengths. All will have weaknesses. All will shine at something. All will drop the ball at times.

No one in a canoe can afford to tell her partner, "Your end is sinking." No one on a softball diamond can afford to ignore the talents of a teammate who bats .900. No individual member of the school team can afford to wander off to minister alone. Nor can the rest of the team ignore the teammate who tries.

Remember, you are a team! Teams work together. Each person has a specific position to fill, a specific role to play.

Some in the church may minimize the importance of job descriptions, considering them unnecessary or even "unspiritual." Yet staff teams function much more smoothly when everyone's responsibilities have been specifically spelled out. Those who write job descriptions should anchor them firmly in the call a worker has received from the congregation. A good job description details both primary and secondary responsibilities.

Each staff member needs to review his or her job description on a regular basis, perhaps once or twice each year. Those who supervise the staff should reevaluate the adequacy and accuracy of each individual's job description. Staff members should ask themselves questions such as the following:

- Does this job description accurately reflect my present duties? If not, what should we add to the document? delete from the document? add to my work load? delete from my work load?
- Does this job description reflect my call? Does it include reasonable expectations? Or does it demand too much? or too little?
- Does anything else in the job description need to change? Why? How could that change happen?

A well-written job description can free workers to concentrate efforts on the kinds of service they do best. It can also free them from the pressure to do everything. It can help protect everyone on the staff from the conflicts that will always occur when two people assume responsibility for the same duty or when tasks remain undone because no one knows who is responsible for them. Finally, it helps to ensure fairness as the congregation, principal, or board distributes the work load among the called workers.

Share!

Picture this. A fifth-grader plays left field. He has a softball glove. The first baseman does not. First inning. The team takes the field. What happens? If the players have committed themselves to one another, and if the team has committed itself to winning, the fielder will probably let the first baseman use his glove—the first baseman likely needs it more.

Picture this. Fifth-graders are playing flag football. Third down and ten. One player figures out a sure-fire way to make a touchdown. What happens? If the players have committed themselves to one another, and if the team has committed itself to winning, the player shares his idea in the next huddle. His teammates listen and evaluate his suggestion on the basis of its merits.

Ideas—information—equipment—schoolyard teams that win share these things. Staff teams that win, share too.

A friend of mine once served in a school large enough to have two seventh-grade classrooms. She taught one of them. Another teacher (let's call her Helen) taught the other. Both teachers used the same textbooks, and they were supposed to use the same supplies.

My friend felt frustrated with her science program from September through February. Her text called for all kinds of experiments that required a variety of equipment—test tubes, beakers, flasks, microscopes, chemicals. She could seldom do the activities recommended in the course because, as Helen kept telling her, the school board would never approve money to purchase all the necessary items.

One afternoon in early spring my friend walked into Helen's classroom unexpectedly. "Nonexistent" beakers boiled merrily away above "nonexistent" cans of Sterno.

My friend told me later, "It was hard to forgive Helen for deceiving me and for cheating my class like that for almost eight months. In the end, I had to remember that she had such a good reputation for teaching science—and such a terrible reputation with her students in just about every other way. I guess science was the one area in which she felt she could excel, and she just could not handle competition in that one area. Until then, we had done a lot of planning together, but even though she apologized, it was hard to think of ourselves as a team any more."

It should go without saying that team members share equipment and supplies with one another. Members of the same team also need to share information. This does not mean staff members gossip with or about one another. It does mean that as they work with people, they confide in one another for the good of the ministry.

Quite naturally, this raises the question of confidentiality. Who should know what and when? And if someone should know, how much should that person know? A good rule of thumb involves the question, "Who needs to know?" If someone on the staff owns a part of the problem, that person should have the information she needs to deal adequately with her part of it. If someone on the staff could potentially provide part of the solution, that person may be consulted.

For example, Mr. Hampton notices that John comes into class every morning and promptly falls asleep. John denies having any particular problems. He tells his teacher, "I'm just tired." Mr. Hampton calls John's home. John's mother seems evasive. After watching John struggle for a week or two, Mr. Hampton might phone Pastor White and say something like, "John Doe just cannot stay awake in class. I'm concerned about him, but I haven't been able to get much help from John's parents. Do you know anything that you can share?"

Pastor White may have no information. On the other hand, he may respond, "The family is dealing with a drug abuse problem right now, and there is, no doubt, lots of disruption at home. Please pray for them."

Mr. Hampton would, of course, keep this information strictly to himself. He would pray for John's family. Knowing something about the situation, he could make allowances for John's behavior, behavior that ordinarily would be unacceptable.

Or suppose the situation would unfold in a different way. Suppose Mr. Doe comes to the church office and tells Pastor White that he has found packages of cocaine in his daughter's jacket pocket. He has suspected for months that something was wrong with Jane, a high school senior. Now the Doe's living room turns into a virtual battlefield every night. Mr. and Mrs. Doe have thought about asking Jane to move out. John and Jane have always been very close, Jane keeping an eye out for her "baby brother" and John adoring his older sister. Now, John cries a lot. Mrs. Doe cries a lot. Jane and Mr. Doe yell a lot.

Pastor White could (and perhaps should) choose to phone Mr. Hampton. He need not describe the problem; Mr. Doe shared it in confidence. But the pastor could ethically tell John's teacher something like this: "The Doe's seem to be having some problems. You may want to keep an eye on John. He can probably use some extra support right now. Pray for the family, too, as the Lord reminds you."

The pastor(s), principal, and faculty members who minister together in a Christian school need to share information like this with one another. Keeping one another informed is not simply a matter of professional courtesy. Information is power—the power to help.

Likewise, good ethics dictate that faculty members share with one another facts that impact a student's learning. For example, as school starts in September, Faith's third-grade teacher could tell Faith's fourth-grade teacher that Faith did not usually bring a lunch last year because Faith's mom struggles with severe depression. That warning would give the fourth-grade teacher time to devise a strategy that would ensure that Faith would get something to eat each day.

Note that even here, though, no other teacher need be involved. Neither does the conversation about Faith take place in the faculty lounge during lunch or anywhere else it might be overheard. Situations like these should never become the topic of general conversation over afternoon coffee or in the teachers' lounge before a faculty meeting—never.

Of course, not every issue of confidentiality lends itself to a quick, easy resolution. When gnarly questions come up, staff members can often unknot the dilemma by asking themselves, "Where is my heart?" This question often clears the way to a God-pleasing decision about when and how much to share.

It is always wrong to pass on information if it makes us feel powerful, or "in the know," or superior to the person about whom we speak. And no matter what the situation, God still expects us to obey His Eighth Commandment. As Luther once wrote, this commandment requires that we "defend (the other person), speak well of him, and explain everything in the kindest way."[3]

Members of the team share equipment and information. They also share their efforts and energies. For example, as the spring basketball tournament approaches, teachers with a heart for team ministry ask themselves, "What *can* I do?" rather than "What *must* I do?" Having a task in mind, they can volunteer instead of waiting for the inevitable draft.

Even if a staff member counts the tournament among her least favorite activities, coming at the task from the angle of volunteering to do the thing she can do most gladly will help her be a better steward of her time and abilities. It will contribute to positive feelings among her colleagues, and it will help her maintain a more joyful attitude as she serves.

Equipment—ideas—information—energy—staff members share all these and one last, most important thing too—faith. Effective ministry teams never let the spiritual aspect of their relationship evolve in a haphazard, hit or miss way. Rather, they plan a strategy. They set aside time—quality time—to pray and to study the Scripture together.

As members of a team, we need to covenant together to be proactive in the Word, rather than reactive to the crises that will always swirl around us. We need to confess our sins to one another, especially when we have hurt one another. We need to forgive one another even as God, in Christ, has forgiven us, and we need to express both our repentance and our forgiveness verbally. We need to share our joys and our faith struggles with one another like the brothers and sisters Christ Himself has made us.

We do everything we can to build team ministry. But when all is said and done, only the bonds of love that our Lord forges for us will remain unbroken by the stresses and strains that will inevitably occur on a multiple-person staff. Our Lord helps us hammer out that unity as we tussle through day-to-day tensions with one another, but He fires and hardens the bonds of love and unity for us as we sit together under His Word, sharing our faith and allowing Him to do His holy work in our hearts.

Cheer One Another On

As most fifth-graders know, players on successful teams encourage one another. On a multiple-person staff this happens as the members pray together and spend time around God's Word with one another. It also happens as God uses us to encourage one another in informal ways:

"I'll pray for your math class. Decimals are never easy!"

"Jesus loves you, Joann, and so do I."

"I read a really powerful Scripture verse last night, Scott. It kind of fits in with what you have been saying. Have you ever noticed 2 Samuel . . .?"

"Your sermon really spoke to me yesterday, Pastor. Thanks!"

"What an interesting bulletin board, Mary!"

Roy Exum, executive sports editor of the Chattanooga *News–Free Press,* tells the story behind the story of the 1977 Orange Bowl. Lou Holtz, who would later go on to great success at Notre Dame, coached Arkansas that year. His team was pitted against purportedly invincible Oklahoma. Two weeks before the game, Arkansas lost four first-string players—Holtz benched three for breaking team rules; the other injured himself.

Odds-makers had Arkansas a 21-point underdog.

Practices the week before the bowl game went abysmally. After the last practice, Holtz called a team meeting. The locker room fell silent, the players awaiting the tongue-lashing they knew they deserved.

Instead, Holtz explained a tradition to them. It seemed that in his family when someone did something well, the rest of the family would sit down with that person and each would share a word of genuine praise with him or her.

Holtz paused for a moment. Then he told the team they were going to take the time, then and there, to do the same thing for one another. In the quiet moments that followed, player after player shared how much each of the other players had done for him, how the others had inspired him and helped him. One or two players choked on their words as they talked about how honored they felt to have played for Arkansas that year. The offensive linemen congratulated the defense. Someone talked about how proud he was to have Steve Little, the nation's best field-goal kicker, on the team. And so it went.

No one from Oklahoma knew it, but the Sooners had lost the Orange Bowl before they ever took the field. Two evenings later, as the fans left the stadium after the game, the magnitude of Arkansas' victory glowed on the scoreboard: the Razorbacks had won, 31 to 6.[4]

We have the power to help one another win. The teacher who says, "I'll care for my kids, but I won't care for my colleagues," is saying in essence, "Your end of the canoe is sinking." We need one another's affirmation. We need one another's accolades. People in ministry serve under stress. Satan wields the weapon of discouragement with great deftness. We can easily fall prey to what someone has called "affirmation deprivation." From where can we get the courage and the will to keep on serving? What will get us through the rainy days when nothing seems to go right?

By God's grace, we can minister His courage to one another. We can look for one another's strengths and celebrate them. We can help one another capitalize on the gifts God has given us. As the apostle Paul once urged God's people, "Encourage one another and build each other up, just as in fact you are doing" (1 Thess. 5:11).

Perhaps you will find this kind of sharing uncomfortable at first, but it becomes easier with practice. Even then, you may hesitate to share affirmation with your principal or pastor, but these members of your ministry team need affirmation and support, too—even if they do not always show it. Our Lord wants to use you as a source of joy in ministry to those who lead your staff. Let Him!

Stick Up for One Another

No one teaches fifth grade for long without understanding something about the fierce loyalty fifth-graders can have for one another. They seem to understand, almost instinctively, the need to close ranks against a common opponent. If someone from another team roughs up someone from *your* team, the offender will likely know the meaning of the word *confrontation* before long.

We must not underestimate the need for loyalty among the members of a team. No matter the position in which an individual serves, opposition never stands far from the door. God puts His people into ministry together partly because He knows we need support from other believers as we fight the battles we will most certainly fight. No army has its soldiers dig trenches for one.

Satan will undoubtedly attack us head-on at times. Then, too, sometimes we get down on ourselves; we attack ourselves for our failures, ineptness, or ineffectiveness. If this were not enough, we sometimes face opposition from other people. As those who have lived through it will testify, criticism almost always hurts worst when it comes from someone whom we have served and whom we love.

197

A wise saint once remarked, "The church is the only army that bayonets its own wounded."

When attacks come, as they inevitably will, we need allies. We long for loyalty from others. Part of cheering each other on involves helping one another handle the criticism that comes to each of us. Regardless of the form the opposition takes, members of a winning team resort, first of all, to prayer. We "stick up for one another," as it were, before the throne of grace.

This kind of prayer goes well beyond the "Dear God, bless the missionaries" genre in which the pray-er expresses general, pious platitudes to God. Paul wrote to the Colossians, "I want you to know how much I am struggling for you and for those at Laodicea" (2:1). The phrase "how much I am struggling" in the original Greek paints a picture of someone straining for victory in an athletic contest.

Paul wrote the letter to the Colossians from prison. How then could he have struggled, strained, or striven for the believers in this congregation? In prayer! And the rest of the epistle makes that clear.[5]

Paul asked God for specific, practical gifts for the Colossians. We honor our Lord when we, too, ask for specific, practical help for our co-workers and for any other individuals involved in a specific conflict. Our prayers also please God and encourage our colleagues when we continue, earnestly praying and waiting for as long as it takes to resolve an issue, steadfast by grace in the faith that God is at work no matter how bleak things may look for the moment.

Very often during times of conflict, Satan tries to stir up smaller pools of dissent in addition to the main event. These swirl around the initial problem and sometimes get sucked up into it, making the original whirlpool even more treacherous than before. The enemy's main weapon in this strategy is gossip.

Parents may come to us with questions. Board members may come with "information." Other staff members may come to us to talk about their concern for the situation. They may want to criticize other staff members. They may want to offer us sympathy—using that as an opening to ferret out what we know. Our response to all this can bring healing or it can exacerbate the hurt.

As professionals and, more importantly, as disciples of our Lord Jesus Christ, we need to ask ourselves questions similar to the ones we ask when we face other issues of confidentiality:

- What reason do I myself have to talk about this or to be involved in it? Do I directly own part of this problem? Has God chosen to use me as part of the solution? How do I know that?
- Where is my heart? Why would I want or need to talk about the problem with the person who has approached me?
- Is the other person directly involved in the problem? Has God chosen to use him or her as part of the solution? How do I know that?

Sorting through these kinds of questions can help us avoid the sin of gossip. It can help us "stick up for" our staff colleagues and for other brothers and sisters in the faith. A process like this can help us thwart Satan's plans for our own lives and his plans to scuttle the ministry God has given the staff on which we serve. The process can help us keep on showing loyalty and love in our staff relationships.

Be Honest!

By God's grace we minister together as brothers and sisters in Christ: We share our joys. We applaud one another. We contribute to the good reputation of our colleagues as we talk with one another, with parents, and with board members. We refuse to gossip about one another. We pray for each other. We listen to each other. We show concern for one another's spiritual welfare. We ask one another, "How's your spiritual life?" In love, we hold one another accountable. In one sense, we agree to allow others on the staff to disciple us, even as they look to us to disciple them. Most of this can be rewarding, even fun.

Yet true loyalty, like genuine love, is never blind. That means we recognize one another's weaknesses as well as one another's proficiencies. Others on the staff—yes, the principal and pastor too—may, at times, say or do things that bruise us personally. What then? Others on the staff may, at times, say or do things that hurt the team. What then?

In some cases, we may in good conscience decide to overlook the offense, to forgive the offender, to let the matter drop without confrontation. To do that without damage to ourselves and to the staff, we must evaluate the situation with stone-cold honesty. We must ask ourselves whether we have truly torn up the IOUs we hold against our colleague as a result of the incident. We must also be able to say before God that the relationship has been repaired and that the memory of the colleague's action will not cause further damage. The Holy Spirit will give us the grace we need to overlook an affront for the sake of the ministry when that course of action is helpful.

Why might we overlook an offense? Every one of us as God's children sees the weaknesses and sins that encrust our own hearts and that keep us from true Christ-likeness. In humility acknowledging the plank in our own eye, we may choose to overlook the speck of sawdust in our brother's eye (Matt. 7:3–5). Paul urges an attitude of humility again and again using words like "Bear with each other and forgive whatever grievances you may have against one another" (Col. 3:13).

Luther once told a story about two goats who met on a bridge over a deep river. Neither could turn back; neither could pass the other—the bridge was too narrow. If they chose to jostle and push one another, both might fall into the water and drown. So, Luther said, if they are wise, one goat will choose to lie down and let the other one walk over him. That way, both can go safely on their way. "Even so," the reformer concluded, "people should rather endure to be trod upon, than to fall into debate and discord with one another."[6]

At times, though, our silence about an offense will cause continuing damage. We may find ourselves unable to forgive. We may catch ourselves nursing a grudge. Sometimes, too, love and loyalty demand that we tell another staff member the truth for that person's own good. Perhaps sometime in your life you have had a friend or teacher or pastor who loved you enough to do this for you and to do it in such a gentle, humble way that you could listen and respond. What a gift from God such servants are! And how rare!

Few among us find this process comfortable—let alone enjoyable. Despite the discomfort, though, the work God does through it can bring a deep sense of satisfaction and a stronger set of working relationships.

Our Lord Jesus gave His church explicit directions about how to deal with conflict between brothers and sisters. A close reading of Matthew 18 reveals much about both the Lord's process and its goals.

The process begins any time a brother or sister "sins against us." Jesus does not reserve the process for certain categories of sin (e.g., "big" ones like murder or grand larceny), rather His words free us to use the method He prescribes to resolve any kind of issue that arises and causes conflict between brothers and sisters in the faith.

The Scriptures insist that we not delay. "In your anger do not sin. Do not let the sun go down while you are still angry, and do not give the devil a foothold" (Eph. 4:26–27). In other words, do not let today become tomorrow before you patch up the relationship. Given time—perhaps not much time—tiny seeds of discontent can grow into grotesque forests of anger and hatred.

In Matthew 18, Jesus tells us to discuss the offense *directly with the offender*. His words imply that we go alone, that we do not hash the situation over with one or two or a dozen other people first. All the while, we keep one goal in mind—winning the other person over, reestablishing the relationship. Reconciliation.

We will seldom feel especially loving or accepting of a colleague who has hurt us. It would be a mistake to say that our feelings do not matter. God cares—deeply—about our feelings. But at the same time, Jesus has freed us from the bondage of having to let our emotions control us.

We need to recognize that we, in fact, cannot work up warm feelings of forgiveness inside our own hearts by simply trying to do that. Our heavenly Father's concern is for the purity of heart and attitude that we need. King David pleaded with the Lord, "Create in me a pure heart, O God!" (Ps. 51:10). The Hebrew word that David used for "create" in this prayer is the same word Moses used in Genesis 1 referring to God who "created the heavens and the earth."

We can ask the Holy Spirit to start from scratch, to bring into existence that which does not now exist. We can ask Him to purify our motives and to give us the willingness to forgive. We can ask Him to make good on His promise—"It is God who works in you to will and to act according to His good purposes" (Phil. 2:13).

When we have given God an opportunity to do this for us, we can then approach our colleague with the problem. Often a nonconfrontational, problem-solving tack will produce results. Henry Ford once told a subordinate, "Don't find fault, find a solution." When God has cleansed our hearts, we find ourselves free to attack the problem, not the person.

We approach the other person in the way we might want to be approached under similar circumstances. Usually, a low-key, but factual statement of the problem is in order. We start off by taking responsibility for our feelings, using "I messages" something like these:

- Francis, I find myself becoming really frustrated when I get to the storage room and find all the construction paper used up. I've had to change my plans for art class twice this month. Could we talk about a way . . .
- Pastor, I'd be happy to talk to you about teaching VBS this summer. But I'm really starting to feel overloaded, almost burdened with responsibilities right now. Could we sit down to talk about . . .
- Ed, I need to chat with you about the boys' soccer team. When they left the gym to go outside to run their laps today, my kindergartners were in the hallway taking off their coats and boots from recess. It gets crowded in the hallway, and sometimes the team members push the little ones out of their way. I am really afraid that one of these days someone will be hurt. Could we talk about a way . . .
- Trevor, I'm concerned about some of the things I heard you say at faculty meeting yesterday. Would you have time to talk for a few minutes after school?

When we find ourselves at odds with others and when, in our best judgment, we cannot overlook an offense, we need to take the responsibility for using Jesus' process. A disciple of the Lord Jesus can never say, "Let her come to me first." Our Lord did not leave that option open for us.

Most of the time, one conversation will clear up a dispute. But occasionally we may have to go back again a second time. Or a third. Or a fourth.

In rare circumstances, it may become more and more obvious that the other person is not going to listen to us. If we reach that impasse, the Lord tells us to take one or two other brothers or sisters along with us. The text implies that these should not be people we recruit with the intent that they take our side. Rather, we look for believers with wisdom and with skills helpful in the reconciliation process. Perhaps as our witnesses listen to both sides, they will conclude that we ourselves need to assume part of the blame. Or even all of it.

If this happens, the Holy Spirit can give us the grace we need to swallow our pride and apologize. At that point, we can also thank Him for sending the third party to tell us the truth. People who have this kind of courage are genuine allies with us in our fight against sin and Satan.

Perhaps reconciliation will occur as the offended party and the witnesses get together with the offender the first time. But if not, Jesus' words imply that we try again. And again.

If a conflict remains unresolved, one conversation is never enough. Relationships in the kingdom of Christ count so much that we keep using the process our Lord has given us, we keep talking and praying, until we reach a reconciliation or until it becomes obvious that no amount of conversation will bring about a resolution.

In an extreme case, Jesus tells us to involve the whole body of believers. The congregation acts together to impress upon the offender the seriousness of a hardened heart. The church acts in love—tough love. It acts with a broken heart and with the goal of restoration, not vengeance, in mind. "Treat him as you would a pagan or a tax collector," Jesus says (Matt. 18:17). Exclude the offender from the family and from the family meal. But remember that Jesus sent us to evangelize the pagans. Remember that Jesus loved the tax collectors. Pray for him. Or her.

Our Lord Jesus has told us not to let our relationships become infected with sin. When that does occur, for it will, He warns us not to let our wounds fester. Obeying Him benefits us—spiritually, emotionally, physically, and in ways we probably cannot imagine. Doing so keeps sin and Satan from weakening the effectiveness of the entire staff's ministry. Doing so also sets a good example for those whom we disciple.

When unresolved anger or mistrust strains staff relationships, our students soon sense it. When those on the staff trust and respect one another, students and parents know that too. For all these reasons, those who minister as part of the team need to guard and nurture their relationships with one another.

Keep On Keeping On!

Staff unity will not sprout up by itself. A short year or two of prayer and cultivation will produce noticeable results, but almost never a bumper crop. Relationships take time. Mutual trust and love will grow, but not overnight. Impatience and unrealistic expectations can destroy the process.

A five-year-old who plants a garden will often dig up the seeds every few days (or every few hours!) to see if anything has happened yet. In the process, the young gardener can easily destroy the possibility of a harvest. Rather than digging around in the garden of staff unity to check on its progress, rather than giving in to discouragement about what we perceive as slow growth, team members can regularly commit one another and their mutual ministry to the Lord in prayer and then draw on His grace as they go about doing what they as individuals can do to nurture the unity God is granting.[7]

Who Is Equal to Such a Task?

If you have read this far, you probably have a big question lurking in the back of your mind right now. If not, you should have! The question? Where does a classroom teacher find time to get to know his students, to listen to them, to minister to members of their families, to establish healthful staff relationships and care for them— to do all that and write lesson plans, design bulletin boards, and coach the cheerleading squad too? The task looks overwhelming, even impossible!

No one has limitless time and money. No one has limitless spiritual, emotional, or physical energy. Because of the nature of the teaching ministry, especially those who teach in Christian schools must learn and practice principles of good stewardship. Chapter 12 outlines some of those principles.

To Think About

1. What factors can get in the way of team ministry? List as many as you can. Which of these are most likely to keep *you* from functioning fully as a team player? How might your Lord want to help you with this?
2. Why do you suppose the Lord Jesus most often chooses to place people in team ministry rather than individual ministry?
3. Rephrase in your own words each of the principles of teamwork given in this chapter. Give an example of each, based on your own experience—in the classroom (as a student or as a teacher), on some other job, or in your family.
4. Which three or four principles of teamwork do you consider most important for the discipling ministry. Why?
5. Explain the concept of confidentiality as you understand it. Why is it especially important in public ministry?
6. Outline the reconciliation procedure Jesus gave his people in Matt. 18:15–20. Why are these principles particularly important for those who serve in public ministry?
7. What expectations do you have about staff unity and teamwork as you think about your ministry? Are these expectations realistic? How do you know? What part can you play in helping to fulfill them?

Notes

1. How beautifully Paul put it in the opening of his letter to the believers in Philippi:
   I thank my God every time I remember you. In all my prayers for all of you, I always pray with joy because of your partnership in the Gospel from the first day until now, being confident of this, that He who began a good work in you will carry it on to completion until the day of Christ Jesus (1:3–5).
2. C. S. Lewis. *The Four Loves* (New York: Harcourt, Brace, and World, 1960), 169.
3. Martin Luther. The Explanation of the Eighth Commandment from *The Small Catechism* (St. Louis: Concordia Publishing House, 1986).
4. This story first appeared in the Chattanooga *News–Free Press* on Oct. 27, 1982. *Reader's Digest* later condensed and reprinted it (September, 1988).
5. Compare, for example, Col. 1:9ff and 2:1–3.
6. *The Table Talk of Martin Luther*, ed. Thomas S. Kepler (Grand Rapids: Baker Book House, 1979), 313.

7. Much more could and probably should be said about team ministry. The reader who wishes to explore further this critically important topic would do well to read *How to Develop a Team Ministry and Make It Work,* by Ervin F. Henkelmann and Stephen J. Carter (St. Louis: Concordia Publishing House, 1985). The authors have packed this small volume with practical examples, tips that really work, and sample documents (e.g., job descriptions) that anyone involved in team ministry should find eminently helpful.

CHAPTER 12

Counting the Cost

If you judge by Hollywood's standards, Jim Jarnish produced his first film, *Mystery Train,* on a shoestring budget. Take, for example, the matter of the camera work.

When professional film crews shoot, they set up multiple cameras so they can record each scene from multiple angles. An editor then splices the film together to create a feeling of immediacy, a sense of movement and excitement. To follow a moving target, professional film crews mount their cameras on carts and use a rail system.

But Jarnish's crew had only one camera and, for the most part, they shot from a fixed position. When they absolutely had to have the camera move—say, for example, when they needed to follow one of the characters walking down the street—they mounted their camera on the hood of someone's car and had six or so crew people push the car alongside the character!

Mystery Train became a Cannes Film Festival winner, despite the difficulties. Yet if you said that to Jim Jarnish, he would probably correct you; he might more likely say, "*Because* of the difficulties, *Mystery Train* became a Cannes Film Festival winner." Interviewed on National Public Radio about his film, Jarnish told the story of its development. Then he offered listeners this bit of advice, "Learn to look upon your limitations as strengths."[1]

What a fantastic reminder: Necessity can be the mother of excellence! Often times, those who stand on the outside looking in can see only the limitations built into the teaching ministry. They see many "never enoughs"—never enough time, never enough money, never enough equipment or supplies, never enough recognition or respect.

Yet as God's Spirit works in our hearts, we can learn to turn our limitations into strengths. Our lives and our service can reflect an excellence worthy of our Eternal King.

My Life, My Stewardship

Say the word *stewardship* inside any church building and many people will instinctively reach for their wallet. The New Testament paints quite a different picture of stewards and stewardship, a much more global one.

In New Testament times, a great and wealthy landlord would sometimes place one of his slaves in a position of authority over his estate. The slave would control the estate in the name of the landlord. He would manage the money, the property, and the work of the other servants. The steward owned none of these things, but he took care of them as though they belonged to him. He managed them for the good of the estate. He had free rein. As you can readily see, a position of stewardship was a position of great trust.

Scripture makes it clear that God gives each one of His people a stewardship. When I say, "I am God's steward," I mean, "I belong to God—everything I am, everything I hope to be." When I say, "I am God's steward," I also mean, "My heavenly Father has entrusted me with many gifts—possessions, abilities, time, opportunities. He has entrusted these things to my care because He loves me. Now He helps me use my life, manage my life, for His glory and for the good of those around me."

The Westminster Catechism asks, "What is the chief end and purpose of man?" It answers that question, "To glorify God and enjoy Him forever." Note both accents—to glorify God *and* to enjoy Him.

Sometimes God's people think of those two purposes as mutually exclusive, as though glorifying God included all kinds of drudgery and very little enjoyment. Or they think of glorifying God as something we do here on earth, and enjoying Him as something we will do only when we get to heaven.

Such thinking distorts God's purpose for us, His stewards.

As a matter of fact, God wants us to enjoy Him and to enjoy being His right now. He has assured us that our lives bring Him glory now and that we will continue to glorify Him into eternity. Our lives, our very existence itself, stands as a testimony to His saving love in Jesus Christ.

When we catch a glimpse of this truth, when we realize what our Lord Jesus has done for us, it sets us free. Free to crawl out from under the "have tos" and "shoulds." Free to serve and to enjoy our service, even as we enjoy our God. Sullen, grudging obedience flies out the window. Gratitude and wonder take its place.

I Am a Steward of My Time and My Abilities

Because we serve our King as His stewards, all our time belongs to Him. All our abilities belong to Him. God could attach all kinds of strings to this part of our stewardship. He could lay on us all kinds of responsibilities and force us to dance to His tune like marionettes. He has not done that, and He never will. He has set us free. Indeed!

Because our Lord has freed us to serve, each of us must answer an important question: "How will you use your freedom?" The question is not so simple as it may look at first blush. We can so easily abuse our freedom and in doing so misuse and abuse ourselves. We can abuse our freedom and in doing so bruise our relationships—with God and with other people.

Some whom God calls to serve in Christian schools fall off freedom's fence on the side of selfishness. Few would express their thoughts aloud, but they allow their attitude and actions to say, "I teach all day long. That's enough. No one can make me do anything else in this congregation."

A servant, a steward of the Lord Jesus, who thinks this way has forgotten a momentous truth:

> For Christ's love compels us, because we are convinced that one died for all, and therefore all died. And He died for all, that those who live should no longer live for themselves but for Him who died for them and was raised again (2 Cor. 5:14–15).

God does not want service that is rendered because we feel we have to give it. He asks us to surrender to Him, to His love, so that He can create within us a heartfelt-attitude of willing service. If we identify selfishness or a you-can't-make-me attitude within our hearts, our Lord invites us to confess this sin to Him. He invites us to admit our need for His cleansing power as we pray, "Create in me a pure heart, O God!" God always honors that kind of prayer. God will change us as we allow His Word to have its way with us.

Some whom God calls as His servants in Christian schools fall off freedom's fence on the other side. They find themselves involved in parish ministry too deeply. They neglect other aspects of their God-given stewardship. They wind up doing things God never expected them to do, things the congregation should not expect either. They become veritable "ministry machines," losing themselves in the process. Although few would admit it, even to themselves, they harbor anger at God and at the congregation for demanding too much. They may not realize it, but they have victimized themselves by their own excesses.

Our Lord says to His stewards, "My primary concern is for you, not for your ministry. I want to help you balance your life, manage your life, care for yourself and for your relationships. I do not expect you to do everything!"

Servants in public ministry who know they tend to overload themselves need to think in global, stewardship-of-life terms as they evaluate whether or not to take on each new responsibility. Remember,

- seeing a need is not enough;
- getting an idea for ministry is not enough;
- having the ability to do a task is not enough;
- having done a particular task last time or having done something like it in a previous parish is not enough;
- having an hour or two, or a day or two, open on your calendar this month is not enough;
- having someone ask you is not enough; and
- pleasing the pastor or board chairperson or principal or president of the PTL is not enough.

Taking on ministry responsibilities for any of these reasons, alone or in combination, will only lead to frustration—for you and for those whom you serve. A servant who continually bases ministry decisions on factors like these cannot claim to be a good steward.

But if these reasons for serving will not float, on what basis *can* a servant of Christ appropriately minister in a specific situation? The apostle Paul answered this question for the Colossians:

Whatever you do, work at it with all your heart, as working for the Lord, not for men, since you know that you will receive an inheritance from the Lord as a reward. It is the Lord Christ you are serving (Col. 3:23–24).

If we serve the Lord Christ, we want His priorities to direct our decisions about when, where, and how to carry out the ministry He has given us. The call documents we have received from our congregation and the job description they have given us based on our call have much to say about God's will for our ministry.

For instance, your congregation may have called you to teach grade eight. Teaching that class with excellence must then be your number-one priority. If you are new to teaching or new to that particular school, you will almost certainly need to focus most of your energy on your classroom at first. You will need to study the curriculum and acquaint yourself with the textbooks you will use. You will need to spend time getting to know parents and building relationships with others on the staff-team. You will need to familiarize yourself with the community and learn about available resources. This includes everything from finding worthwhile places for field trips to exploring the community-based counseling services we talked about in chapter 9.

It may turn out that during the first year, or even two, you cannot take on congregational duties outside the classroom and still perform your classroom responsibilities with excellence. You may need to remind yourself and others of that, in some cases more than once.

Perhaps you find yourself teaching a first-grade class, heading up the high school youth program, and leading the primary department of the Sunday school. You may find yourself floundering under the work load, especially if the high school youth program begins to evolve in such a way that you are spending several hours each week counseling with individuals. If your job description includes both teaching responsibilities and youth work, you may need to talk with your supervisor about jettisoning your Sunday school tasks.

Love knows when to say no. Love knows how to set limits so that you can serve with both excellence and joy as God's faithful steward. It is the Lord Christ you are serving!

Balance—An Attitude of Excellence

Christians who sit down to think about life's priorities often rank them something like this:

- God
- Family (others)
- Myself

It sounds pious. But it seldom turns out to be a practical guide for decision-making. If we want a God-pleasing balance in our lives, our Lord must take the central place in our hearts. Other facets of life can then take their rightful place as circumstances dictate. The proportion of time we spend on any given area will vary from day to day, from year to year.

To serve faithfully, a first-year teacher may well spend a large portion of her week becoming familiar with the curriculum and writing careful lesson plans. In subsequent years she may add parish duties outside the classroom.

To serve faithfully, an experienced teacher may well devote a large proportion of time to upgrading the parish evangelism program or the evening weekday school which the congregation conducts for public school students. She may also coach the girls' soccer team or the boys' basketball team—or both! And enjoy it.

To serve faithfully, a teacher whose parents are experiencing failing health may need to drive several hundred miles home two or more weekends each month to care for them.

As our Lord helps us balance our lives, we need to think of ourselves as His stewards in several areas:

- *Family*—At times, the most godly thing I can do is to read a story to my nephew; at times, the most godly thing you may do is take your wife out to eat or help your husband wash and wax the car.
- *Self-care*—At times, the most godly thing I can do is to head for the Nautilus center to lift weights; at times, the most godly thing you may do is take off your tie, pull on your jeans, and go for a walk through the park.
- *Recreation*—At times, the most godly thing I can do is to sit back and watch a Star Trek rerun; at times, the most godly thing you may perhaps do is sort through your baseball card collection or go out to see a movie.
- *Social*—At times, the most godly thing I can do is to invite friends over for a barbecue; at times, the most godly thing you may do is volunteer to take your children, or the neighbor's children, to the Dairy Queen.

- *Work*—At times, the most godly thing I can do is to plan the Board of Education agenda so I will be ready to chair this month's meeting; at times, the most godly thing you may do is write a math test or phone a parent about a classroom problem.

Remember,

Whatever you do, work at it with all your heart, as working for the Lord, not for men, since you know that you will receive an inheritance from the Lord as a reward. It is the Lord Christ you are serving (Col. 3:23–24).

Practical Tips for Good Time Management

Time management books almost all agree on certain basic principles and practices. They describe specific skills that we can learn. As God's stewards, we do well to invest time reading something about this and then learning to apply the basic principles.[2] Most experts will emphasize points like these:

- *Make lists.* Before you leave the classroom each evening, make a "To Do" list for the next day. Then rank the items on the list according to their importance. The next morning, do task 1 first and so on. At the end of the day, add any unfinished tasks from the list for day one to the list for day two. Then rank the new list.
- *Set goals and identify intermediate milestones.* If your class or choir will present this year's spring musical, jot the date on your planning calendar. Then work backwards to decide what you must do and when to make the presentation. Note that many time management experts suggest that you fill only about 50 percent of the available time; they counsel that the rest of your calendar will fill itself as tasks take unanticipated time and as emergencies arise.
- *Group similar activities through the day.* For instance, plan to make all your phone calls at one time, perhaps after school. You can have the phone book at hand and you will not have to wait for someone else to finish making a call. Write all of next week's lesson plans at the same time, or try planning two weeks at once. As you make one bulletin board, think about making two. You will need to find the stencils, the stapler, and the other equipment only once.

213

- *Organize supplies and keep them where you will use them.* If you write lesson plans at home, you may want to keep a copy of your teachers guides there. Dedicate one classroom cabinet to science equipment, another to math manipulatives, another to art supplies. If storage space is at a premium, ask your school to invest in stackable plastic baskets (available at most discount department stores). Use them to organize and store your classroom equipment. Have your students help you keep storage areas neat.

- *Recycle.* Keep copies of parent letters and reuse the ideas in them from year to year. File handouts and worksheets you consider worth reusing. Store bulletin boards you could use again in cardboard "under the bed" storage boxes. (Note that construction paper fades when exposed to sunlight or fluorescent lights, but ordinarily a display can be used twice before it must be discarded. Even then, think about using the old one as a pattern for a new version.)

  Keep copies of the Bible studies you lead for, let's say, Sunday school teachers' meetings. You may be able to recycle them later for an adult Bible class. But be sure to note your original audience on the handout, and verify whether your new audience includes the same or different folks.

  Jot notes to yourself in the margins of your teachers guides about activities that worked well, and those that did not. Update, revise, and reuse your ideas as you plan the next time around.

- *Delegate.* If your students show the necessary maturity, you can ask them to exchange homework assignments and correct one another's papers. Think through the most productive ways to use any parent helpers your principal makes available to you. Talk with other members of your staff about exchanging duties. If you enjoy teaching music, perhaps a teacher down the hall would teach your art class twice a week in exchange for two music classes.

- *Ask for help.* If you find yourself overwhelmed and overburdened, do not ignore your dilemma. It will not resolve itself. Sit down with a paper and pen to brainstorm solutions. Perhaps you will find it helpful to talk with your principal or with a trusted colleague. Ask that person to sort through the facts and to brainstorm with you. Use the allies God has given you to help you hone your skills as His steward.

I Am a Steward of My Financial Resources

Few people have become wealthy on the salary that teachers in Christian schools earn—that is, wealthy by the world's standards. Our Lord expects all His people to exercise good financial stewardship. But if we recognize that the Lord has led us to serve Him in a Christian school, and if we respond to the call of His church to serve Him in that capacity, we must pay even closer attention to managing our finances as His stewards. If we neglect to manage our money, we will soon find ourselves locked in the grip of financial crisis. Make no mistake! Satan will quickly pounce on that crisis and use it to squeeze the joy of serving out of our hearts.

As Christians think about money, we begin with a basic truth: God is the Giver. He gives because that is His nature, His character. He wants to bless His people. Giving brings Him pleasure. God blesses us with many intangible gifts—the forgiveness of our sins, peace, joy, His love. God also blesses us with material gifts:

> I believe that God . . . has given me my body and soul, eyes, ears, and all my members, my reason and all my senses, and still takes care of them.

> He also gives me clothing and shoes, food and drink, house and home, wife and children, land, animals, and all I have. He richly and daily provides me with all that I need to support this body and life.[3]

Some world religions deny the goodness inherent in material things. They elevate the "spiritual" and denigrate the physical. Christians, however, know from the Scriptures that God approves of material things; after all, He created them. As Giver, God delights in seeing His people enjoy the material gifts He gives.

For that reason, He offers us principles we can use to maximize our enjoyment of His good gifts. These principles are sprinkled throughout the Scriptures. The Bible has much to say about money, possessions, and their use, far more than even most Christians realize and certainly far more than this chapter can spell out. You will probably recognize the basic biblical truths outlined below in broad strokes:

- *God has made us stewards of all our possessions.* Just as He has made us stewards of our time, He also asks that we use the money and the material things He entrusts to us as His caretakers or managers. He wants us to handle our money in His name as we believe He would use it if He Himself collected our paycheck and paid our bills. As we manage what He has given us, we may ask Him for wisdom, knowing that money does not manage itself.

- *"Godliness with contentment is great gain" (1 Tim. 6:6).* Our Giver reminds us again and again that material things will never make us truly happy. He gives us things; He wants us to have them; but He does not want our things to have us. When we allow God to give us a contented heart, our contentment frees us to enjoy the material possessions He has given us. We can live free from the slavery of always looking for fulfillment in acquiring things.

- *God does not measure our worth by how much money we make. Neither need we.* If we doubt our true worth, we need only look at the cross. Satan would like nothing better than to get us to take our eyes off that cross and to focus instead on our pay stub. Our culture tends to reinforce the enemy's lie; when we apply for a loan, for instance, the application blank will include a worksheet to calculate our "net worth." But remember, God thought you were worth the life blood of His only Son. No one on this earth has a calculator big enough to estimate that kind of "net worth"!

- *God shares with us the joy of giving.* God has an open heart, an open hand. As His grace works in our hearts, He opens our hearts and our hands too. Listen as Paul describes the way the believers in Macedonia gave:

> Out of the most severe trial, their overflowing joy and their extreme poverty welled up in rich generosity. For I testify that they gave as much as they were able, and even beyond their ability. Entirely on their own, they urgently pleaded with us for the privilege of sharing in this service to the saints. And they did not do as we expected, but they gave themselves first to the Lord and then to us in keeping with God's will. (2 Cor. 8:2–5)

Did you catch it? Overflowing joy plus extreme poverty produced rich generosity. But first these saints "gave themselves to the Lord." God was at work in them. The Creator of the universe did not need their money. He does not need ours either. He never has and He never will need anything from His creatures. The thought is ridiculous.

God does want something from us, though. He wants our hearts. The gifts we offer Him serve as an outward indication of His internal work. As we allow God to work the grace of giving in us, we will find ourselves giving Him our firstfruits, not our leftovers. We will set aside for Him gifts proportional to the income He has enabled us to earn (1 Cor. 16:2).

Some believers have assumed that God demands 10 percent of their income. Some have even gone so far as to say that God will not bless a believer who gives less. That notion, of course, grows out of a legalistic understanding of the new covenant.

Other believers through the centuries have looked at tithing through the lens of grace. They have found the 10 percent figure helpful as a guideline; they have seen it as a floor rather than a ceiling. Even under the Old Covenant, God's people brought Him "tithes *and* free-will offerings" (e.g., 2 Chron. 31:12, emphasis mine).

But whether we give 2 percent or 10 percent or 28 percent, God wants our gifts to come from joyful hearts, hearts made willing by the Holy Spirit as He empowers us to "excel in this grace of giving" (2 Cor. 8:7). As we grow in this grace, we will learn more and more to trust our Provider's promise:

> God is able to make all grace abound to you, so that in all things at all times, having all that you need, you will abound in every good work. . . . Now He who supplies seed to the sower and bread for food will also supply and increase your store of seed and will enlarge the harvest of your righteousness. You will be made rich in every way so that you can be generous on every occasion, and through us your generosity will result in thanksgiving to God (2 Cor. 9:8, 10–11).

All grace . . . in *all* things . . . at *all* times . . . having *all* that you need . . . you will be made rich in *every* way so that you can be generous on *every* occasion! As we rely on God our Provider, He will see to it that we have the resources we need both to sow into the lives of others and to furnish our own "bread for food." He will supply the resources we need to care for our own needs.

No wonder Paul preceded this promise with the statement, "God loves a cheerful giver" (2 Cor. 9:7)! The word the apostle used here for *cheerful* is the Greek word from which we derive the word *hilarious*. We can give with almost reckless joy, knowing that God has revealed Himself as our Provider.

God expects His people to live within their means. He commands us to pay our debts (e.g., Rom. 13:8), to pay the legitimate taxes we owe (e.g., Rom. 13:7), and to provide for our own needs unless we are incapable of doing so for some reason (e.g., 2 Thess. 3:10).

Free to Spend: Budgeting

If you already know how to set up a budget, and if you already handle your income in this way, the next few paragraphs—even the rest of this chapter—will probably seem elementary to you. If, however, you have not developed a budget and put it into regular use, you may find the next few pages helpful.

Whether you earn $10,000 or $100,000 annually, you need a budget. A few people have the kind of memory for detail and mind for figures that enables them to plan their spending without committing their plan to paper. Most of the rest of us need to write it down.

Basically, a budget is a financial plan. It lists all the various ways you intend to use the money you earn in a given year. As you begin writing a budget, make a list of the categories for which you need to plan. For example,

- Church and charitable contributions
- Rent/house payment
- Utilities (heat, light, water, sewer, garbage removal, telephone)
- Car expense (including gasoline, estimated repair costs, and car payment if you have one)
- Clothing and personal care items (e.g., dry cleaning, laundry, toothpaste, cosmetics)
- Groceries
- Student loan repayment
- Savings (e.g., "rainy day," retirement, vacation)
- Continuing education

- Health care (insurance premiums and/or deductible fees and any medical services not covered by insurance—e.g., eyeglasses)
- Gifts (e.g., Christmas, birthdays)

If you are married, you need to write a unified family budget. Husband and wife both need to sit down together to agree on a financial plan. Scripture knows no such thing in marriage as "my money" and "your money." When God joins a man and woman as "one flesh" (Gen. 2:24), it means among other things that all the money is "our money," or more accurately "God's money" given to the family members to manage for their good and His glory.[4]

Some expenses on your list will be fixed or nearly so. The rent a landlord charges her tenants will not ordinarily change more than once (or perhaps twice) a year. Many utility companies allow customers to opt for a "budget payment plan" so that the cost of air conditioning does not drive the electric bill out of sight in summer or the cost of home heating into orbit in winter.

Other items on this list are less predictable, but usually more discretionary. If the budget gets too tight, last year's raincoat will probably meet this year's needs.

Wisdom dictates that you look at your "big ticket" items first as you make basic lifestyle decisions. You may have to repay a student loan. You will need a place to live, and housing is usually costly. You may need a car. Keep all these things in mind as you plan.

Before you sign a lease on an apartment or assume a car loan, take a prayerful look at your overall financial picture. Ask God for wisdom as you make important decisions like these. He wants you to succeed. He wants to help you use the resources He has given you to the best advantage—both for your own benefit and for the good of others.

Ask the Lord for grace to be realistic! Most financial counselors recommend that housing, for example, should not take more than 25 percent of one's income. Add utilities and the bill should amount to no more than a third of total earnings.

Your budget may be pinching already at this point. If so, look at it from a problem-solving perspective. On a sheet of paper brainstorm all the options you can think of. Ask a trusted friend for ideas. For example, if you want to rent a small condominium by yourself, you may need to take the bus to work or walk rather than buying a car. If you need a reliable car, you may opt for a studio apartment with smaller rent payments and utility expenses.

You may find a talk with your principal helpful. Chat with some of the other teachers. Find out what they do to live within their means in the community you serve.

After you have locked in your major expenses, estimate the rest as closely as you can. Write these estimates down. If you estimate on a monthly rather than on a yearly basis, you will likely find your budget more helpful as a spending guide from week to week. Some expenses will show up only once or twice a year though (e.g., car insurance payments). Be sure to build enough flexibility into your plan that you can absorb these.

As you follow your budget for the first few months, plan to adjust it to fit reality. You may find groceries cost more than you had anticipated or that you have not spent as much on gasoline as you had thought you would. Then, every few months evaluate your situation. Readjust as circumstances change. Allow your budget to guide you, not to bind you.

Fair warning! By all means find a way to save for emergencies. Whether you are barely squeaking by or enjoying the luxury of some discretionary dollars, you may find it hard to save. My own acquisitive tendencies in our consumer-oriented society often tempt me to spend everything I earn, or most of it. Falling for that temptation is a mistake.

Financial planners advise their clients to stash away at least 45–60 days of income for use in a crisis. This financial storm shelter needs to be readily accessible (e.g., a passbook savings account). No one likes to think about it, but the refrigerator could blow up. The fuel pump on the car could go out, or the landlord could suddenly decide to raise the rent by 20 percent. Emergencies don't send a 60-day advance notice. As good stewards, we trust God. But we can also pray that the fruit of self-control will evidence itself in our lives in such a way that we are able to save a few dollars from every paycheck until we have stockpiled a financial cushion.

As you can see, the discipline of writing down a budget and recording expenditures helps us keep better control of the financial resources with which God has blessed us. It can help us distinguish between a reasonable and an unreasonable debt load. It can help us identify and plug holes that might be siphoning off our cash flow.

In short, our Lord can use a budget to teach us how to exercise better financial stewardship.

Free to Save: Hatching a Nest Egg

This chapter began with a word of advice from Jim Jarnish: "Learn to look upon your limitations as strengths." People who know they must live within a limited budget can plan carefully. They can evaluate purchases with an eagle-eye toward value. They can let God teach them the difference between needs and wants. By God's grace, financial limitations can become a strength. Sometimes, though, that wisdom comes only through experience.

During my junior year of college, I bought a 1956 Mercury Monterey sedan for $300. To my chagrin, my family christened it "The Peach" for its relative shape, as well for its color scheme (two-tone—white and, well, peach).

Although my sister Gail swore—with ample justification—that this behemoth had cast iron bumpers, I managed to squeeze 20 or so miles from every gallon of gasoline. All in all, the automobile treated me very well; I remember only one or two repair bills, and minor ones at that. Dad went so far as to throw around the term cream puff. Gail responded, "Yeah! A peach cream puff." Comedians, all.

In May, two years later, I graduated from college and was assigned to my first parish school. The Peach celebrated its 16th birthday that year. It wore its age well. The odometer displayed only 35,000 miles—and I had added 10,000 of those myself. I could have coaxed another 50,000 miles from it. Quite easily, as a matter of fact.

But I had my pride, and I had had my fill of peach jokes. So that summer I said good-bye to The Peach. As I walked off the used-car lot having made a deal on a different vehicle, I felt great. After all, I now carried keys to a car that better bespoke my position as a college graduate.

Two days later, I awoke to the fact I had traded The Peach for a lemon.

For the next year, I wrote regular checks for $20, $40, $80 to the garage, and that in addition to monthly car payments. Even then, I could never pull out the highway without wondering whether the radiator was about to spring a leak or worrying about some whoos-amajigit or other that might be about to blow a gasket.

By the end of my third year of teaching, I had traded cars three times. That summer the Lord led me to another teaching assignment in a different part of the country. I bought a fourth car—a new one this time. I found myself finally free from repair bills, but I chafed under the saddle of a much higher monthly car payment. As my seventh year of teaching ended, I awoke to the fact that I had been making car payments every month during my entire career.

The seven-year milestone took on special significance, because at that point in my life I first learned about "the miracle of compound interest," as financial advisors fondly call it. It works like this. If a person who graduates from college can

- Invest $2000 a year (roughly $83 per pay check, for someone paid twice a month);
- Save that amount each year consistently for seven years;
- Find a savings instrument or institution that will pay on average 8 percent interest over the years (a reasonable expectation based on what has happened to interest rates during the past two decades or so);
- Leave the money in the account, adding nothing to it and withdrawing nothing from it until retirement at age 65;

the original $14,000 investment will have grown to $1 million. It's as good as winning the state lottery—and a much, much surer thing, I might add!

The day I heard this explained, I sat down with a paper and pencil to do a little figuring. I discovered that my car payments at the time totaled somewhat more than $83 per paycheck, and they had for some time. Instead of a nest egg, I had a fistful of receipts and a car (my fourth) that had depreciated to less than half its original value.

Is having a car wrong? Of course not—not in and of itself. And borrowing money to buy a car is not inherently wrong either. But still today I wonder what God might have done for me had I drawn up a financial plan with long-range goals at that point in my life.

The "miracle of compound interest" stalks both sides of the street. When we make house payments, car payments, credit card payments, or buy things on any other installment plan, our creditor gleans the advantage.

When we save—even amounts that seem insignificant at the time—we take advantage of the "miracle." Investing a small amount each month on a consistent basis may seem hardly worthwhile at the time. But God can use this practice to etch wise habits on our hearts: the habit of delaying gratification, so rare in our instant society; the habit of planning ahead to meet future needs and to provide for future joys; and the habit of thoughtful, rather than impulsive, spending.

New graduates may find it impossible to begin a long-range savings plan during the first few years of their ministry. If you cannot set aside even a few dollars at first, be at peace. God holds us accountable for what we have, not for what we do not have. But as you budget, plan some long-range financial goals anyway. Most people who set goals eventually find themselves in a position to implement them. On the other hand, those who have no goals . . .

A Special Note about Tax Law and "Ministers of Religion"

If the Internal Revenue Service rules allow you to claim "minister of religion" status for tax purposes, you can take advantage of several major tax benefits.[5] But you will need to adjust your financial plan somewhat to meet the government's regulations.

For example, the law requires that congregations withhold Social Security tax for staff members who do not qualify as "ministers of religion." The law does not require that they withhold the corresponding self-employment tax for those who do qualify. If your congregation does not withhold self-employment tax for you, you will need to file a declaration of estimated taxes with the IRS, telling them the income you expect to receive for the year. You will then also have to make estimated tax payments each quarter.

If you receive a housing allowance, you will owe self-employment tax on it. If you live in a house or apartment furnished by the congregation, you will owe self-employment tax based on the fair-rental value of the housing you receive—in other words, on what you would pay if you rented it yourself.

If your congregation tells you that you qualify for "minister of religion" status, and if you do not thoroughly understand the tax ramifications, hire an accountant. Folks who wander innocently into this thicket without a guide almost always find themselves being eaten alive. Can it be all that serious? Yes! If you do not know what you are doing, find someone who does—and do it now![6]

I Am a Steward of My Spiritual Walk

God has made us stewards of the time and of the financial resources He entrusts to us. Our stewardship extends into many other segments of life too; into all other segments, as a matter of fact. The most important of these, of course, is our own personal relationship with our Savior.

In one sense, to claim to take care of one's own spiritual life is the height of foolishness. God holds onto us; He keeps us in the faith. We do not keep ourselves there. By the same token, God works through His Word and the sacraments. If we choose to avoid the means He uses to strengthen His people, we weaken ourselves both personally and professionally. If we walk down the path of that kind of rebellion long enough, eventually our faith will die.

Everyone who serves the Lord Jesus in public ministry knows this truth. But how easily we forget or even deliberately ignore it. At times, we find ourselves feeling nibbled to death by the demands placed on us. We get so busy caring for others that we feel we simply have no time or energy left to spend with God or to care for our own souls. But even when we practice good time-management techniques, even when we carry a reasonable work load, we can trip over the temptation to neglect our spiritual lives.

No one will notice at first. We may not notice the difference ourselves. But sooner than we would like to think, we lose the edge we need—the edge we personally need to face the challenges of life and the edge we need to minister to others. The danger is so insidious, and so deadly.

On the positive side, the blessings of a rich, full, devotional life always spill over into everything else we do. As we spend time with our Lord, He promises to give us the vision and the strength we need to do His will and to do it His way. His strength makes it possible for us to live in victory despite our problems. His strength makes it possible for us to march onto Satan's turf and overpower his minions and their schemes.

Christians choose to structure their devotional lives in many different ways. The format matters much less than the content. What counts is that we spend time listening to God speak to us through His Word and that we allow ourselves time to respond to Him in confession, intercession, worship, and praise.

How much time? My own experience tells me not to trust programs with such promising titles as "Spiritual Fitness in 10 Minutes a Day." Some days, I find I need at least the first 10 minutes just to slow down, to quiet the thoughts that stream through my mind, to arrive at the point I can listen to my Lord. Although I sometimes miss my own mark, I aim at setting aside 20–25 minutes of uninterrupted time with Jesus each day. That way, after the Holy Spirit has stilled my heart, I have about 15 minutes of quality time left in which to listen to Him and to pray.

For the most part, our habits determine our lives. Unless you find a way to make devotional life a habit, you will probably always struggle to find time. Make an appointment with the Lord Jesus. Pick a time you can use consistently each day. Ink it in on your planning calendar. Be sure to choose a time you will find comfortable and inviting.

For the past decade or so, for example, I have eaten breakfast with the Lord Jesus at McDonalds or Hardees. Seldom does another meeting compete for my time, because few people feel like discussing business at 6 a.m. Along with my raisin biscuit or scrambled eggs, I study God's Word. On occasion, the Lord has even used my presence in a fast-food restaurant to create an opportunity to witness. What better opening for witness could anyone invent than the question I am sometimes asked: "Are you reading the *Bible*?"

Early morning works best for me; you may find that you enjoy using your lunch period or the time before you go to bed.

Again, the format matters much less than the content and the consistency. Make an appointment and ask God to help you set the habit so firmly in your heart that you break it only in the case of war, pestilence, or earthquake—and perhaps not even then.

Expect opposition, both at first and later on too. Satan hates to see God's people sit at His feet and draw strength from Him. That kind of behavior depresses the devil; he has a much harder time defending himself against believers who pick up the sword of the Spirit each day and let God teach them how to use it. If Satan hates it, so does our sinful flesh. When Jesus urged His disciples to pray in the Garden of Gethsemane, He explained their reluctance this way—"The spirit truly is ready, but the flesh is weak" (Mark 14:38 NKJV).

Often I find my mind wandering. Sometimes I find myself distracted by conversations around me in the restaurant. Sometimes I just get sleepy. But over time, the Lord has taught me more about how to concentrate. He has also taught me that staying awake in the morning is easier if I crawl into bed on time the night before. My time with Jesus has become so important to me that I seldom mind missing the late newscast anymore. Perhaps He has worked this kind of need in your heart, too. But if not, He will. You need only ask.

Sometimes people who start a program of personal Bible study think they must begin in Genesis and read straight through the remaining 65 books. Sometimes that works, but most of the time they make it as far as Leviticus and then throw up their hands in defeat, puzzled beyond frustration over an obscure ceremonial law. Leviticus paints a beautiful portrait of the work of the promised Messiah. Yet it is not a portrait that a believer who is relatively inexperienced in Bible study is likely to see at first. During the first months or even years of study, most Christians find the New Testament easier to read and to understand. You may want to start there. Or perhaps the Lord will lead you to begin in Psalms or one of the Old Testament historical books. Ask Him and then settle on a plan you believe reasonable.

Because I find myself so easily distracted, I often write as I read. The past several weeks, for example, I have been studying Colossians. Each day as I begin my devotional time, I skim through the four chapters of the book—they are rather short. Then I go back to the place I left off the morning before and jot notes to myself and to the Lord about what I have read.

Sometimes I write words of worship, sometimes words of confession. Sometimes I note ideas or concepts I do not yet understand. Whatever you choose to write, remember that the Holy One of Israel (as Isaiah so often and so beautifully calls Him) interacts with us as we interact with His Word. We can expect Him to touch us, to change us—He has promised to do that. (Excerpts from the notes I made today as I read in Colossians appear elsewhere in this chapter; perhaps some readers will find them of value.)

Helpful Ways to Do Personal Bible Study

We can approach Scripture in many different ways. God's Word contains such riches that no believer need ever find Bible study anything less than the high point of the day. If you do find your spiritual daily bread getting stale, you might consider varying your methods. For example:

Underlining and annotating the text. Use colored pencils or watercolor markers to underline verses that treat specific topics. My own color scheme works something like this:

Red—verses that promise God's forgiveness for my sins

Blue—verses that spell out God's other promises to me

Orange—verses that talk about sanctification

Gray—verses that tell about Satan and his schemes

Purple—verses that tell about Christ's second coming and the End Times

Pink—verses that tell about giving and about Christian financial stewardship

Green—verses that tell about the Holy Christian Church and my part in it

Yellow—verses that especially seem to draw my heart into worship

Besides underlining, you may want to make notes to yourself in the margins. Your notes could include cross-references to other Scripture passages, exclamation marks next to words or concepts you find especially meaningful, and words that summarize an insight you gained during your study that day, and so on.

Character study. Use a good concordance or a tool such as the Concordia Self-Study Bible's "Index to Subjects" or the Open Bible's "Biblical Cyclopedic Index" to find all the texts that deal with a specific person in the Bible. Study the texts for a week or two, or a month or two, depending on how many you find. Remember as you study that the *only* hero in Scripture is God! Ask yourself, "How was the Lord at work in this person's life?" and then,

Notes from Colossians

3/30   Colossians 2:6-7 (NKJV)

Verse 6 —

" As you have therefore received ⨯
Jesus the Lord ... " How did I receive
Him? In Baptism, by His grace, by
the Holy Spirit's power at work in
my ♡. Not by "trying hard" to earn it.
    Jesus has come into my ♡, into
my life as Lord to rule and reign.
A concept foreign to our culture
that wants to bow to no authority;
a concept also foreign to my heart.
Still, He is King of kings and, by
His grace, my Lord. He didn't wait
for me to come to Him; He came
to me as my Servant, my Servant-
King, and He won me with His love.
Praise You, Lord Jesus!
    " ... so walk in Him, rooted and
built up and established in the faith,
as you have been taught, abounding
in it with thanksgiving."
    My walk so often becomes a stumble
or a fall. How did I receive Him?
By grace. As I received Him, so I
am to walk in Him — by grace.
How I need that grace, Lord Jesus!
Teach me to walk by grace each day!

"What does this mean to me?" You may want to keep a notebook at hand to jot down the discoveries you make.

In-depth verse or chapter study. Use a Bible with extensive cross-references like the center column references in the Concordia Self-Study Bible. Read a verse and write it into your Bible study notebook. Then read all the cross-references given for it. What new insights has God shown you? What light do the cross-referenced texts shed on the verse you are studying? You will probably find studying a whole chapter in this same way rewarding!

Through the Bible in a year. If I am honest, I must say that this method of Bible study changed my spiritual life and continues to transform it. Twelve years ago, the Lord Jesus led me into a through-the-Bible program, a program I have followed ever since. Each time I finish the book of Revelation, I find myself astonished at how much more "living and active" (Heb. 4:12) the Scriptures have been this year, compared with the year before.

The Book becomes more clear and yet somehow more mysterious the more I get to know it. While, on occasion, I take detours along the basic Genesis through Revelation path to keep my daily study fresh (as per the comments above on Colossians), I still cherish the way God has fed me and continues to feed me as I walk through one book of Scripture after another, chapter by chapter, book by book.[7] (See appendix C for a Bible-reading outline that will take you through the entire Scripture in a year and through the Psalms twice.)

Memorizing Scripture. When we memorize portions of God's Word, the Holy Spirit can bring verses back to our minds at times when we need to remember a specific truth. The psalmist once wrote, "I have hidden Your Word in my heart that I might not sin against You" (119:11). Verses we have memorized serve us as a deterrent to sin. They also help us when we witness—to a distressed student or family member, to someone who does not know the Lord Jesus, to someone who comes to us for counsel.

Perhaps you will want to select a "Verse of the Week" from the Scriptures you are studying. Write it on a note card and post it on your desk at school or on your bathroom mirror. Meditate on it "when you sit at home and when you walk along the road, when you lie down and when you get up" (Deut. 6:7). If Moses wrote this admonition today, he might tell us, "Think about it when you find yourself stalled in traffic and as you wait in line at the grocery store, when you eat your lunch and after the 11 p.m. newscast." Let God continue through the day what He begins during your devotional time. Memorizing—it's not just for children anymore!

A Word about Public Worship

"The body of Christ"—the more I study Scripture, the more wonderful and mysterious this concept becomes. God meets with His gathered people and touches us together in a way somehow different from the way He meets with us as individuals. Jesus told His disciples, "Where two or three come together in My name, there am I with them" (Matt. 18:20).

In public worship, we confess our sins to God and to one another. In public worship, we join our fellow saints in praising our God for His goodness. In public worship, we sit together under His Word, allowing that Word to do its piercing and healing work in our hearts. In public worship, we collect our petitions and our gifts and offer them to God. In public worship, we celebrate the Holy Supper:

> The day of the Lord's Supper is an occasion of joy for the Christian community. Reconciled in their hearts with God and the brethren, the congregation receives the gift of the body and blood of Jesus Christ, and, receiving that, it receives forgiveness, new life, and salvation. . . . The fellowship of the Lord's Supper is the superlative fulfillment of Christian fellowship. As the members of the congregation are united in body and blood at the table of the Lord so will they be together in eternity. Here the community has reached its goal. Here joy in Christ and His community is complete.[8]

We all know this. So why say it all here? Because I know how easily my own heart falls into the trap of worshiping "professionally." Rather than coming as a little child to my Father's house to crawl up into His lap and let Him tell me of His love, I often come as a teacher, as an editor, as a writer, as one in public ministry.

I come into God's house, but I have not come home. I have not dropped the pretense of personal proficiency. I have not lowered the mask of my own competence. I have not opened the bandages that hide my hurts so that God can touch and heal them by His Word spoken through His people.

As God's people meet together in worship, God wants to do just that. He wants to minister to us—to serve us! He wants to touch and heal us. If we forget this, if we look on public worship as one more duty, as one more line item in our job description, or even as one more chance to set a good example for our students, we lose. We lose the sense of anticipation God wants us to have as we look forward to worship. We lose the joy in meeting with our family in our Father's house. We lose the impact He intends His Word to make on our hearts.

Every time—*every time*—the body of Christ comes together, our Lord wants to share Himself with us. He invites us, "Come! Eat at My table. Hear My absolution. Listen to My Word for your lives. Let Me love you through your brothers and sisters. Let Me strengthen you and prepare you for even larger service." What an invitation! What an opportunity! What a Savior!

Sometimes I Feel Like a Failure

God wants to be for us a perpetual spring of Living Water. He wants to refresh us. At times, though, we who have set aside our lives to serve Him feel as dried up as an old stick. Perhaps we see our ministry for Him as nothing but a long string of failures.

At times like that we need to ask ourselves, "What does God think? What is success? What is failure? How does my ministry measure up?"

The closing chapter of this book addresses those questions.

To Think About

1. Explain the term *stewardship* as the Scriptures use it. What does the term have to say to us about our use of time? of money? of our relationship with our Lord?
2. What valid reasons does someone in public ministry have for taking on a new task or for declining to do that task?
3. Describe a situation in which you managed your time well and one in which you managed your time not so well. What made

the difference? Why is time management an important skill for those in public ministry?

4. Which of the time management principles cited in this chapter have you used? Comment on how effectively they worked for you. Are there some techniques you have never tried? If so, which ones? Do they sound helpful or not? Explain.

5. List the principles for financial management given in this chapter. With which of these do you agree? disagree? Explain.

6. What plan do you now follow to spend time with the Lord Jesus in His Word and in worship? Rate your satisfaction with that plan on a scale from 1–10. How may God want to lead you to a plan that will give you deeper satisfaction?

7. Have you ever found yourself worshiping "professionally" rather than personally? What factors contribute to that tendency? How can confession/absolution help you conquer this temptation?

Notes

1. The interview took place on the NPR program "Fresh Aire" on Dec. 20, 1989.

2. Two time management books I have found helpful are the following:

What to Do When You Can't Do It All by Carol Von Klompemburg (Minneapolis: Augsburg, 1989). The author deals with her topic from a very practical, but spiritual perspective. Her book helped me work through some of my own struggles with time management.

The Tyranny of Time: When 24 Hours Is Not Enough by Robert Banks (Downers Grove, IL: InterVarsity Press, 1983). Banks writes in a more scholarly style, but also gives much practical advice. He speaks especially to those in church leadership positions, addressing not just their personal concerns, but also ways they can help those they lead to manage their time better.

In addition, I recommend:

Keeping the Sabbath Wholly by Marva J. Dawn (Grand Rapids: William B. Eerdmans, 1989). Dawn's work has challenged me to see myself as a steward of my time and abilities in a deeper way than I have before. She lends a unique perspective that defies my ability to even describe in a few words the concepts with which she works. Reading this book helped me take a fresh look at my worship patterns, my relationships with other believers, my place in God's creation. I highly value her scholarship and her insights.

In *Search of an Excellent Leader,* a video seminar for those in positions of parish leadership, includes an excellent tape on the stewardship of time and setting Scriptural priorities. Howard Hendricks leads the seminar. It is produced and distributed by Dallas Seminary Video Ministry, 3909 Swiss Avenue, Dallas, TX 75204.

3. From Martin Luther's explanation of the First Article of the Apostles' Creed. *The Small Catechism,* (St. Louis: Concordia Publishing House) 1986.

4. A friend of mine who does pastoral counseling with families often remarks, "Financial divorce is a precursor to legal divorce." No marriage needs that kind of stress. If one or both marriage partners serve in the church's public ministry, it is especially important that in making financial plans they help each other remember that a person's worth cannot be measured by the size of his or her paycheck. If they do not do this, all kinds of attitudes and behaviors destructive to both the marriage and the ministry can arise.

5. The IRS has coined the term *minister of religion* and uses it in a strictly defined administrative sense. Ask your principal if you meet IRS requirements. Or consult with the treasurer of your school or congregation.

6. Two helpful resources come to mind:

   The Church and Clergy Tax Guide uses fairly simple language to explain tax policy, especially as it affects congregations and church workers. It is updated every year and is available from Christian Ministry Resources, P.O. Box 2301, Matthews, NC 28106.

   Church Law and Tax Report is a newsletter published bimonthly and alerts readers to those changes in the law likely to affect churches. The articles in it deal with, but are not limited to, tax law. It is available from Christian Ministry Resources, P.O. Box 1098, Matthews, NC 28106.

7. The eight books of *Light for the Way* by Frank Starr (St. Louis: Concordia Publishing House, 1986, 1987) guide the reader through the entire Bible in two years. Starr adds helpful insights, especially Law and Gospel insights, in his devotional comments on each day's reading. I also find his daily prayer suggestions helpful.

8. Dietrich Bonhoeffer, *Life Together* (San Francisco: Harper and Row, 1954), 122.

CHAPTER 13

Success and Failure
An Epilogue

Hurricane Hugo roared onto the beaches of South Carolina in the fall of 1989, collapsing buildings, uprooting century-old trees, and flinging semitrailer trucks like Matchbox toys around parking lots. The media warned of Hugo's approach and of its destructive fury for over a week before the storm's arrival. About six hours before the killer hurricane hit land, a network news reporter interviewed one coastal resident. The interview went something like this:

Reporter: *The United States Weather Service has determined that Hugo will arrive just a few short hours from now. The Weather Service has also told us that the storm will almost surely hit this particular beach with full fury. Have you made plans, ma'am, for what you'll do during the storm?*

Resident: *No. Not really.*

Reporter: *Your home stands back there along this beach, right? Where will you go when the storm hits?*

Resident: *I don't know.*

Reporter (incredulous): *You've made no plans! What will you do?*

Resident: *I don't really know.*

Reporter (shaking his head): *How long have you lived here, ma'am?*

Resident: *Twenty-seven years.*

A few hours later, Hugo screamed, "Ready or not . . ." and came ashore. The storm devastated a wide strip of land along the eastern coast of the United States. After the hurricane had blown itself out, the Weather Service ranked it as the most destructive hurricane to have hit the nation in two decades. The authorities had done a good job. Residents of the area heard plenty of warnings, and they heard

234

them in plenty of time. Nonetheless, some people faced the storm unprepared. They had no place of shelter.

We live in an unsafe world. Sin and Satan rage all around us. And if that were not enough, death destroys dreams and collapses the hopes of millions of individuals and families every day. Our planet relentlessly turns toward the day of final judgment. Still, many—probably most—people have no shelter, no place of refuge.

Christian schools can stand as beacons in the gathering darkness. Christian schools can point people to the only place of refuge: Jesus Christ.

When those who serve in Christian day schools ask the Lord's help to see, and when they seize the opportunities He gives, great things can and do happen. Jesus wants to touch the hearts of our students. Jesus wants to touch the hearts of parents and of all the members of each school family. He wants to touch their lives forever.

Lest we in ministry forget, though, Jesus wants first and foremost to touch us individually and personally:

*God's main concern for your life is not primarily your ministry; what concerns God most of all is **you!***

The chapters of this book have explored some of the many ways those who teach in Christian schools can structure their lessons, their classrooms, their witness, their time, and their relationships to maximize the growth of those they disciple. The philosophy of Christian education, the skills, and the techniques God helps us develop can and do play an important role as we serve our Redeemer-King.

Even so, I pray that as you finish reading this book you take one fundamental fact away with you. I pray that the Holy Spirit will burn a single concept deeper and deeper into your heart and soul so that you can say with more conviction than ever before: Jesus loves *me*!

That you know the self-sacrificing love for you that fills the heart of Jesus is the number one goal the heavenly Father has for your life. That you cling to that love, trusting your Lord to cling to you even when your strength and courage fail—that sums up His primary objective for you. That accurately states the reasons behind everything He has done throughout earth's history and everything He will do in the future.

Yes, your Lord treasures the service you give His people and offer up to Him. But God does not draw you closer to Himself and deepen your discipleship primarily as a means to some other end—not even a commendable one, like your increasing ability to serve Him better in your public ministry. No. One clear note reverberates throughout the Scripture: God gave up His Son into death for you so that He could enjoy an eternity of fellowship with you. He looks upon His relationship with you—with you personally—as the most precious and important thing in the entire universe. *The most precious and important thing!*

When the Storms Hit

As we serve our Lord, as we disciple others, storms will strike. We cannot hold them back any more than the Weather Service could keep Hugo off the beaches of South Carolina.

When that first-grader walks out of your classroom in June, still unable to read or add . . .

When that third-grader comes in from the playground for the 79th time, unable to master the interpersonal skills he needs to play kickball with his peers for 10 minutes without starting a fight . . .

When a former student's name flashes through a network news story about soldiers missing in battle, and questions about his relationship with Jesus march through your mind . . .

When that fourth-grader's mom calls to say, "You never have cared about the children in your classroom. I've seen that from day 1! . . ."

When that dad walks into a third-quarter parent conference and chokes out the details of the cancer killing his 27-year-old wife . . .

When that principal or pastor or veteran colleague seems to criticize your ministry at every turn, no matter how hard you try . . .

When that sophomore from your geometry class winds up in jail for shoplifting or illegal possession of drugs or worse . . .

When storms like these break, you will need to draw upon your Lord's grace and strength, even as you do on days of warm sunshine and crisp sea breezes. When storms hit, you need a place of shelter—the only place of shelter, Jesus Christ. As the winds rage outside, let your Savior quiet your heart. Let Him remind you of the truth, the truth that has set us free and that keeps us free indeed as we serve:

- Remember, your Lord loves you! In times of stress and worry and failure, God's love for you—for you personally—does not change.

- Remember, you can always come home to your Father! He is the Rock of refuge, the Rock to whom we may continually flee (Ps. 71:3). Don't run from Him, run to Him! Pour out your heart and your hurt at His throne of grace.

- Remember, your Lord will never, ever turn you away! Even if you have caused your own trouble by your own sin, you can confess that sin and open your heart to receive His forgiveness. God always forgives our sins, even sins we commit in ministry. Your Lord is the God who cleanses you and who gives His servants a second chance (and a third and a tenth and a ten-thousandth). Just as the Holy Spirit has used you to assure others of that, let Him assure you too.

- Remember, failure is not fatal to future service! God did not call you into public ministry because of your great talents. He called you because He wanted to bless you with the chance to serve. He equips and gifts you for your service. If something that looks like failure has shown you that you need more knowledge, better skills, or further training to improve your effectiveness, ask your King about providing those things for you. He wants to help you grow—personally and professionally.

- Remember, you are almost certainly not the best judge of your own performance! Sometimes a set of circumstances may look like failure, walk like failure, even quack like failure, and yet not be failure—not in the end. God does not give up on people, not easily anyway.

  Years from now, that student, that parent, that colleague may remember something you have said or done, and God will use the memory to jump-start the work He has begun now. If you do not see results right away, and even if you never see results at all, you dare not conclude nothing has happened. The weapon you wield—the Word of God—is mighty through God (2 Cor. 10:4)!

- Remember, most things take time. From Ex. 2:1 through 14:9, Moses' ministry looked like a disaster. Yet not many verses later, God's people danced to the words, "I will sing unto the Lord, for He has triumphed gloriously!" While Israel waited, God had been at work. All the pieces needed to fall together; then the Lord acted in a single night.

- Remember, success is not up to you. God has given people free will. He will not force anyone to believe or to respond to His Word in the right way. The Lord holds you responsible for the faithful proclamation of His Law and His Gospel. He assumes responsibility for the crop that seed of the Word produces.

Grace, Grace, and More Grace

Satan sometimes joins forces with our flesh to suck us into a law-driven approach to our service for God. An insidious thought starts to tug at the back of our mind, a thought which, left to grow in the darkness, will poison our life with God and our ministry for Him. The lie goes something like this:

> If only I were a better servant (teacher, choir director, coach, counselor), God would love me just a little more.

> If only my students achieved at a bit higher level, if only my technique for working with parents were more polished, if only I would pray a little harder, produce a little more, or work a little longer each day, then God would be more pleased with me and with my service for Him.

These kinds of Law-driven thoughts soon push us over the brink into Law-driven behaviors. Such thoughts and behavior block the peace and joy with which God wants to flood our lives. We lapse, almost imperceptibly, out of the grace-base that characterizes effective kingdom service.

When you feel you have failed, you need to tell yourself the truth. Your Lord loves you—right now—just as much as He will love you in all eternity. God delights in you—right now—every bit as much as He will when He comes to take you home to live with Him in heaven. God cherishes you—right now—as much as He did at noon on Good Friday as He watched the sky grow dark in anticipation of the death of His Son.

This truth sets us free to serve. It sets us free to fail while still steadfastly refusing to believe Satan's lie that we are failures. It sets us free to free others. The hallmark of our freedom, of our service? The grace of God!

Whatever you do, work at it with all your heart, as working for the Lord, not for men, since you know that you will receive an inheritance from the Lord as a reward. It is the Lord Christ you are serving (Col. 3:23–24).

First Aid for Bruised Servants

- When I need wisdom—James 1:2–5
- When I want to give up—1 Cor. 15
- When I feel incompetent—2 Cor. 3
- When someone has attacked me—2 Cor. 4
- When I have sinned—1 John 1
- When I see no results from my work—Matt. 13:1–23; Is. 55:10 –11
- When Satan seems to be winning—John 10
- When I am worn out—Is. 41:8–10
- When I need to worship—Ps. 145

To Think About

1. When do you find it easiest to accept the truth of our Lord's love for you? When do you find it more difficult? How might the Holy Spirit help you deepen your realization of His compassion and commitment to you? How could a deepening realization of this help you personally? How could it add more power and peace to your ministry?
2. Think about times you have confronted failure in the past. What is your usual pattern of response? What aspects of that pattern are helpful? harmful?
3. Why do you suppose Satan uses discouragement so frequently in the life of God's servants? How can you counter this temptation?
4. What truths do you think might help you most in times you feel you have failed in your ministry? Why would these be helpful?
5. Memorize Col. 3:23–24. How could these words help you as you face success or failure in your work for the Lord Jesus and for His people?

Ministering to the Whole Child of God: Home Visits

(The material that follows is for use with chapter 10. It has been abbreviated and adapted from materials developed by the faculty and staff at Christ Lutheran School in Norfolk, NE. Many thanks to them for sharing it!)

Preparing Our Hearts

I would like to briefly sketch what home visits can accomplish as we go out as Christ's ambassadors, modeling and reflecting all that He is. You see, we go not just as teachers, but as His messengers, commissioned and burning with a message of Good News. We go out not to share ourselves or the subjects we will teach, but instead to share Jesus Christ and all that He will accomplish in our school this year. Do you see the difference?

Our Lord's call changes your classroom into a pasture rich with His presence and the goodness of His Word. It changes you from a teacher into a shepherd to whom the Holy Spirit has given the compassion of the Chief Shepherd and the task of caring for His lambs. These changes make our school a ministry, rather than a private academy with a smidgen of religion thrown into the stew for good measure.

Before the Visit

1. Read John 13:1–17. As you do, pray that the Lord Jesus would make you a better servant.
2. Thank the Lord Jesus for your Baptism and for the new life He has given you through His death and resurrection. Thank Him for counting you worthy to be used to proclaim the treasures of

His Word. Thank Him for the high calling of your ministry. Pray for a positive, Christlike attitude, one that genuinely looks forward to each visit in the homes of your students.

3. Review what you will tell families about Christ and about the ways you will structure your classroom so that He will be at the very center of everything you teach each day. Think of ways to impress on the family what a Christian education truly involves.

4. Pray for each child and for each family in the days and weeks before you visit their homes. Pray for courage to be a good witness to Jesus in word and deed. Pray for the power of the Holy Spirit in your words.

5. Anticipate the home visit as a time of planting seeds. Anticipate the victory you will celebrate—the joy of opening the door to each home for further ministry throughout the rest of the school year.

6. Pray for each family and for what you will say as you set up each family appointment. Let the person on the other end of the telephone line hear Jesus' joy in your voice and your sincere desire that your visit will be a blessing.

During the Visit

1. As you drive to each student's home, think about what God in His grace would like this family to become as they grow in His Word. Pray about how you can best nurture this student and witness to the student's family throughout the year.

   For example: *Lord, go with me now and guide me through this visit. May the members of this family see You and hear You through me. May a relationship of ministry to this family begin today, a relationship that will refresh each of us throughout this school year. Let's ring the doorbell together, Lord! Amen.*

2. During the visit, "walk by faith, not by sight." Begin by praying with the family members.

   For example: *Dear Father, we thank You today for new life in You. We thank You for the blessing of this family and for the fact that you have led them to enroll their child/children in Christ Lutheran School so they can grow in their faith and be equipped for service in Your kingdom. Bless our time together today that*

241

*You may be honored and praised in all we do and say. In Jesus'
name we pray. Amen.*

3. Talk about your plans for the school year. As you do, share (specifically) how Christ will be central to everything that happens.

   Warning: It will be easy at this time to fall into the trap of talking about yourself, lunch tickets, homework, recess, and so on. Do not let that happen! You have a mission! Don't forsake it! Focus your words and thoughts on the eternal!

4. Share thoughts from Deut. 6:4–9. It deals with the responsibility of Christian education God has given to the parent/parents in the family. Share the fact that you have also been called to help them with this task. Walk through these verses with gentleness and assurance.

   Warning: Do *not* become legalistic! Show how these verses give us the honor and the privilege of carrying out our Lord's will. Yes, He commands that we do this, but we obey not out of fear but out of love. He provides the power and wisdom we need. Rely on the Lord to lead you through this.

5. Stress team work between the home and school. Encourage the family in their prayer life, their devotional life, their worship life, and in their church and Bible study attendance. Take along the aids you yourself use in your own spiritual life. If they need help finding or obtaining materials, tell them that we at the school will see, by the Lord's power, that they receive them.

6. Ask if they have questions or concerns. Remember always to tie their questions and concerns back to the love of Jesus and the mission of the Christian school.

7. Thank them for the opportunity to visit with them. Close with a prayer together.

   For example: *Dear heavenly Father, thank You for being with us during this visit. We are excited about beginning a new year of growth in Jesus Christ. Strengthen this family in their desire to please you and to grow in Your Word. In Jesus' name we pray. Amen.*

   (Note: As you pray, add to your prayer any specific concerns, joys, or sorrows the family shared with you. Personalize the prayer.)

8. As you get back into your car, pause before you start the engine. Offer a prayer of thanks to Jesus for this family and for His help during the visit.

Sample Notes Home

Dear Parents,

As you will see from this week's note, we will be a busy class for the next five days. Although it can get hectic, we can rejoice that the Lord has blessed us with so many opportunities to grow and learn.

Memory

This week we will be memorizing the First Commandment and its meaning. You may want to discuss some of these ideas listed during dinner or family devotions.

1. What are some Bible stories that talk about false gods?
2. What are some of the things that adults or children put before God?
3. What are some ways that TV tries to make us think that God isn't very important?
4. We all feel guilty when we put things before God, but we can feel confident that Jesus' death on the cross has paid for all our sins. Look up Rom. 3:23–24. What does this mean for you?

Science

Test on Thursday

Singing

The students will be singing at late service this Sunday. Church starts at 10:30 a.m. but we would like the students here at 10:15 a.m. so that they can warm up and get organized. I hope that you and your family can be there to listen to the children share God's special message of love and forgiveness with the congregation.

Field Trip

Oates Museum on Friday. Permission slips due Thursday.

Basketball Game

Tuesday at 6 p.m. in our gym.

I pray you have a week filled with our Lord's joy and hope. Let me know if I can help you or your child in any way.

In Jesus' love,

Adapted from *Vision for Witness Kit* by Debbie Fitzpatrick, Board for Parish Services, The Lutheran Church—Missouri Synod.

First

Dear Parents,

Have you ever wondered what is in your child's head? What is he thinking? How does she learn? Does he really know or understand what we adults are trying to say?

Modern psychologists tell us that children must actively explore their environment in order to learn effectively. To many adults, this active involvement looks like play time. As a matter of fact, children "fool around" with things and people in God's world in order to learn. Your child needs many opportunities to explore and discover.

You can give your child opportunities to explore and discover the world. Suppose your child has never seen snow. She will not learn what snow is from pictures in a book, on TV, from snapshots, or from your description of snow. She may remember some attributes of snow, but will not *know* about snow until she sees it falling from the sky and can touch the cold substance.

Young children also construct knowledge about God. Again, they may be able to remember some facts we tell them about God, but they do not truly understand God's love until they experience love from significant people in their lives. They cannot understand God's forgiveness unless they experience forgiveness from people in their lives. Through the power of the Holy Spirit, they begin to understand God's love and care through the love and care shown them by important adults. You, as parents, and we, as teachers, can nourish the faith of your child through our words and actions.

Adapted from *Insights and Ideas* by Marilynn Beccue, Board for Parish Services, The Lutheran Church—Missouri Synod, March 1991.

APPENDIX C

Daily Lectionary

This outline is a devotional reading plan that covers the entire sacred Scriptures each year. The selections are based on ancient models and are generally in harmony with the liturgical church year. The average reading is three chapters daily. A seasonal canticle is assigned for each month and is scheduled to replace the psalm on the first and last days of the month. All of the psalms are read twice a year.

The lectionary is in accordance with Martin Luther's suggestions: "But let the entire Psalter, divided in parts, remain in use and the entire Scriptures, divided into lections, let this be preserved in the ears of the church." Also, "After that another book should be selected, and so on, until the entire Bible has been read through, and where one does not understand it, pass that by and glorify God."

December

1	Luke 1.46-55 Revelation 1—2	12	Psalm 11 Isaiah 10—12	22	Psalm 21 Isaiah 40—42
2	Psalm 1 Revelation 3—5	13	Psalm 12 Isaiah 13—15	23	Psalm 22 Isaiah 43—45
3	Psalm 2 Revelation 6—8	14	Psalm 13 Isaiah 16—18	24	Psalm 23 Isaiah 46—48
4	Psalm 3 Revelation 9—11	15	Psalm 14 Isaiah 19—21	25	Psalm 24 Isaiah 49—51
5	Psalm 4 Revelation 12—14	16	Psalm 15 Isaiah 22—24	26	Psalm 25 Isaiah 52—54
6	Psalm 5 Revelation 15—17	17	Psalm 16 Isaiah 25—27	27	Psalm 26 Isaiah 55—57
7	Psalm 6 Revelation 18—20	18	Psalm 17 Isaiah 28—30	28	Psalm 27 Isaiah 58—60
8	Psalm 7 Revelation 21—22	19	Psalm 18 Isaiah 31—33	29	Psalm 28 Isaiah 61—63
9	Psalm 8 Isaiah 1—3	20	Psalm 19 Isaiah 34—36	30	Psalm 29 Isaiah 64—66
10	Psalm 9 Isaiah 4—6	21	Psalm 20 Isaiah 37—39	31	Luke 1:46-55 Mark 1
11	Psalm 10 Isaiah 7—9				

January
1 Luke 1:68-79
  Mark 2
2 Psalm 30
  Mark 3
3 Psalm 31
  Mark 4
4 Psalm 32
  Mark 5
5 Psalm 33
  Mark 6
6 Psalm 34
  Mark 7
7 Psalm 35
  Mark 8
8 Psalm 36
  Mark 9
9 Psalm 37
  Mark 10
10 Psalm 38
  Mark 11
11 Psalm 39
  Mark 12
12 Psalm 40
  Mark 13
13 Psalm 41
  Mark 14
14 Psalm 42
  Mark 15—16
15 Psalm 43
  Genesis 1—3
16 Psalm 44
  Genesis 4—6
17 Psalm 45
  Genesis 7—9
18 Psalm 46
  Genesis 10—12
19 Psalm 47
  Genesis 13—15
20 Psalm 48
  Genesis 16—18
21 Psalm 49
  Genesis 19—21
22 Psalm 50
  Genesis 22—24
23 Psalm 51
  Genesis 25—27
24 Psalm 52
  Genesis 28—30
25 Psalm 53
  Genesis 31—33
26 Psalm 54
  Genesis 34—36
27 Psalm 55
  Genesis 37—39
28 Psalm 56
  Genesis 40—42
29 Psalm 57
  Genesis 43—45
30 Psalm 58
  Genesis 46—48

31 Luke 1:68-79
  Genesis 49—50

February
1 Luke 2:29-32
  Exodus 1—3
2 Psalm 59
  Exodus 4—6
3 Psalm 60
  Exodus 7—9
4 Psalm 61
  Exodus 10—12
5 Psalm 62
  Exodus 13—15
6 Psalm 63
  Exodus 16—18
7 Psalm 64
  Exodus 19—21
8 Psalm 65
  Exodus 22—24
9 Psalm 66
  Exodus 25—27
10 Psalm 67
  Exodus 28—30
11 Psalm 68
  Exodus 31—33
12 Psalm 69
  Exodus 34—36
13 Psalm 70
  Exodus 37—38
14 Psalm 71
  Exodus 39—40
15 Psalm 72
  Leviticus 1—3
16 Psalm 73
  Leviticus 4—6
17 Psalm 74
  Leviticus 7—9
18 Psalm 75
  Leviticus 10—12
19 Psalm 76
  Leviticus 13—15
20 Psalm 77
  Leviticus 16—18
21 Psalm 78
  Leviticus 19—21
22 Psalm 79
  Leviticus 22—24
23 Psalm 80
  Leviticus 25—27
24 Psalm 81
  Numbers 1—3
25 Psalm 82
  Numbers 4—6
26 Psalm 83
  Numbers 7—9
27 Psalm 84
  Numbers 10—12
28 Luke 2:29-32
  Numbers 13—15

March
1 Isaiah 64:1-9
  Numbers 16—18
2 Psalm 85
  Numbers 19—21
3 Psalm 86
  Numbers 22—24
4 Psalm 87
  Numbers 25—27
5 Psalm 88
  Numbers 28—30
6 Psalm 89
  Numbers 31—33
7 Psalm 90
  Numbers 34—36
8 Psalm 91
  Deuteronomy 1—3
9 Psalm 92
  Deuteronomy 4—6
10 Psalm 93
  Deuteronomy 7—9
11 Psalm 94
  Deuteronomy 10—12
12 Psalm 95
  Deuteronomy 13—15
13 Psalm 96
  Deuteronomy 16—18
14 Psalm 97
  Deuteronomy 19—21
15 Psalm 98
  Deuteronomy 22—24
16 Psalm 99
  Deuteronomy 25—27
17 Psalm 100
  Deuteronomy 28—30
18 Psalm 101
  Deuteronomy 31—34
19 Psalm 102
  Luke 1
20 Psalm 103
  Luke 2—3
21 Psalm 104
  Luke 4—5
22 Psalm 105
  Luke 6—7
23 Psalm 106
  Luke 8—9
24 Psalm 107
  Luke 10—11
25 Psalm 108
  Luke 12—13
26 Psalm 109
  Luke 14—15
27 Psalm 110
  Luke 16—17
28 Psalm 111
  Luke 18—19
29 Psalm 112
  Luke 20—21
30 Psalm 113
  Luke 22
31 Isaiah 64:1-9
  Luke 23—24

248

DAILY LECTIONARY

April

1 Isaiah 25:1-9
   Romans 1—3
2 Psalm 114
   Romans 4—6
3 Psalm 115
   Romans 7—9
4 Psalm 116
   Romans 10—13
5 Psalm 117
   Romans 14—16
6 Psalm 118
   1 Corinthians 1—3
7 Psalm 119:1-8
   1 Corinthians 4—6
8 Psalm 119:9-16
   1 Corinthians 7—9
9 Psalm 119:17-24
   1 Corinthians 10—11
10 Psalm 119:25-32
   1 Corinthians 12—14
11 Psalm 119:33-40
   1 Corinthians 15—16
12 Psalm 119:41-48
   2 Corinthians 1—4
13 Psalm 119:49-56
   2 Corinthians 5—7
14 Psalm 119:57-64
   2 Corinthians 8—10
15 Psalm 119:65-72
   2 Corinthians 11—13
16 Psalm 119:73-80
   Galatians 1—3
17 Psalm 119:81-88
   Galatians 4—6
18 Psalm 119:89-96
   Ephesians 1—3
19 Psalm 119:97-104
   Ephesians 4—6
20 Psalm 119:105-112
   Philippians 1—2
21 Psalm 119:113-120
   Philippians 3—4
22 Psalm 119:121-128
   Colossians 1—2
23 Psalm 119:129-136
   Colossians 3—4
24 Psalm 119:137-144
   1 Thessalonians 1—3
25 Psalm 119:145-152
   1 Thessalonians 4—5
26 Psalm 119:153-160
   2 Thessalonians 1—3
27 Psalm 119:161-168
   1 Timothy 1—3
28 Psalm 119:169-176
   1 Timothy 4—6
29 Psalm 120
   2 Timothy 1—2
30 Isaiah 25:1-9
   2 Timothy 3—4

May

1 1 Samuel 2:1-10
   Titus, Philemon
2 Psalm 121
   Hebrews 1—4
3 Psalm 122
   Hebrews 5—7
4 Psalm 123
   Hebrews 8—10
5 Psalm 124
   Hebrews 11—13
6 Psalm 125
   James 1—3
7 Psalm 126
   James 4—5
8 Psalm 127
   1 Peter 1—2
9 Psalm 128
   1 Peter 3—5
10 Psalm 129
   2 Peter
11 Psalm 130
   1 John 1—3
12 Psalm 131
   1 John 4—5
13 Psalm 132
   2 John, 3 John, Jude
14 Psalm 133
   John 1—2
15 Psalm 134
   John 3—4
16 Psalm 135
   John 5—6
17 Psalm 136
   John 7—8
18 Psalm 137
   John 9—10
19 Psalm 138
   John 11—12
20 Psalm 139
   John 13—14
21 Psalm 140
   John 15—16
22 Psalm 141
   John 17—18
23 Psalm 142
   John 19
24 Psalm 143
   John 20—21
25 Psalm 144
   Acts 1—2
26 Psalm 145
   Acts 3—4
27 Psalm 146
   Acts 5—6
28 Psalm 147
   Acts 7—8
29 Psalm 148
   Acts 9—10
30 Psalm 149
   Acts 11—12
31 1 Samuel 2:1-10
   Acts 13—14

June

1 Isaiah 12:1-6
   Acts 15—16
2 Psalm 150
   Acts 17—18
3 Psalm 1
   Acts 19—20
4 Psalm 2
   Acts 21—22
5 Psalm 3
   Acts 23—24
6 Psalm 4
   Acts 25—26
7 Psalm 5
   Acts 27—28
8 Psalm 6
   Joshua 1—5
9 Psalm 7
   Joshua 6—8
10 Psalm 8
   Joshua 9—11
11 Psalm 9
   Joshua 12—16
12 Psalm 10
   Joshua 17—21
13 Psalm 11
   Joshua 22—24
14 Psalm 12
   Judges 1—3
15 Psalm 13
   Judges 4—6
16 Psalm 14
   Judges 7—9
17 Psalm 15
   Judges 10—12
18 Psalm 16
   Judges 13—15
19 Psalm 17
   Judges 16—18
20 Psalm 18
   Judges 19—21
21 Psalm 19
   Ruth
22 Psalm 20
   1 Samuel 1—3
23 Psalm 21
   1 Samuel 4—6
24 Psalm 22
   1 Samuel 7—9
25 Psalm 23
   1 Samuel 10—12
26 Psalm 24
   1 Samuel 13—15
27 Psalm 25
   1 Samuel 16—18
28 Psalm 26
   1 Samuel 19—21
29 Psalm 27
   1 Samuel 22—24
30 Isaiah 12:1-6
   1 Samuel 25—27

GO AND MAKE DISCIPLES

<table>
<tr><td>

July
1   Deuteronomy 32:1-4
    1 Samuel 28—31
2   Psalm 28
    2 Samuel 1—3
3   Psalm 29
    2 Samuel 4—6
4   Psalm 30
    2 Samuel 7—9
5   Psalm 31
    2 Samuel 10—12
6   Psalm 32
    2 Samuel 13—15
7   Psalm 33
    2 Samuel 16—18
8   Psalm 34
    2 Samuel 19—21
9   Psalm 35
    2 Samuel 22—24
10   Psalm 36
    1 Kings 1—2
11   Psalm 37
    1 Kings 3—6
12   Psalm 38
    1 Kings 7—8
13   Psalm 39
    1 Kings 9—11
14   Psalm 40
    1 Kings 12—14
15   Psalm 41
    1 Kings 15—17
16   Psalm 42
    1 Kings 18—20
17   Psalm 43
    1 Kings 21—22
18   Psalm 44
    2 Kings 1—3
19   Psalm 45
    2 Kings 4—6
20   Psalm 46
    2 Kings 7—9
21   Psalm 47
    2 Kings 10—12
22   Psalm 48
    2 Kings 13—15
23   Psalm 49
    2 Kings 16—18
24   Psalm 50
    2 Kings 19—22
25   Psalm 51
    2 Kings 23—25
26   Psalm 52
    1 Chronicles 1—5
27   Psalm 53
    1 Chronicles 6—10
28   Psalm 54
    1 Chronicles 11—15
29   Psalm 55
    1 Chronicles 16—20
30   Psalm 56
    1 Chronicles 21—25
31   Deuteronomy 32:1-4
    1 Chronicles 26—29

</td><td>

August
1   Habakkuk 3:2-19
    2 Chronicles 1—3
2   Psalm 57
    2 Chronicles 4—6
3   Psalm 58
    2 Chronicles 7—9
4   Psalm 59
    2 Chronicles 10—12
5   Psalm 60
    2 Chronicles 13—15
6   Psalm 61
    2 Chronicles 16—18
7   Psalm 62
    2 Chronicles 19—21
8   Psalm 63
    2 Chronicles 22—24
9   Psalm 64
    2 Chronicles 25—27
10   Psalm 65
    2 Chronicles 28—30
11   Psalm 66
    2 Chronicles 31—33
12   Psalm 67
    2 Chronicles 34—36
13   Psalm 68
    Ezra 1—5
14   Psalm 69
    Ezra 6—10
15   Psalm 70
    Nehemiah 1—3
16   Psalm 71
    Nehemiah 4—6
17   Psalm 72
    Nehemiah 7—9
18   Psalm 73
    Nehemiah 10—13
19   Psalm 74
    Esther 1—3
20   Psalm 75
    Esther 4—6
21   Psalm 76
    Esther 7—10
22   Psalm 77
    Job 1—3
23   Psalm 78
    Job 4—6
24   Psalm 79
    Job 7—9
25   Psalm 80
    Job 10—12
26   Psalm 81
    Job 13—15
27   Psalm 82
    Job 16—18
28   Psalm 83
    Job 19—21
29   Psalm 84
    Job 22—24
30   Psalm 85
    Job 25—27
31   Habakkuk 3:2-19
    Job 28—30

</td><td>

September
1   1 Chronicles 29:10-13
    Job 31—33
2   Psalm 86
    Job 34—36
3   Psalm 87
    Job 37—39
4   Psalm 88
    Job 40—42
5   Psalm 89
    Proverbs 1—3
6   Psalm 90
    Proverbs 4—7
7   Psalm 91
    Proverbs 8—10
8   Psalm 92
    Proverbs 11—13
9   Psalm 93
    Proverbs 14—16
10   Psalm 94
    Proverbs 17—19
11   Psalm 95
    Proverbs 20—22
12   Psalm 96
    Proverbs 23—25
13   Psalm 97
    Proverbs 26—28
14   Psalm 98
    Proverbs 29—31
15   Psalm 99
    Ecclesiastes 1—3
16   Psalm 100
    Ecclesiastes 4—6
17   Psalm 101
    Ecclesiastes 7—9
18   Psalm 102
    Ecclesiastes 10—12
19   Psalm 103
    Song of Solomon 1—4
20   Psalm 104
    Song of Solomon 5—8
21   Psalm 105
    Jeremiah 1—3
22   Psalm 106
    Jeremiah 4—6
23   Psalm 107
    Jeremiah 7—9
24   Psalm 108
    Jeremiah 10—12
25   Psalm 109
    Jeremiah 13—15
26   Psalm 110
    Jeremiah 16—18
27   Psalm 111
    Jeremiah 19—22
28   Psalm 112
    Jeremiah 23—25
29   Psalm 113
    Jeremiah 26—28
30   1 Chronicles 29:10-13
    Jeremiah 29—31

</td></tr>
</table>

October		November	
1	Jonah 2:2-9	1	Exodus 15:1-18
	Jeremiah 32—34		Hosea 8—10
2	Psalm 114	2	Psalm 122
	Jeremiah 35—37		Hosea 11—14
3	Psalm 115	3	Psalm 123
	Jeremiah 38—40		Joel
4	Psalm 116	4	Psalm 124
	Jeremiah 41—43		Amos 1—5
5	Psalm 117	5	Psalm 125
	Jeremiah 44—47		Amos 6—9
6	Psalm 118	6	Psalm 126
	Jeremiah 48—50		Obadiah, Jonah
7	Psalm 119:1-8	7	Psalm 127
	Jeremiah 51—52		Micah 1—3
8	Psalm 119:9-16	8	Psalm 128
	Lamentations 1—2		Micah 4—7
9	Psalm 119:17-24	9	Psalm 129
	Lamentations 3—5		Nahum
10	Psalm 119:25-32	10	Psalm 130
	Ezekiel 1—3		Habakkuk
11	Psalm 119:33-40	11	Psalm 131
	Ezekiel 4—6		Zephaniah
12	Psalm 119:41-48	12	Psalm 132
	Ezekiel 7—9		Haggai
13	Psalm 119:49-56	13	Psalm 133
	Ezekiel 10—12		Zechariah 1—5
14	Psalm 119:57-64	14	Psalm 134
	Ezekiel 13—15		Zechariah 6—10
15	Psalm 119:65-72	15	Psalm 135
	Ezekiel 16—18		Zechariah 11—14
16	Psalm 119:73-80	16	Psalm 136
	Ezekiel 19—21		Malachi
17	Psalm 119:81-88	17	Psalm 137
	Ezekiel 22—24		Matthew 1—2
18	Psalm 119:89-96	18	Psalm 138
	Ezekiel 25—27		Matthew 3—4
19	Psalm 119:97-104	19	Psalm 139
	Ezekiel 28—30		Matthew 5—6
20	Psalm 119:105-112	20	Psalm 140
	Ezekiel 31—33		Matthew 7—8
21	Psalm 119:113-120	21	Psalm 141
	Ezekiel 34—36		Matthew 9—10
22	Psalm 119:121-128	22	Psalm 142
	Ezekiel 37—39		Matthew 11—12
23	Psalm 119:129-136	23	Psalm 143
	Ezekiel 40—42		Matthew 13—14
24	Psalm 119:137-144	24	Psalm 144
	Ezekiel 43—45		Matthew 15—16
25	Psalm 119:145-152	25	Psalm 145
	Ezekiel 46—48		Matthew 17—18
26	Psalm 119:153-160	26	Psalm 146
	Daniel 1—3		Matthew 19—20
27	Psalm 119:161-168	27	Psalm 147
	Daniel 4—6		Matthew 21—22
28	Psalm 119:169-176	28	Psalm 148
	Daniel 7—9		Matthew 23—24
29	Psalm 120	29	Psalm 149—150
	Daniel 10—12		Matthew 25—26
30	Psalm 121	30	Exodus 15:1-18
	Hosea 1—4		Matthew 27—28
31	Jonah 2:2-9		
	Hosea 5—7		

251

Index